ADMINISTRATION IN BU
Made Simple

Ronald R. Pitfield, ACIS, MBIM

Made Simple Books
HEINEMANN : London

Printed and bound in Great Britain
by Richard Clay (The Chaucer Press) Ltd,
Bungay, Suffolk
for the publishers William Heinemann Ltd.,
10 Upper Grosvenor Street, London W1X 9PA

First Edition, April 1980
Reprinted, December 1982

British Library Cataloguing in Publication Data
Pitfield, Ronald R.
  Administration in business made simple.—(Made simple books)
  1. Management
  I. Title   II. Series
  658   HD31

ISBN 0-434-98562-7

Preface

This book is specifically designed to accord with the module entitled 'Administration in Business' in the Business Education Council scheme for National Awards. Its structure is based on that of the module and in writing it the object has been to express the learning philosophy established by the Council. In this respect the subject has been recognised as being a practical one, so that it is treated in as realistic a manner as possible. This has meant that principles and theories have been interpreted by giving examples of business life as it really is.

Each chapter concludes with a list of 'Key Points' which summarise the content of the chapter in a stylised format. The intention is that these will serve to bring together the most important aspects in order to make understanding easier and also to provide material which can be used in pre-examination revision.

Appendix 1 contains a lengthy list of assignments, some of which can be undertaken by individual students while others are intended for groups. All the exercises have been designed to call for a practical approach, so that learning is facilitated by relating it to real situations. It is hoped that students and teachers will find them of interest and benefit.

In writing the book, the requirements of other students have also been borne in mind. It should be of value to those studying for professional examinations which call for a knowledge of administration and office management. The bodies concerned include the Institute of Cost and Management Accountants, the Institute of Administrative Management, the Institute of Chartered Secretaries and Administrators, the Society of Company and Commercial Accountants, the Association of International Accountants, the Institute of Commercial Management and the Institute of Administrative Accounting.

Those engaged on relevant modules in schemes for BEC Higher National Awards should also find the book useful.

I am grateful to the many people and organisations who have been of assistance in the writing of this book. The help of those who have provided illustrative material is acknowledged in the appropriate places. I would like to express my thanks in particular to the companies listed overleaf.

RRP

Acknowledgements

Adler Business Computers Ltd
Datasaab Ltd
D. D. Lamson Ltd
IBM United Kingdom Ltd
ITT Consumer Products (UK) Ltd
Kalamazoo Ltd
Kodak Ltd
Nashua Copycat Ltd
Philips Electrical Ltd
Rank Xerox (UK) Ltd
Roneo Vickers Ltd
Texas Instruments Ltd
Thorn-Ericsson Telecommunications (Sales) Ltd
Wiggins Teape (Mill Sales) Ltd

Contents

SECTION 3—THE EMPLOYEE WITHIN THE ORGANISATION

SECTION 1

ORGANISATIONAL STRUCTURE

1

THE NATURE OF ORGANISATION

1.1 The Function of Organisation

Every formally constituted body is established in order to achieve objectives. These objectives and any quantification of them are first determined at the highest level of the concern. For example, it may be decided by a business to manufacture and sell a specified quantity of a product at a stated cost and selling price; a professional body may aim to increase its membership by, say, 500 in the course of the ensuing year.

These targets will be set for management to achieve. Top management will then allocate to different groups of people the responsibility of carrying out specified sections of the total work. Each group must consist of a sufficient number of people to do the work in the time allowed and those people must be specially qualified for the type of work required. A person must be in charge of each group and be directly accountable to his superiors for carrying out the duties imposed on the group. In turn, that person will allocate work to his subordinates in the group, again choosing those most suitable for each section of the group work.

It is now possible to specify the management concepts which have emerged from the above account:

(*a*) **Objectives.** The overall objective is set at the highest level. Top management then determines the groups which must be involved and sets objectives for each group.

(*b*) **Delegation of responsibility.** First, top management is made responsible for achieving the overall objective. Then each group leader is given the responsibility of achieving his group objective. The leaders may subdelegate some of their responsibilities to subordinates within their groups.

(*c*) **Authority and direction.** If a person is to have responsibilities he will require to have authority. He must be given such power as is necessary for him to play his part. In so doing, he will make decisions as to how he will perform his functions; this planning and the consequent giving of orders is known as **direction**. The extent of each person's authority will be determined by the superior who delegates the related responsibility.

(*d*) **Accountability.** Every person who is given responsibility is accountable for his actions to the person bestowing the responsibility. From the lowest level, each person is accountable to his immediate superior. At the highest level, top management is accountable to those who gave it the responsibility for achieving the global objective.

(*ε*) **Division of activities.** The allocating of responsibilities to different groups means that the various activities within the whole are divided into specialist groups. Within a group there may be further divisions.

Summary. It can therefore be established that 'organisation' is a process of dividing work into logical sections with links of responsibility and account-ability within and external to the sections, the whole being coordinated to achieve the global objective.

Organisation is therefore a **method** and should not be confused with '*an* organisation', which is a term referring to a cohesive body established for a specified purpose.

1.2 The Strata of Management

It will thus be seen that organisation entails the establishing of tiers of authority and responsibility and of accountability, with each person (except those at the extremes) having levels above and below him. The simple prin-ciple is that

(*a*) authority and responsibility are passed *downward*, and
(*b*) accountability is passed *upward*,

between the same persons.

This is sometimes known as the 'strata of management' and can be por-trayed in the form of an **organisation pyramid**. Fig. 1.1. illustrates the principle and shows the levels of management, with lines of authority and responsi-bility and lines of accountability travelling in converse directions. The illus-tration relates to a company, with the directors establishing the objectives and the managing director, as the chief executive officer, being given overall administrative responsibility. He plans the operation by allocating responsi-bility for specified areas to the senior executives, and the pattern continues as the triangle widens.

The whole represents a system of continuous delegation and because it depicts vertical relationships it is sometimes referred to as the **scalar process**.

1.3 Further Aspects of Organisation

The general principles of function specialisation and the hierarchical aspect having been considered, it is now necessary to add other factors which are required to make an organisation effective.

(*a*) **Coordination.** The activities of all the functional areas must be co-ordinated in such a manner as to focus on the attainment of the objective. There must be relationships between groups other than those which are immediately superior and inferior. Therefore, relationships must be horizontal as well as vertical. Coordination must also exist *within* groups so that the group objectives are attained.

(*b*) **Communication.** There must be systems whereby each group can consult with related groups. Controlling groups must be made aware of the degree of achievement of each of its subsidiary groups and of any problems being encountered. Top management must be kept informed of the progress being made by each group.

Procedures must be established so that communication routes are deter-mined and the information to be provided is specified. Intelligence will flow in the form of meetings, literary and statistical reports, formal returns, etc.

(*c*) **Planning and control.** The overall plan will be made by the policy-makers, and contributing to this will be sectional plans. This in itself would be inadequate unless arrangements were made to compare what had been achieved at any one stage with what had been planned. Controls must therefore be established so that comparisons of performance against forecasts can be made.

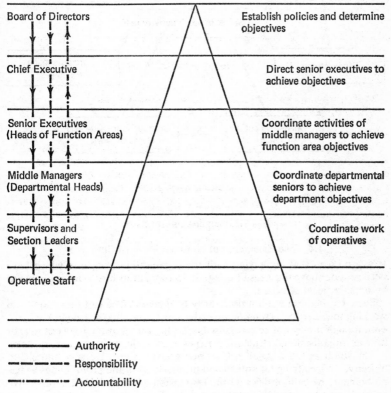

Board of Directors — Establish policies and determine objectives

Chief Executive — Direct senior executives to achieve objectives

Senior Executives (Heads of Function Areas) — Coordinate activities of middle managers to achieve function area objectives

Middle Managers (Departmental Heads) — Coordinate departmental seniors to achieve department objectives

Supervisors and Section Leaders — Coordinate work of operatives

Operative Staff

——————— Authority

— — — — Responsibility

—·—·—·— Accountability

Fig. 1.1. The strata of management.

This form of checking must be continuous so that any deviation may be identified without delay, thereby allowing corrective action to be taken before the deviation has a cumulative effect. There must therefore be arrangements for 'feedback' of data to enable the comparisons to be made.

The illustration of a planning-control chart (Fig. 1.2) could relate to the global objective or the objective of a functional area. It will be seen that the objectives are first set and that the work is then planned to include forecasts for each stage. The performance figures for each stage are compared with the forecasts and any action necessary to reconcile the two sets of figures is taken. On completion of the whole operation the total performance figures are compared with the target figures which were compiled when the objectives were set.

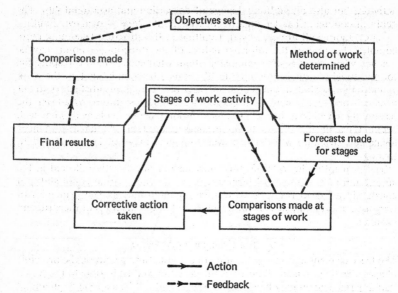

Fig. 1.2. Planning-control chart.

1.4 The Emergence of an Organisational Structure

It will be seen that complying with the organisation principles which have been set out above must result in a pattern of relationships. This is known as an **organisational structure**.

Such a structure need not necessarily be *designed*. The fact that people are working together for a common objective must mean that a structure *exists*— even though it may not be recognised as such. The following is an example of how an organisational structure emerges at even the most elementary stage.

Mr Smith opens a small self-service grocery shop. He sets himself an objective by specifying his anticipated turnover, costs and profit, but as he has no manager he cannot delegate the responsibility of attaining the objective; he is his own 'top management'.

He employs Miss Brown to be in charge of the check-out desk, on the understanding that when there are no customers she will assist him in filling the shelves. Immediately he does so he effects a *division of activities*, by dividing the work between himself and Miss Brown. He also *delegates responsibility* to his assistant and gives her the necessary *authority*. In so doing, he makes her *accountable* to him for the performance of her duties. Because he makes the decision as to how the work is to be divided and allocates specific duties to her, he performs the function of *direction*.

The business grows and Mr Smith appoints another assistant, Miss White. The newcomer is mainly engaged in shelf-filling but is also required to operate a second check-out desk when circumstances make it necessary. Miss Brown remains in general charge of check-outs, so that Miss White becomes Miss Brown's subordinate. Thus, there is now not only a further division of activities but also an additional stage of delegation and accountability. The chain of command has lengthened to Miss White–Miss Brown–Mr Smith.

Later, more staff are employed, resulting in the structure becoming more complex. Because of the informal nature of the direction, a point may be reached where there is some confusion about what each person is responsible for and to whom she is accountable. There may be complaints that the work is unevenly distributed. One employee may prove to be unsatisfactory in her present work and it may be necessary to change her duties. Whatever the reason, there will be a time when some decision must be made as to what each person is responsible for and to whom she is accountable. At that stage a more formalised structure will emerge, even though it may not be committed to writing.

The principles illustrated in this short history are directly reflected in the largest and most complex of business concerns. Organisation is not static: it constantly alters in response to changing circumstances. The principles of organisation will always exist, however, even though the form of the structure changes.

1.5 The Grouping of Activities

The basic element in dividing the total of activities into groups is the principle of **specialisation**. In a small business the grouping will be flexible to the extent that any one person may have various duties and not be a specialist in any of them. In the nature of things, however, a degree of specialisation may show itself. For example, one person may have an aptitude for figure work and may spend some time dealing with the small amount of quantitative work which exists. *Complete* specialisation will not come into being, however, until there is work of a particular kind sufficient wholly to occupy one person.

As a business expands, there will be more and more specialist jobs which demand full-time work. Subsequent increases in work will result in specialisation being practised by whole departments instead of by individuals. At an even later stage of development the work of some departments will be divided, so that each new division will specialise in one aspect of what was once the complete responsibility of a department. Thus, the *range* of work in an area becomes narrower as specialisation is intensified. For example, a single accounting department may be split so that the calculation and payment of wages becomes the responsibility of a separate department. Other refinements may follow. If it becomes necessary to pay more attention to, say, costing and budgeting, then those areas will be 'hived off' to become new departments.

The advantage of specialisation is that those concerned can concentrate on a narrower range of expertise. This result should lead to greater efficiency. A possible danger is that it will produce a narrowness of outlook by the specialists. A person concentrating on a limited range of work may overlook the fact that he is merely a contributor to a wider expertise and he may thereby have an unbalanced attitude. Specialisation also often results in people being congregated into small working groups and this can lead to a parochial attitude.

Continuing the example of the accounting function, it must be recognised that no matter how extensive and complex the degree of specialisation is, the accounting function *as a whole* remains a single unit. All the divisions which are made result only in the creation of subfunctions, the total of which constitutes the accounting function. Each subfunction would have a leader who would head his group hierarchy, but, in turn, he and his group would be a lower level of another hierarchy—that is, the general accounting function group.

There must therefore be a direct relationship between each subgroup and its leading group to form the total functional area. In many cases there will also be relationships *between* subgroups but with all such joint activities focusing on the major group.

This constant splitting of functional areas into more specialist areas must of necessity lengthen the 'chain of command'. Primary subgroups will be accountable to the main group, but will also be responsible for any secondary subgroups; and the same principle will continue *within* groups.

1.6 The Principles of Effective Organisation

The style of organisation may differ among undertakings and only experience will show which is the most effective. Generally, an organisation structure *develops* and therefore precepts may change as circumstances indicate the necessity for doing so. However, certain principles have universal application.

(*a*) **Unity of purpose.** All functional areas should contribute to the global objective and conform to accepted policy. There is no justification for any part of the undertaking 'doing its own thing' contrary to the general aims. There is therefore a requirement for integration which leads to the common goal. There must also be central control to ensure that this is being done.

(*b*) **Operational efficiency.** Each function and subfunction must operate in the most efficient manner possible. This entails study in order to reduce costs, to shorten the time for completion of tasks, to reduce the incidence of errors and to increase the rate of success in attaining objectives. Numerous management techniques are available to assist in these respects.

Overall efficiency must also be constantly striven for. For example, it is necessary to ensure there is no duplication of work by two or more function areas. There may be circumstances in which one activity can be eliminated or some of them merged into a single group. The lengthening of the chain of command may bring with it the dangers of 'remoteness' and an increasing impersonalisation in staff relationships. Lines of communication may lengthen to the extent that delays and misunderstandings become more frequent. Consequently, there must be frequent reviews of the working of the structure.

(*c*) **Responsibility and authority** should be given to those best suited to accept them. It should be bestowed only on those who not only have the necessary expertise but who also have the character not to abuse their authority or fail in their responsibilities.

(*d*) **Flexibility.** In large undertakings (such as branches of the Civil Service) there is the danger of an organisational structure becoming rigid. There must be acceptance of the principle that if experience indicates some failure of coordination or of inefficiency, then the structure must be altered to solve the problem. Slavish adherence to the structure with the refusal to change it may lead to bureaucratic practices of sometimes farcical proportions.

(*e*) **Inter-relationships.** The vertical line of authority must be unambiguous. Each person should know who is his immediate superior, what the extent of his authority is, what he is responsible for and who his subordinates are.

The horizontal relationships are not so rigid. There must be some positive links but, as will be shown later, in practice there will also be 'informal' relationships.

Flows of information must progress on defined lines of communication which reflect the inter-relationship links.

1.7 The Human Factor

An inescapable fact is that all aspects of management involve human activity. Each person is unique and in many instances human reaction is unpredictable. For example, it is generally accepted that, with efficient planning, two people working together can achieve more than twice what could be achieved by either of them working alone. Management experts may decide that if the team was increased to four persons by adding another equally efficient pair there would be an even greater improvement. In practice, however, the reverse may apply. The theory may have been scientifically justified but the consequent increased relationships may cause personal friction with a resulting decrease in efficiency. The mathematical concept of the law of increasing returns may be disproved because of the vagaries of human nature.

Increased mechanisation frequently leads to a reduced amount of human activity but, perversely, it can sometimes result in increased personal problems.

Key Points

1. *An* organisation is a body, such as a company. **Organisation** is a *method* of coordinating activities to achieve an objective.

2. A *global* objective is divided into *group* objectives, each contributing to the whole. This requires **direction** by passing *downward* **responsibility** and **authority**. **Accountability** flows *upward*.

    Division of activities means allocating *group* responsibilities and responsibilities *within* groups.

    These principles are known as the **strata of management**, establishing a **hierarchy**.

3. The achievement of the global objective also requires

    (*a*) overall and group **planning and control**;
    (*b*) **coordination** between groups and within groups;
    (*c*) **communication** between groups, and between groups and the directing body.

4. An **organisational structure** shows a *pattern of relationships* in achieving an objective. It always exists, consciously or not.

5. **Specialisation** means

    (*a*) giving work to those *best suited to perform it*;
    (*b*) reducing the *range* of each person.

    It results in *increased efficiency* but can lead to a *narrowing of outlook*.
    Functional specialisation lengthens the chain of command.

2

FORMALISING THE STRUCTURE

2.1 The 'Unconscious' Structure

In the previous chapter we saw that the congregating of people at work established areas of activities, that people had individual duties and that they occupied different levels of seniority. We also saw that such a series of relationships was not necessarily drafted as a plan, because positions were taken up as a natural consequence of day-to-day work. In such a situation, people are *unconsciously* part of a structure. At a very early stage the pattern of responsibility and seniority becomes apparent, but rarely is it set out in diagrammatic form.

When staff has grown to a certain number it may be necessary to come to an understanding as to the responsibilities of each member and their interrelationships. The agreement may be roughed out on a piece of paper and if this is done there then exists an **organisation chart** in its most elementary form.

If the shop which was given as an example in the previous chapter now had five employees, Mr Smith may decide that Miss Brown and Miss White would be fully engaged on the check-out desks, Miss Brown being the senior. Mrs Grey would be responsible for shelf-filling and be assisted by Miss Green. The storekeeper would be Mr Black. The business has therefore been divided into three functional areas and a hierarchical system has been established. In drafting his rough plan, Mr Smith would probably set it out in what to him is the most obvious style—the genealogical table which everyone understands. His effort would appear as shown in Fig. 2.1.

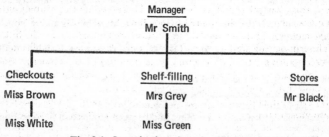

Fig. 2.1. Organisation chart (small shop).

2.2 The Purposes of Organisation Charts

An organisation chart is an attempt to portray the various relationships *as they are*. As will be shown later, there are limits to its effectiveness but the purposes can be illustrated by referring to Mr Smith's piece of paper.

The responsibilities of the staff are clearly shown as being split into three areas of activity. The persons directly responsible to Mr Smith for each area

10

are shown to be Miss Brown, Mrs Grey and Mr Black. In each of the first two areas, the chain of command is extended by one link in that Miss White and Miss Green are directly accountable to Miss Brown and Mrs Grey respectively and not to Mr Smith. The two senior ladies are, however, accountable to Mr Smith for the *whole* work content of their areas, including that performed by their subordinates.

The chart therefore achieves its objective in showing the vertical and horizontal relationships, and the focusing of all activities at the coordinating point occupied by Mr Smith.

2.3 Study of a Large Organisation Chart

Fig. 2.2 shows an organisation chart of a manufacturing company. It will be seen that it essentially conforms to the same principles as Mr Smith's somewhat rough plan. The following observations may be made upon studying the chart.

(*a*) The main functional areas are identified as follows:

Company secretarial
Purchasing
Production
Marketing
Accounting
Personnel
Office services

With the exception of the Company Secretary, the head of each main function is directly accountable to the General Manager. The Company Secretary is not directly engaged in the operational activities of the company. He is secretary to the directors and is involved in specialist duties. He is therefore accountable to the board and not to the General Manager.

(*b*) The General Manager (who may be known as the Managing Director if he is a member of the board) is the chief executive officer of the company. He is in charge of the whole administration area and provides the link between the board and the staff in respect of the work processes. Policy is decided and objectives are set by the directors. It is the duty of the General Manager to put into effect the decisions of the board by passing instructions to the function heads and coordinating their activities.

(*c*) Each function area is divided into subfunction areas, the latter being those most logically related to the former. In this respect there can be said to be **functional organisation** in that the whole is divided into broad areas of specialisation which are supported by subsidiary specialisms. For example, the Chief Accountant has various types of expertise available to him.

(*d*) The hierarchical structure is apparent, showing the immediate and ultimate superiors and subordinates. The vertical relationships indicate what is known as **line organisation**. A more indicative title may be 'military organisation' in that it appears to be similar to the strict stage-by-stage relationship between private, corporal, sergeant, etc. In practice, the rigidity is tempered by allowing complaints, etc., to travel along more expeditious routes, but the

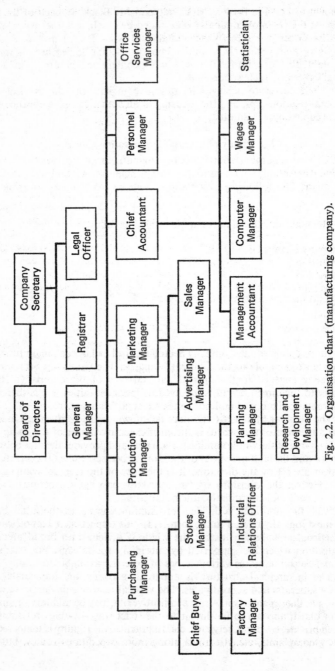

Fig. 2.2. Organisation chart (manufacturing company).

system has the advantage of clearly identifying the chain of command and facilitating the delegating of authority.

(*e*) The functions actively engaged in trading are:

Purchasing
Production
Marketing

These three must work closely together as they constitute the 'front-line troops'. They are supported by the following functions:

Accounting
Personnel
Office Services

These are not directly engaged in trading but they provide services to the others. Although each is a self-contained unit, they all offer essential facilities to the whole undertaking. They are therefore often referred to as **staff** in that they provide specialist support (*staff.* stick or pole as support—OED). Within each of these groups there is, of course, a line structure because of the essential element of delegation. There is also a functional structure as is shown by the specialist departments under the Chief Accountant.

It is for these reasons that the structure of a large company, as shown in Fig. 2.2, is usually **line and staff organisation.**

2.4 Inadequacies of a Large Organisation Chart

It is necessary to reiterate that an organisation chart can only be an attempt to delineate the realities of responsibilities and relationships. An examination of Fig. 2.2. will indicate the following inadequacies of the method:

(*a*) It indicates only the heads of the function areas; there is no identification of their subordinates. The justification for this is obvious. If every employee was to be named and given a place in the structure the complexities of the chart would reach ridiculous proportions. If it was thought necessary to give such detail it could be done only by drafting a chart for each department.

(*b*) The chart does not record the full functional responsibilities relevant to each post. It shows the *position* of the Marketing Manager, for example, but does not state exactly what his duties and powers are. This can be achieved by specifying them elsewhere (see Section 5.11).

(*c*) In practice, the authority and responsibilities of a staff officer will often go beyond the confines shown on the chart. A staff officer's facilities are available throughout the undertaking and this must mean that his responsibility and authority is wider than indicated. For example, the Office Services Manager would be responsible for, among other matters, supplying office equipment. If the Chief Accountant asked for, say, a new typewriter, a decision that he could not have it will be made by the Office Services Manager. This might be because he is limited by his budget but, whatever the reason, he has in this instance authority over an officer who would be senior to him.

(*d*) The chart does not show the coordinating relationships between function areas. The obvious example is that production could not commence until there had been consultation between the Production Manager and, at the least, the heads of the purchasing and marketing functions.

(e) Any structure requires to have channels of communication. These are not set out in the chart because of the complexity which obviously would result. *Separate* procedure plans would be required, such as those relevant to budgeting operations, committee schedules, staff reports, etc.

2.5 The Value of Organisation Charts

Having considered the inadequacies of organisation charts, it may be thought there is some doubt that they have any value at all. Many managers tend to have this opinion, but a balanced evaluation of their worth to a particular undertaking must take account of the following factors:

(a) A chart can provide only an historical record. It shows the position as it was when the chart was drafted. Organisations change and often a chart soon becomes outdated. In this respect one must also take account of the time and money spent in compiling a chart. It can be a lengthy operation and it may be considered that the cost of providing a record of something which may now be in the past is unjustified.

(b) If a chart is reasonably up to date it can be examined to identify anomalies and contributions to inefficiency. If a large-scale reorganisation is contemplated then certainly one must start with a diagrammatic presentation of the current structure.

(c) In any business activity there will be relationships which cannot be shown on a chart. Such relationships are legitimate and come into being when normal working indicates their logicality. They cannot be portrayed because of their complexity and the fact that many such relationships are transitory.

(d) A chart can be useful to show a new employee a broad outline of the composition of the undertaking.

(e) A chart can contribute to a rigidity of outlook by the staff. The placing of people in neat 'boxes' can induce a too-conscious recognition of boundaries. Staff may interpret the chart narrowly and become involved in wasteful disputes about demarcation lines. To the extent it does not damage discipline, some flexibility in interpreting spheres of activity should not be discouraged.

(f) Fixing the position of people on vertical lines can lead to problems with those who are 'status conscious'. The determining of relative positions means committing comparisons to paper and can result in unfortunate human reactions.

It is also common for staff to misinterpret the significance of vertical positions on a chart. Fig. 2.2 shows the Office Services Manager on the same level as the Chief Accountant. The latter would be very much senior to the former; all the chart intends to show is that both officers are directly answerable to the General Manager. Other areas of possible misinterpretation are apparent.

The net result of some of these considerations is that many companies deliberately refrain from publishing organisation charts to the staff. Charts can be of assistance to management, however. A chart which shows the staff composition by departments can be useful in determining staff allocations, promotions, etc. If the grades of staff and the particular expertise contained in a department were charted it would facilitate the attainment of a more balanced staff structure.

2.6 Detailed Organisation Charts

The lack of detail which must be a feature of a 'total' chart has been discussed above. More information can be provided if a smaller area is analysed.

Fig. 2.3 shows a chart relevant to a major function. This particular Company

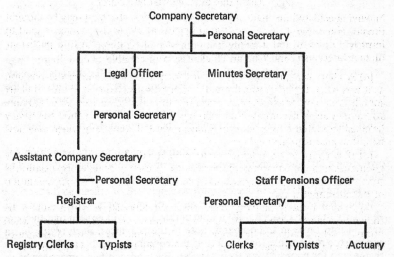

Fig. 2.3. Organisation chart (company secretarial function).

Secretary has overall responsibility for legal matters and staff pensions and is directly responsible for the statutory duties of such an officer.

Fig. 2.4 shows the organisational structure of a department, indicating the gradings composition of the staff.

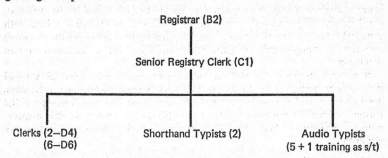

Fig. 2.4. Organisation chart of a department, showing numbers of staff by grades.

2.7 Charting Specific to Industries

The style and content of organisation charts will differ between different types of undertakings. The chart shown in Fig. 2.2 illustrates the distinctive features of a manufacturing company—that is, the buying of raw materials and components, the converting of them into marketable products and the selling of the finished goods. Such a structure may be compared with those relevant to other forms of business activity, such as those discussed below.

2.8 Charting a Servicing Unit

Fig. 2.5 shows the organisation chart of a company which is a *servicing* business. Firms classed as service industries are those which are not engaged in buying and selling, but which obtain their income from fees earned by providing services. The example is that of a staff employment agency, engaged in providing office staff (mainly 'temporary' typists) for its clients. The basis of such a business must be an efficient system capable of handling a large volume of small transactions with the minimum of delay. It demands sophisticated systematisation to facilitate the recording of personal details and the movement of staff. An essential feature is efficient communication to provide fast links, not only with clients and staff but also between offices, so that, where necessary, enquiries can quickly be switched from one office to another.

The success of such a business therefore depends upon its reputation for providing a fast and efficient service and the organisation must be designed to that end.

A feature of this type of agency must be a network of offices, so that service can be provided within reasonable reach of employers. For the sake of simplicity the chart does not list all the offices, but it will be seen that they are divided into those in London and those in the provinces. Each region has a supervisor, responsible for overseeing the running of each branch within a region and for coordinating their services. Each branch has a manageress.

It will thus be seen that the emphasis of the organisation is the provision of services through the branches. The Offices Manager has overall responsibility for this most important of areas. He is accountable directly to the General Manager and is that person's most senior officer. This area of activity also has the support of a Servicing Manager. His function is to attend to the physical aspects of the offices. He is in charge of converting newly acquired premises, the decorating and furnishing of them, the provision of equipment, etc. It is essential that the 'shop window' be attractive and patently efficient, and this accounts for the importance of this post.

All the other functions are supporting ones. The accounting area includes one department responsible for calculating salaries and another for collecting fees from clients. Because of the number of employment transactions, many of them for short periods, and the complexities of income tax and insurance, a sophisticated system is essential.

The presenting of a 'good image' to the outside world is very necessary and this is part of the duties of the Promotions Manager. Heavy Press advertising is a feature of such a business and is the responsibility of a department subsidiary to the Promotions Department. The Promotions Manager is required to 'sell' the business by visiting prospective clients and, with the assistance of the Advertising Manager, plan mailing shots and other forms of publicity. An important part of his work is to investigate complaints by clients and attempt to repair any damage to the company's reputation.

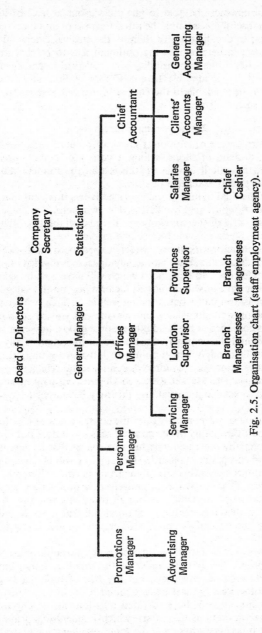

Fig. 2.5. Organisation chart (staff employment agency).

Such a business must be able to analyse various aspects of its activities. This would be useful in assessing the attractiveness of an office in one area as against others; in deciding where there is the strongest demand for certain types of worker; in determining the optimum fees to be charged, etc. This important function is the responsibility of a Statistical Department. Although the department is accountable to the Company Secretary, the service it provides would be available to the Offices Manager because he is the person who requires such analyses.

2.9 Charting a Retail Chain

Fig. 2.6 illustrates the organisation chart of a retailing undertaking. The company has a chain of shops, selling a variety of goods purchased from manufacturers. Essentially, therefore, this is a buying and selling business and the form of its structure reflects this.

Because of the dual nature of the firm's activities it is vital that the buying and selling functions are highly efficient. The two factors which determine the success or otherwise of the company are the marketability of the goods and the differences between buying and selling prices.

The buying therefore requires a widely experienced staff. Because of the expertise needed it will be seen that the buying team is divided into specialists. The general objective is to buy goods which will have a ready sale and therefore the buying pattern will be largely determined by the sales force. Each store manager is aware of what is selling well in his area (which may include goods not selling well elsewhere) and his analysis will be supported by the sales statistics compiled at the head office. Some goods, however, have a short popularity life and the company must be quick to recognise any irreversible 'tailing off' in demand. When it comes to introducing untried products an element of uncertainty is encountered. Again, some reliance upon the sales force is necessary. The Market Research Department may make a survey in an attempt to assess the potential and this may be supported by some form of promotion.

The reputation of the company (and the consequent size of sales) is largely dependent upon the quality of the goods it sells. As it does not produce those goods, the company must take measures to ensure that its suppliers provide products of an acceptable standard. The company will be buying most goods in large quantities and is therefore in a strong position to impose conditions on its suppliers. It is usual for an entirely new product to be subjected to appropriate tests by the retailer before an order is given and to make later tests to ensure that the quality is maintained. The responsibility for this would belong to the Chief Technical Officer, who would be provided with the requisite facilities.

The selling price which would be acceptable to the public must be measured against the price paid by the retailer to the supplier. Large buying orders would provide reduced unit costs, but the risk of ordering large amounts which may not sell easily must be recognised.

The example shows 16 shops, divided into four areas. The extent of the shops and the varying buying pattern which frequently appears in different regions make it necessary to divide the total retailing area. Overall, however, there are commonly accepted selling policies. The data and opinions for

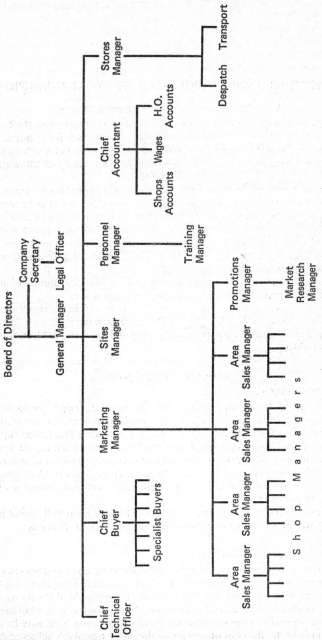

Fig. 2.6. Organisation chart (chain of retail shops).

forming these flow back from the shop managers via the area managers to the Marketing Manager.

The Sites Manager is responsible for the decorating and equipping of the shops, bearing in mind that most chains adopt a uniform and recognisable style. The replanning and conversion of shops are also among his duties.

The company requires to have a highly efficient system for receiving goods from its suppliers. The general aim is for goods to be in store for the least possible length of time. Sophisticated methods are therefore required for recording shop requirements, for 'breaking down' the incoming goods into loads for the shops, for their despatch, for quickly compiling complex and extensive records, and for maintaining and operating a fleet of delivery vehicles. Almost certainly, all this would be facilitated by computerisation.

Because of the number of staff there is a large Personnel Department. As part of that team, the Training Officer is responsible for all forms of training, from induction programmes to management training schemes.

Key Points

1. An **organisation chart** shows an *existing* situation but it *can* be used in order to devise a new structure.

   It cannot show the *realities* of human relationships.

   It can rarely be up to date.

   If it is *published* it can lead to demarcation disputes and a rigidity of outlook.

   Two names on the same horizontal line does *not* indicate equality of seniority.

   It will be impracticable if it is *insufficiently* detailed or *too* detailed.

2. **Functional** organisation shows the areas of *function specialisation*.

   Line organisation is *strictly vertical*.

   Staff organisation relates to specialist *support*.

3. The *types* of departments and their *relative importance* vary according to the type of business.

3

FUNCTIONS SPECIFIC TO THE MANUFACTURING AREA

3.1 Coordination in Production Planning

The types and quantities of goods to be manufactured are determined by the extent of orders or of anticipated orders. When the demand is in the form of a special order from a customer there is no uncertainty; it is then merely necessary to ensure that production costs are below the quoted price. In other instances, however, production must be based on estimates made in the Marketing Department of the extent of sales. Where the same types of goods are sold regularly in an established market, the requirement is to produce at a rate equal to normal demand and to ensure that sufficient goods are held in stock to provide a 'buffer' against any fluctuations in normal demand. Where the demand is not so assured, however, there exist the alternative dangers of having large stocks in store when demand is less than expected or being unable to meet an unexpectedly high demand.

In planning production there must therefore be close coordination between the Production Planning Department, the Marketing Department and the Stores. Each must be constantly aware of the current and anticipated situations of the others.

The Marketing Department will provide figures of regularly-selling goods expected to be required within a certain period, taking account of those already in stock, or it may accept a special order. The feasibility of those figures will, however, depend upon the ability of the Production Department to produce that number of goods in the time required. If production is already so committed to earlier orders as to be unable to meet the new demand, the Marketing Department cannot fulfil orders it has or anticipates. Similarly, the Stores may be short of some stock and then discover that it is not possible to replenish from production.

Unless there is a constant interchange of information between the three areas a serious imbalance between supply and demand may result. In a situation contrary to the example given above, the Marketing Department and the Stores may be unaware that currently the Production Department has spare capacity. Knowledge of that fact would have allowed the Marketing Department to make attempts to increase sales so as to keep the Production Department fully employed. An even more serious situation would be one where the demand for goods was not being fully met because the Marketing Department did not know that production could be increased. If the Stores was cognizant of the production situation, it could have taken the opportunity to 'stock-pile' when circumstances made such an action reasonable.

The requirement is to not merely know the *current* situation in each department. It is necessary that future production commitments, anticipated sales and expected demands for stock be known to all so that forward planning can be coordinated.

21

The problem is complicated by the time required to produce goods; products cannot be made immediately available for sale except from stock. Also, except in the case of special orders, all calculations are based on *estimates* of the demand. There may be an over- or under-estimation of sales; the demand for *types* of products may change; costs and competing selling prices may alter after the calculations are made.

A further factor which may upset plans is that raw materials (and, possibly, components) have to be ordered. Production cannot commence until these are available and, consequently, an allowance must be made for the time required for delivery. There is also the possibility that there may be difficulty in obtaining some of the supplies. As a result of these complications, the Purchasing Department is added to the other three departments which must work in close collaboration.

The total requirement, therefore, is for **constant flows of information** between all the departments and **coordinated planning**. Any one department not acting in concert with the others will result in failure of the whole

There are circumstances in which the problems of aligning supply and demand are easier to solve. For example, where sales are on a regular basis (as they would be when standard goods are supplied to well-established markets), purchasing will be a continuous, almost routine, procedure, in the same way that the goods flow out at a steady pace. In such circumstances, the only problem would be the necessity to adjust the rate of purchasing, producing and storing to accord with any variation in sales. Where the variation is due to seasonal demand for the goods (such as, for example, ice-cream), such changes can be forecast to a large extent and plans to cope with them can be made in advance. (There may, of course, be fluctuations within the seasonal variation—for example, bad summer weather affects the sale of ice-cream.) If the *product* is seasonal, planning can take account of that fact. Thus, fruit and vegetable canning must operate within a fairly predictable timetable.

3.2   The Production Process

The necessary stages in a production programme are outlined in Fig. 3.1. As mentioned above, the impetus will derive from a special order placed by a customer, from the Marketing Department or from Stores.

The particulars will be passed to the Production Planning Department which will decide how the goods are to be produced. Except in the case of a special order, the techniques will already have been established, but calculations must be made to facilitate integration of the required processing into manufacturing which is already in hand. The availability of the necessary manpower and plant, the time required for delivery of materials and many other factors must be taken into account. Having done this, it will be possible to state a delivery date for a special order. In other instances, the Stores or Marketing Department will know when the goods will be available and they can make forward plans accordingly.

The Purchasing Department will be instructed to obtain the requisite materials and components, and the Production Department will be told the methods to be used when supplies arrive.

On completion of the production process the goods will be passed to the Finished Goods Store and then delivered.

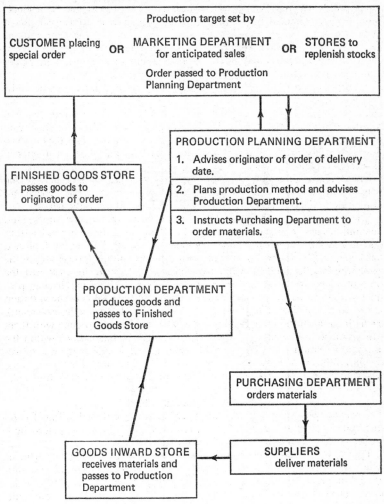

Fig. 3.1. The production process.

3.3 Areas in the Production Function

As with any other form of organisation, it is necessary to divide the total of the production activities into main fundamental areas and to group related specialisms within each area. Before making a study of the objectives and activities of each department it is necessary to note the logicality of such groupings and their integrated contribution to the production process. Fig. 3.2 shows the functions which are brought into operation after the decision to produce has been made.

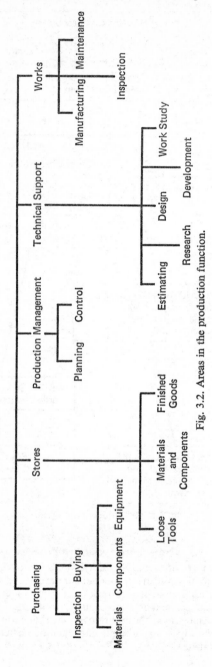

Fig. 3.2. Areas in the production function.

3.4 Production Management

This major area is concerned with all the planning and processing necessary to meet production targets, and to that end uses various management techniques. As mentioned above, the Production Planning Department will determine how the manufacturing is to be organised and what delivery dates can be promised. In so doing, management establishes targets, with the result that in addition to planning it also has the responsibility of ensuring the targets are met.

(*a*) Targets and standards will be set for every stage of the processing, so that a system of continuous control exists. This dual function of **planning and control** means that throughout the process the level of performance must be measured against the set targets. These will be on a *time basis* so that specific stages are completed within the established periods, and on a *quantity basis* so that output equals the budgeted figure. To facilitate this there must be systems which provide performance data as a basis for comparisons with targets. Checks can be made on the factory floor by 'progress chasers' who can take any available action to remedy a situation where failure to meet the objective appears likely. These 'trouble shooters' may be required to deal with such matters as machine malfunction, delays in receiving supplies or tools, staff shortages, etc.

Management will be required to deal with other causes of falling performance. If the fault cannot be quickly remedied it will have to rearrange the total work pattern. This may mean giving priority to some orders over others; arranging for overtime to be worked; contracting out some of the work; transferring work from one machine to another, etc.

(*b*) Although the purchasing and manpower functions are the responsibility of specific departments, production management has overall responsibility for ensuring that supplies are received in time to go into production and that the requisite amounts and types of labour are available. It must also ensure that the necessary plant and tools are provided and adequately maintained.

(*c*) There must also be a firm control on *quality*. This covers several stages, each requiring its own form of inspection. First, all materials and components to be used in production must be examined to ensure they are of the required standard. Tests must also be made during the work process, so that any failure to achieve the required standard is identified at the earliest possible stage. Finally, the finished goods must be examined for quality. This examination may be functional (such as running a domestic appliance or carrying out a circuit test) and/or visual (such as looking for blemishes).

3.5 The Purchasing Department

It will be seen in Fig. 3.2 that the Purchasing Department is responsible for providing the 'ingredients' required in production—that is, raw materials which are to be converted and, where relevant, components which are to be assembled. A section of the department would be charged with obtaining equipment and materials not be to absorbed into production, such as tools, fuel, cleaning material, etc.

Market intelligence. The broad objectives of a Purchasing Department are to ensure that the requisite items are available when needed and to buy at the most economical prices. Both requirements make it necessary to have an intimate knowledge of the supply market. There must be intelligence allowing the department to be aware of future shortages and price changes, of new techniques relevant to the products, of the availability of 'bargains', etc. In a large undertaking there must therefore be a degree of specialisation between buyers because no one buyer would have expert knowledge about every type of supply.

The department must be knowledgeable about the reputation of suppliers in respect of quality, prices and delivery. To this end the department will keep records of the performance of all those it has dealt with, and this would be supported by a library of specifications and price lists issued by suppliers. All this information must be made available to the Production Planning Department when production schedules are being drafted because of the effect it will have on costs and the length of time within which production can be completed.

Records. There must be an efficient system for recording all the activities of the department. An example of this aspect is given in Chapter 8.

Price. The department should aim to buy supplies at the lowest available price, provided this advantage is not lost by poor quality or unreliability of promises about delivery dates. Bulk buying usually results in a reduction of unit cost and the advantage of buying more than is immediately required must be set against the cost (and possible risk) of storing an unusually large amount.

In establishing the price to be paid, the department may, in the case of large orders or the purchase of a special item (such as a machine), invite suppliers to submit **tenders**. Another method is to buy under **contract**, whereby the purchaser agrees to accept a certain quantity over a period (e.g. fuel oil for a year) at a fixed price. The buyer is thereby assured of supplies and the price is fixed. **Spot** purchases are those made at the point of sale, such as buying a machine at a showroom or ordering cleaning materials from a visiting salesman. If the manufacturer buys commodities, they may be in a market where the tradition is to deal in **futures**. Tea, coffee, cocoa, etc., are bought at fixed prices on the understanding that delivery will be made at a future date. The system is speculative, particularly as the price is frequently fixed before the amount and quality of the crop is known.

3.6　The Stores

It is well noted from Fig. 3.2 that there are three types of store, each fulfilling a different function. Materials and components enter via the Goods Inward Store and the completed products leave via the Finished Goods Store, as shown in Fig. 3.1 and Fig. 3.3. In both cases, therefore, storage is transitory, the goods either awaiting processing or despatching. The waiting period must be as short as possible because of the expense of storage.

The official in charge of the Goods Inward Store has the responsibility of ensuring that the amount of stock is the *safe* minimum. Levels must not be so reduced as to result in a shortage and, accordingly, he will require to know the future requirements of production. In his calculations, he must also take account of the time it will take to obtain further supplies. The operation therefore requires fine judgment and sophisticated control methods. Motor vehicle manufacturers, for example, have the general objective that all components are used in production within 24 hours of being received from the suppliers. Consequently, the Stores manager must maintain records which will immediately indicate the amount of each item in stock, the amount awaiting delivery and future requirements. There must also be procedures for receiving items and issuing them. These operational aspects are considered in Chapter 8.

Special orders will, of course, be passed from the Finished Goods Store to the buyer immediately, but the length of stay of goods for general sale will depend on the strength of immediate demand. Again, the principle previously stated concerning cooperation between departments is vital. An imbalance between sales and the amount held in stock will result in either a loss of sales or expensive stock-piling.

Such principles do not apply to the Loose Tools Store, which contains equipment used in production. There must also be facilities for storing such items as fuel oil, lubricants, cleaning materials, etc.

A further responsibility of the storekeeper is to preserve those items which are in stock. They must be stored in such an appropriate manner as to protect them against heat, cold, damp, etc; suitable equipment must be available to prevent damage in handling; certain items must be inspected regularly for signs of deterioration. Security measures are essential to prevent theft and to reduce opportunities for pilfering by staff.

3.7 Technical Support

We have seen that the areas responsible for producing, purchasing, marketing and storing must work in close coordination and that the executives in charge of them have defined duties. A study of those supporting functions which are specific to the manufacturing area can now be made. (Those supporting functions which are relevant to the marketing aspect are referred to in Chapter 4 and those which are applicable to business generally are discussed in Chapter 5.)

Estimating. The function of an Estimating Department is to calculate the cost of making a product as a basis for fixing the selling price or for submitting a tender. If the product is one which has been made before or is a regularly selling one, the cost can be based on historical figures, allowance being made for any changes in costs. If the product is new, the estimators must calculate the cost of the materials (based on the amounts of materials forecast by the Design Department), the cost of the labour involved (as estimated by the Production Planning Department), and the amount to be included for overheads (as set by the Costing Department). To these costs will be added the profit required. The composition of the price will therefore be as follows.

> Direct labour
> Direct materials
> Production overheads
> ──────────────
> *Factory cost*

Administration overheads
Profit margin

Price

═══════════════

Allowance will be made for the fact that above a certain quantity of units produced, the cost per unit will fall.

Design. If a company manufactures articles, then it has the responsibility of designing them (except where an order includes the buyer's design). The designer is faced with the problem of reconciling objectives which often conflict. For example, a functioning object (such as a domestic appliance) must, obviously, operate efficiently. As a technician, the designer would prefer to include refinements so as to ensure operating perfection, but to do so may make it so costly to produce as to result in a price unacceptable to buyers. The inclusion of such refinements may also make the production method unduly complicated and so result in much spoiled work.

Against this, the designer must recognise that a domestic appliance, to take the same example, may be subject to a degree of abuse by the buyer. The user may not necessarily treat the machine with the same respect a technician would and therefore the design must aim for a high level of durability. The problem would be the extent to which the design should allow such protection to increase costs.

There are other reasons for not planning for a very high degree of durability. The longer an article lasts the fewer the replacements which will be required. Thus, most articles are designed to have a limited life span—that is, they have a **built-in obsolescence**. Such a principle also benefits the consumer because it reduces the cost of the article. A buyer is satisfied if an article provides a service which is commensurate with its cost, an extreme example being 'throw-away pens'. Also, if a buyer has an article which refuses to wear out (and he has paid highly for that 'advantage') he may eventually own something which is unfashionable and which, practical though it still is, does not have recent refinements. An obvious example is a motorcar.

The appearance of a product can have a very important bearing on its marketability. The sales of even such a practical article as a typewriter will be largely influenced by its styling. For some products, such as lipsticks and even some low-priced furniture, appearance is the major influence on customer-acceptance.

The consequences of error in design are serious. Losses can ensue if production costs are higher than estimated; the price may be beyond what the public will pay; complaints may be received of malfunction or lack of durability; or the public may reject the design.

Research and development. Because of the nature of their products, some companies must engage in research. Pharmaceutical companies have extensive laboratories but facilities are necessary for *any* business which has to search constantly for new or improved products and better methods of production.

It has to be accepted that much money may be spent on research which shows no return. Research means finding out if something is feasible and the answer may be affirmative or negative, but only by spending money can one discover that something *cannot* be done. The financial justification is that the gains resulting from successful research must compensate for the cost of unsuccessful research.

Some research, successful or unsuccessful, results in discoveries which are not those that were sought. Some incidental knowledge may be gained in pursuing an investigation and this is sometimes known as 'spin-off'.

Research may establish that a certain idea has practical application. The fact that something 'works' does not, however, necessarily mean it is commercially viable. It is known, for example, that electric light bulbs can be made so that they have a very long life, but the manufacturers claim that the selling price of such bulbs would be prohibitive. Cars can be made to run on batteries instead of petrol but the operational difficulties arising from the limited life of batteries and the technical problems caused by their weight are daunting.

If research does indicate the possibility of commercial viability then the investigation continues to the **development** stage. This would aim to identify any manufacturing problems by producing the article in normal factory conditions. This would also enable the cost of manufacture to be ascertained. It would then be necessary to test the *application* of the product by using it in conditions similar to those which would apply in the market. This would identify the efficiency and durability of the articles in normal usage. If the product is intended to be sold generally (e.g. a new soap powder), it may be introduced to a limited market in order to assess the public's response.

3.8 Location of Departments

Those departments directly engaged in the production process must be arranged in such a way that the items being handled travel in a continuously forward direction and that the distance between each stage is as short as possible.

This principle is demonstrated in Fig. 3.3. It will be seen that incoming materials are first inspected for quality. Some then go directly into the main production line and proceed through the whole process. Other materials are used to make parts which, after inspection, are placed in store until required. It will be seen that Part A joins the main production line at the fourth stage and Part B at the sixth stage.

In-work inspection takes place at the third, fifth and seventh stages and the completed product is subjected to a final inspection.

Key Points

1. The **amount to be produced** is influenced by:

    (*a*) anticipated sales and the stock in hand;
    (*b*) the availability of production facilities;
    (*c*) seasonal fluctuations;
    (*d*) any necessity to have a 'buffer stock'.

2. If increased sales are anticipated the answers to the following questions should be *already available:*

    (*a*) Marketing to Production—at what rate can you produce?
    (*b*) Marketing to Stores—what stocks have you of finished goods?
    (*c*) Purchasing to Production—at what rate are you consuming materials?

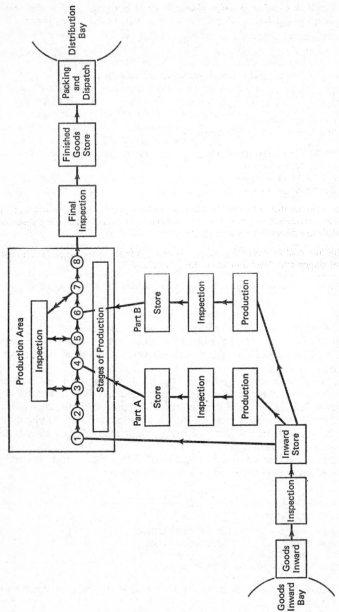

Fig. 3.3 Location of production departments.

(*d*) Purchasing to Stores—what materials are in stock?

(*e*) Stores to Purchasing—how long will it take to get further supplies?

3. **Production planning** involves integration of functions.

Targets must be set for stages of production; against these must be measured *performance*; *corrective action* must be taken if there are deviations.

There must be control of *quantity*, *quality* and *time spent*.

4. Efficient **purchasing** requires:

(*a*) knowledge of the market;

(*b*) economical buying;

(*c*) firm control on delivery dates.

5. Economical **storage** requires that

(*a*) demands can be met;

(*b*) not too much is stored;

(*c*) stock must be protected.

6. **Design** often involves a conflict between production cost, production method and aesthetic considerations. Once a design has been agreed the producer is committed, so that *design errors* can be very costly.

7. Usually, the cost of **research** cannot be exactly related to the benefits. The subsequent stages are: development; testing; production.

4

FUNCTIONS SPECIFIC TO THE MARKETING AREA

4.1 Incidence of Marketing Activity

In the previous chapter it was explained that the derivative of production was orders received by means of the marketing function. Marketing exists, however, at every link in the chain by which finished goods reach the ultimate buyers. Fig. 4.1 illustrates this concept and may be explained as follows:

(*a*) The producers of raw materials supply them to the manufacturers of final products. Other manufacturers produce components for assembly by final manufacturers and in turn obtain their supplies from the providers of raw materials. In each of the three transactions there is marketing activity.

(*b*) Manufacturers of final products may sell direct to the public, as is the case with mail order business. The same link exists when a product is made for a buyer's special order. They may sell to wholesalers, who then sell to retailers, who, in turn, sell to the ultimate consumers. Because of the decline in wholesaling as a separate activity in recent years, however, they are more likely to sell direct to retailers for onward sale to the ultimate consumers. Again, at every stage there will be marketing activity.

It will thus be seen that every line in the chart represents the incidence of marketing activity. This must therefore be a part of every trading business but, obviously, its importance and its methods will vary between different types of trader. For example, the marketing activities of a company which leases

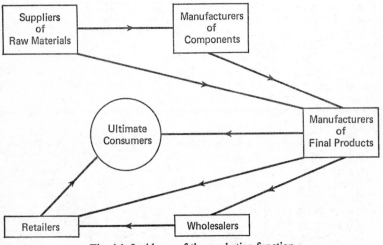

Fig. 4.1. Incidence of the marketing function.

earth-moving equipment to road builders would be largely confined to increasing its business by personal contact. The number of possible users would not be large but each contract would be a sizeable one. At the other extreme, a manufacturer of household detergents would be aiming to sell to a considerable number of people and each sale would be a minor transaction. Its marketing methods would therefore include most of those generally available *except* personal contact with the ultimate buyers. A further aspect is that although the manufacturer has a direct link with wholesalers and retailers and must sell to them as his outlets, the promotion of his product is directed at the buying public. His marketing therefore operates on two separate planes.

4.2 The Marketing Department

The titles of departments vary between businesses, but it can be accepted that the responsibilities of what may be generally called the Marketing Department differ from those of what is usually known as the *Sales* Department. The latter is concerned with actual selling and as such constitutes part of the total functional area of the former. The responsibilities of the Marketing Department include the following:

(*a*) It will assist the directors to determine marketing policy, and will provide expert advice and statistics to facilitate the making of relevant decisions. **Marketing policy** means the determination of the most advantageous methods of using a firm's resources in order to increase profits from sales. It must be decided *what* to sell and *in what markets*. It may be decided, for instance, to increase sales of an already popular item or to make efforts to increase sales of another which is not selling well. A decision may be made to introduce a new item. It may be the board's opinion that a market may be changed or a new one added. For example, if an item is selling in an 'exclusive' market it may be decided to go 'down market' by selling it in mass outlets.

Any decision to change must be based on forecasts of its effectiveness and the consequences. The amount of existing or possible competition must be considered; the methods of distribution may have to be altered if the market is changed; different methods of promotion may be required; the amount of production, and perhaps its methods, may have to be altered.

(*b*) The marketing policy having been determined, the Department then has the responsibility of implementing it. This must be done within any financial constraints imposed by the board and related to targets which have been set. The carrying out of this responsibility requires the department to do the following:

(*i*) If the company is a manufacturer there must be liaison with the Production Planning Department so that the plans agreed to in respect of the amounts and types of product to be made are coordinated with the sales programme. If the company buys the goods it sells, close cooperation with the suppliers is necessary. There must be continuous interchange of information to facilitate any alteration of plan which circumstances may dictate.

(*ii*) The plans to promote sales would be finalised and put into effect.

(*iii*) There would be consultation with the Sales Department about the marketing policy so that the staff would be able to work to any new objectives. The sales staff would be made aware of any new strategy which is to be used. It would also be fully informed of any change in the products they are to sell so that they may be knowledgeable when talking to customers.

(*iv*) The progress of the sales programme would be continuously monitored. Derived information would be passed to the board from time to time in case circumstances indicated the necessity to amend the marketing policy.

(*c*) Additionally, the Department will have continuous responsibility for the following.

(*i*) To carry out market research.
(*ii*) To prepare sales budgets.
(*iii*) To control personnel engaged in selling, clerical duties and store-keeping.
(*iv*) To oversee all aspects of warehousing, distributing and transporting.

4.3 Components of the Marketing Function

Fig. 4.2 shows the elements usually contained in the marketing function. These are considered individually later in the chapter but at this stage the broad divisions can be identified. The Sales Department obtains and processes

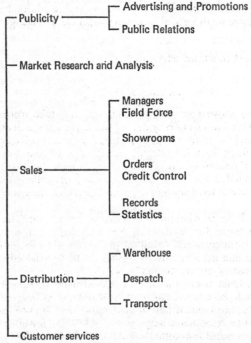

Fig. 4.2. Components of the marketing function.

orders, and maintains the requisite records. The functions *prior* to sales are those in the publicity and market research areas. The functions brought into existence *subsequent* to sales come under the headings of distribution and, where relevant, customer services.

4.4 Relationships of the Marketing Department

In fulfilling its responsibilities, the Department must work in relationship with other areas of the business.

(a) As previously stated, there must be close cooperation with production planning if the company manufactures the goods it sells. If it is a buyer of goods it sells then it must work closely with the Purchasing Department. There must be a regular flow of marketable goods and the purchasing staff must keep the marketing staff constantly informed of conditions in the supply market and pace its buying to that of selling.

(b) The sales section must work closely with the accounting department in respect of customers' accounts. All sections will be concerned with the implementing of budgeting policies and will have to provide such statistics as are called for.

(c) The clerical aspects of each section will bring it into contact with the Office Services Department and, possibly, the Organisation and Methods Department.

(d) The Personnel Department will be involved in all staff matters and therefore will have relationships with every aspect of the Marketing Department.

(Those support functions which exist in most businesses are discussed in Chapter 5.)

4.5 The Sales Force

Apart from any showroom staff, active selling will take place outside the premises. How the sales team is organised will depend upon the nature of the products sold and the number of sales outlets. A company selling consumables in constant demand to a lot of retail outlets (e.g. biscuits to grocers) will probably have a nation-wide market. Calls by salesmen will be numerous in fairly concentrated areas. This will require a large selling team and the division of the whole territory into areas and, possibly, their subdivision into branches.

This practice is not so widespread as it may at first appear. The major share of the grocery trade, for example, is taken by large companies operating supermarkets. In these cases, almost all the buying is done centrally so that there is a direct link between buyers and sellers on the respective head office staffs, with no selling on the shop premises.

When the product is not one in constant demand by numerous buyers, the structure will be entirely different. A company selling, say, technical equipment to factories would have a lesser concentration of customers, and salesmen would therefore have larger territories. The number of sales would be comparatively small but with a higher value of each sale. The salesmen would be technicians, able to speak to potential buyers in their own language.

Many of the sales would require periods of negotiation and perhaps demonstration before they are completed.

4.6   Organisation of the Sales Department

The head of the Sales Department would be a 'desk officer', controlling those in the field from his office. Where relevant, tiers of authority would extend downward through area and branch officers to salesmen operating in their territories. Where such a structure exists, control will follow the same pattern. Thus, targets will be set for areas which are then subdivided into branches, and, finally, there may be individual targets for salesmen. Policy will be communicated and implemented, and information fed back, through the same channels.

Such control requires the provision and analysis of data. As information is received, the office staff will process it. Figures will be required of the sales of each type of product and these will be analysed into area, branch and salesman achievement. Such information will serve as the basis for future market policies. Thus, a company marketing nation-wide would be able to detect the popularity of one product in a certain area as against its acceptance in others. Any weakness of one part of the sales force as compared with others could be identified.

There must be efficient procedures for dealing with orders. This requires systematised links with the Accounting Department, the Stores and the Despatch Department. (A demonstration of such procedures is given in Section 7.10.)

The department will be responsible for servicing the sales force so that it has the literature, equipment and facilities (such as cars) it requires. It will also be responsible for training the sales force, including the provision of 'refresher courses' within the company and, perhaps, arranging for staff to attend salesmanship courses provided externally.

Arrangements must be made for corresponding with customers who write directly to the department. It must do all possible to augment the goodwill built up by those staff working close to the customers.

4.7   Credit Control

Orders must not be gained regardless of cost. A customer who does not pay provides a company with a loss instead of a gain. There must therefore be measures to ensure this risk is reduced to the minimum.

It must first be accepted that almost all business is done on credit. There will therefore be a time allowed for payment of accounts, and that period will be the one generally prevailing in the particular type of business. A common discount rate for early settlement also operates in most businesses of a like nature.

A new customer will be required to establish his 'credit-worthiness' before being granted credit. This can be obtained from credit enquiry agencies and may be supported by references from a bank and from other traders.

Every customer is given a **credit rating**, showing the extent to which he may have credit. As his reputation with the company is built up that rating may be increased, so that a customer of proven reliability may be offered more credit if he requires it.

A vital aspect of credit control is close liaison with the department maintaining customer accounts. Undue slowness in paying will be apparent only in that department and it must pass a warning to the Sales Department immediately there are danger signs. If more sales are made to the customer in ignorance of the state of his account, the position will worsen. Of considerable value is the prompt despatch of customers' statements. A month-end statement not sent out until the middle of the following month loses impetus and the customer will probably put it aside until he gets the next month's batch from his more efficient creditors.

Management should establish and firmly apply a **bad debts policy**. This will prescribe the amount of latitude which may be given to debtors in the form of requests for payment. Where there is no response after a specified number of requests the matter should automatically be referred to the creditor's solicitors. This would provide the responsible officer with a clear authority (and duty) to act at the appointed stage. Such an attitude has a salutory effect on other debtors when they recognise the firm line being taken.

4.8 Publicity

Advertising is a specialist activity and would therefore be undertaken by advertising agents from outside the business. The Publicity Manager, operating within the marketing policy and financial constraints, will discuss plans with the agents. The final decision as to the methods and philosophy of the advertising will be made within the company, but because of the expertise of the agents it will be their views which will prevail. The reputation of an advertising agent depends upon the success of the plans he implements and a campaign that fails will probably result in his losing the 'account'. Consequently, the company should understand that an agent will refuse to embark on an advertising programme with which he fundamentally disagrees.

Sales promotion is a general term for any method of attempting to increase sales, but in practice is usually regarded as excluding advertising. It refers to such exercises as special offers, competitions and special displays. It is therefore confined to the domestic consumer market.

Public relations refers to activities designed to project a good public image. A large company may have its own department handling such matters but smaller concerns may use an agent. Whatever the practice, however, there should be an official *on the staff* who can personally deal with complaints and enquiries from the public and who can speak to the Press when necessary.

The work includes any activity which can improve the reputation of the company (and, in unfortunate circumstances, attempt to maintain it) and make the company's name more widely known. A department would be responsible for distributing literature about the company and its products to anyone requesting it; it could make information available even when it may not directly influence sales (e.g. a central heating company replying to a member of the public or the Press asking for technical information); Press releases can be made of newsworthy items favourable to the company; Press conferences can be held to launch new products; exhibitions can be held and entries made in trade fairs. Even the sponsoring of sporting events and concerts are forms of public relations, provided the name of the company is made prominent.

In recent years the public has become very sensitive about the damage which has been done to, and which still threatens, the environment. A company which even appears to be guilty in this respect can have its 'image' badly damaged. A business whose activities have a bearing on the environment must make every effort to show it is 'ecology conscious'. If a company has to defend its activities it may probably be too late to do so effectively. It must therefore promote recognition by the public that it has a genuine concern about such matters before the possibility of attack arises.

4.9 Market Research

It is pointless to try to sell goods which the public will not buy. This very obvious statement was not always recognised as being such, because in the past some producers paid little regard to what the public wanted. The general aim was to produce goods of acceptable quality at as low a cost as possible. This laudable principle (which still obtains) often ignored the fact that the particular product, or the form in which it was presented, was not what the public wanted. A company with such an attitude may be said to be **product-orientated**.

There is now general recognition that the customer is king; products must not necessarily be those which appeal to the manufacturer or which are the easiest to make, but those the public wants. For example, if the public shows a preference for an appliance which has 'gimmicks' that add little or nothing to its efficiency or an object in a particular colour, the manufacturer must design and produce accordingly, no matter what his views are. This attitude is known as being **customer-orientated**. Viable products can also include those the public can be *persuaded* to want, by means of advertising.

Investigation must therefore be made to attempt to assess the preferences of the public or the possibility of conditioning the public's attitude.

The first aim of market research is to discover if there is a potential market for a new product and, if there is, the probable extent of that market and the price the public would be prepared to pay. Setting up production of any new article is a very expensive operation and if subsequent events show that sales are poor because of inadequate public response the financial outlay will be wasted.

There must be further and continuous research after a product has been placed on the market to determine the public's opinion of it. Producers of established products may become complacent and then realise, too late, that public preference has changed (perhaps to a competitor) and that sales are falling rapidly. Also, without research a producer may miss the opportunity of *increasing* sales because he has misinterpreted the public's attitude. This is known as **consumer research** and entails determining the buying habits of the public (how often they shop; what size packets they buy, etc.) and their preferences and prejudices. For example, there is no additional benefit derived from using a toothpaste because it has coloured stripes or a detergent because it produces a lot of foam, but both factors influence sales. Research must identify such examples of bias (which is often unconscious) and direct production and advertising accordingly.

Such research can be carried out only by asking the public. To do this a standard list of questions is compiled, the answers are recorded, and the total of answers to each question is analysed. The questioning must, obviously, be widespread in order to get a representative average. The choice of day and place of questioning may also be important. For example, the opinions of few elderly shoppers will be available on a wet day; the social classes of shoppers may be affected by where the survey is made.

Other research may be internal and is generally known as **market analysis**. The company's own sales records will give some indication of the comparative popularity of its products, perhaps influenced by geographical location. 'Grass roots' reports by the sales force of its customers' attitudes would be very valuable. Official statistics and those provided by trade associations, etc., can provide information about distribution of age groups and income groups, the proportion of householders by geographical areas, spending patterns, etc.

Market research must be recognised as being an *aid* to management and that the major task of business is to produce and sell. No matter how expert the forecasting by the researchers was it will be of little avail unless management, having set targets based on the research, concentrates on achieving the objectives. If the research showed that the objectives were attainable then only exceptional circumstances could make it no longer so. A management which changes its plans after accepting the results of market research makes such research pointless. A 'dithering' attitude of constantly changing plans and losing sight of objectives indicates lack of corporate confidence and is conducive to failure.

4.10 Distribution

The responsibilities of the Marketing Department do not end until the goods are in the hands of the buyers. Although all the functions of distribution are within the province of specialists, overall responsibility rests with the controlling department.

The warehouse is the name usually given to the outward store. Where there is multiple distribution, such as applies when despatching goods to a large number of retail stores or when the company has many selling branches, there must be a sophisticated system for assembling goods into delivery loads.

The general principles concerning storage mentioned in the previous chapter are applicable.

Transport. Unless the company's transport requirements are small, it will use its own vehicles. This provides the advantages of not being dependent upon the reliability of contractors and of economy. It entails administration of the fleet operations, including the provision of maintenance facilities.

Scientific planning is necessary if deliveries are made frequently to many points in order to reduce the incidence of 'empty return' loads and part loads. Multiple deliveries must be so routed and timed as to avoid 'back-tracking' and duplication.

4.11 Customer Services

A company which ignores its customers after securing a sale damages its reputation and endangers further sales. There must be a department (often known as a **Customer Relations Department**) which can deal with any complaints or suggestions from buyers. The staff involved must exercise tact and, particularly when a customer is unreasonable, patience. If a complaint is unjustified it must be dealt with diplomatically—any attempt to 'score' over a customer must be strongly resisted. If a complaint is justified, then the company must admit it gracefully and make generous recompense.

Such a department plays a particularly important part if after-sales service is provided. Any undertaking to recondition or to provide new parts must be firmly adhered to. Bad after-sales service cannot cancel a sale which has already been made but future sales to that customer and those he acquaints of the incident will not be forthcoming.

Key Points

1. A **marketing policy** decides:

(a) *what* to sell		(a) market research
(b) *how* to sell		(b) competition
(c) *where* to sell	based on	(c) production capacity
(d) the *price*		(d) production cost

2. The **Marketing Department**

    (a) implements the marketing policy;
    (b) relates to Sales, Stores and Despatch Departments;
    (c) sets targets and compares with performances;
    (d) carries out consumer research;
    (e) controls publicity.

3. The **Sales Department**

    (a) is answerable to the Marketing Department;
    (b) controls and records sales;
    (c) services and trains the sales force;
    (d) exercises credit control by liaison with the Accounts Department.

4. A manufacturer must produce what the public wants at a price it is prepared to pay, irrespective of the manufacturer's views. This is known as being **customer-orientated** and can be contrasted with **product-orientated**.

    To determine buying attitudes requires **consumer research** and **market analysis**.

5. A company's **image** can be projected by *public relations* exercises, *advertising* and a *Customer Relations Department*.

5

SUPPORTING FUNCTIONS AND THE EXECUTIVE STRUCTURE

5.1 Introduction

A study having been made of those functions which are specific to certain undertakings, consideration may now be had of the other functions which exist in most firms and which operate as support groups. The division of activities into specialisms means that functional areas must have leaders, thereby creating an executive structure. The efficient working of this structure is largely influenced by the personal qualities of those comprising it.

5.2 The Accounting Departments

It is first necessary to distinguish between the two divisions of accounting. Briefly, **financial accounting** is concerned with recording transactions which have taken place. **Management accounting** functions as an aid to management and includes the elements of forecasting, analysis and control.

The Financial Accounting Department is required to maintain records of events of a financial nature *as they occur*. Accounts must be kept of all debtor and creditor transactions and of all money paid to or by the company. The payments of wages and salaries will also entail the allocating of sums due in respect of deductions for income tax and national insurance, and the transferring of amounts to staff pension funds, etc.

It is also required to make *periodic* recordings, such as the following:

(*a*) The **annual accounts** must be prepared in order to produce a profit and loss account and a balance sheet which is acceptable to the auditors. In the case of a company, these must be in the form and disclose the information prescribed in the Companies Acts. The accounts and specified statements must be filed with the Registrar of Companies and placed on file so as to be available for public inspection.

(*b*) Accounts must be prepared in a form acceptable to the Inland Revenue for the purpose of assessing corporation tax. At specified times, transfers must be made to the tax authorities of sums due by the company.

(*c*) From time to time the department must provide the board of directors with financial statements. These can take various forms, such as: totals of debtors and creditors; the amount of cash expected to be available in the ensuing period, allowing for anticipated income and expenditure; the valuation of investments held, etc. Some companies produce monthly 'final accounts'—that is, drafts of profit and loss accounts and balance sheets as they would appear if taken out at the month end.

(*d*) Asset valuations must be adjusted to allow for depreciation.

(*e*) Amounts must be transferred to and from reserves.

Financial accounting is therefore concerned with internal matters but much of its activities extend outside the business.

The **Chief Accountant** is invariably a senior member of the staff. His expertise is required not only within his department but must also be available to the board. Every activity of a business depends upon adequate finance and it is the accountant's responsibility to see that the firm is financially viable. He must not only ensure that records are compiled which accurately show the current and anticipated position but he must also be capable of advising the directors about financial strategy. He must therefore have a close relationship with the directors and frequently is a member of the board.

Management accounting, on the other hand, relates only to the internal affairs of the business. It analyses data and presents information and forecasts to the board to provide a basis for decision-making. Because of its concern with costs it was known as **cost accounting** but the above title is now in general use as being more indicative of its purpose as a management aid.

Operating systems of **budgetary control**, it sets standards of achievement and limits on spending for the various aspects of the business. Comparisons can be made to identify deviations from planned expenditure, economies can be effected and forecasts made.

Costing is a separate skill from financial accounting and each has its own place in administration.

The Cashier's Department is a subdivision of the Accounting Department. It is concerned with all transactions involving cash, such as small purchases, any wages paid in cash, and received cash. It is concerned to a larger extent with receipts and payments other than in cash, such as cheques, bank transfers, etc. Money received from debtors will be received by the Cashier Department, recorded and banked, and then the necessary information passed for another department to record in the debtors' accounts.

The extent to which the department makes payments will depend upon the company's practice. Large payments, such as for purchasing equipment or investments, would normally be made in the Accounting Department. All cheques drawn by the Cashier Department and all money it receives should therefore pass through a bank account which is used specifically for those purposes. A reconciliation between the bank's record and the department's would thereby be possible.

This department must work closely with the **Wages Department**. The latter calculates remuneration due to employees, based on data emanating from other areas. Salaries do not alter frequently but wages may change weekly because of the hours worked by each employee and any bonuses earned. The data for calculating wages will derive from the Works Department. Deductions will be made for income tax, insurance, etc. The resulting 'take home' pay will be notified to the Cashier Department which will then either draw cash from the bank or transfer the amounts through the banking system to the employees' bank accounts.

The auditors are not part of the staff. They are appointed by the company in general meeting in accordance with the requirements of law. Basically, the responsibility of the auditors is to the *shareholders*—not the company or the directors. The members have no legal right to see the company's books and as they delegate to the directors the authority to manage the company's affairs the auditors act as 'watchdogs'. The auditors are also required to ensure that the accounts have been properly prepared in accordance with the Companies Acts and to certify that in their opinion a 'true and fair' view is given. Only accountants with certain qualifications may act as auditors of public companies. Audited accounts are also required by the Inland Revenue.

A business may have **internal auditors** on its staff. These would carry out checks on various accounting aspects and would be particularly concerned with checking for defalcations by cashiers and any other persons handling cash.

5.3 The Personnel Department

A vital necessity for any sizeable business is an efficient Personnel Department. The responsibilities of the department, which is usually headed by a qualified officer, include the following:

(*a*) **Recruitment.** The required staff will be sought and interviews arranged. Recruitment will be planned as part of a policy which determines allocations of staff and which will be influenced by future requirements, promotions and retirements. The usual arrangement is that the head of the department which has a vacancy will specify the sort of person required. The Personnel Department's responsibility will be to make the necessary arrangements. The interviewers would be the departmental head concerned and, usually, a member of the Personnel Department. The choice of any other members of the interviewing team will depend upon the nature and importance of the post.

(*b*) **Training.** This is a specialised area and in a large firm would be the responsibility of a **Training and Education Officer**. The facilities provided can include induction training, whereby junior newcomers are 'introduced' to the business; technical training for the job; supervisory and management training; management and technical courses provided from outside the business.

(*c*) **Staff appraisal.** The department may administer a system whereby staff are regularly assessed. Such a scheme has a bearing on promotions and transfers of staff. The department's task would be to facilitate these operations within the company's personnel policy. Decisions about individuals would be made by the departmental heads concerned, subject to any overall policy.

(*d*) **Salary structures.** The department will advise on and implement policies concerning levels of remuneration.

(*e*) **Welfare.** The department will administer a section (which in a large concern would be headed by a **Welfare Officer**) providing facilities for the staff. These vary considerably between firms but often include medical facilities, opportunities for sport and recreation, social counsellors, transport to and from work, etc. Under this heading may be grouped any 'fringe benefits' such as pensions, assistance with house purchase, discounts on company products, etc. It may also be claimed that the term includes the provision of favourable working conditions and measures to protect the health and safety of the staff. In respect of these there is extensive legislation, which most employers regard as setting minimum standards.

(*f*) **Records.** The department is responsible for maintaining records of employees. As they contain personal information, such records must be regarded as being confidential so that security precautions are necessary. Statistics must be compiled for use by management and returns have to be made to Government departments from time to time.

All administration depends upon human activity and where there is staff discord there is inefficiency. The Personnel Department can make a major contribution to the creation of the required 'atmosphere' in a business, although it must be recognised that the ultimate factor is the personnel *policy* of the business.

5.4 The Labour Relations Officer

This officer may be said to be part of the personnel function but his services would be required only if the employer had a fairly large labour force. His duties generally relate to those employees who are not of managerial level and who are not office workers. His main concern is with industrial relations and he would be involved in negotiations with trade union officials in his capacity as a representative of the management. Where necessary, he would take part in dispute procedures.

5.5 The Office Services Manager

The duties of the person in charge of clerical functions vary considerably between firms, largely because of the different sizes of the undertakings. In a small business he may be known as the **Office Manager** and would combine the relevant duties of such a post with others. For example, an accountant may also be in charge of all office work.

In larger businesses, the position is recognised as being one demanding specialisation. The person concerned, supported by a specialist staff, would be responsible for clerical work generally. Each departmental manager would, however, control the clerical staff in his own department. The duties of an Office Services Manager are, therefore, to *advise and coordinate*. For example, the Sales Manager would be in charge of his own clerical staff and would plan their work, but the Office Services Manager, as a staff officer, would be able to provide specialist help and, where his authority allowed and the circumstances made necessary, give directions.

Clerical procedures and the relevant principles are dealt with in Section 2 of the book, but at this stage the scope of this officer's work can be summarised as follows:

(*a*) To advise departmental managers in the planning of work processes and the layout of offices, and to assist in the implementation of any new schemes.

(*b*) To advise on and supply office equipment.

(*c*) To advise on and supervise clerical training.

(*d*) To analyse office procedures and introduce new methods of working, including the integration of the procedures of more than one department.

(*e*) To standardise procedures, forms, stationery, etc.

(*f*) To provide and maintain general services, such as those relevant to the post, telephones, stationery and equipment supplies, and to provide central-ised services (where required) for typing, filing, duplicating, etc.

(*g*) To advise management on procedures and equipment; to provide statistics as required; to implement company policy; to operate within budget limits.

The grouping of a department's operations may be as illustrated in Fig. 5.1.

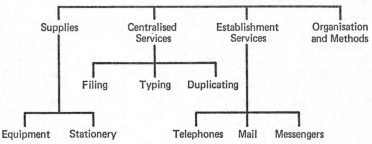

Fig. 5.1. Functions of the Office Services Department.

5.6   The Computer Manager

A Computer Department would provide a centralised service in that it would use the company computer to process work from different departments. A study of computer processes is provided in Chapter 14, but at this stage it can be stated that the Computer Manager would liaise with the Office Services Manager about the design of departmental records so that they would be in forms acceptable to the computer. He would also be required to schedule his work-loads in order that processing for departments would be so arranged as to complete all the work within each department's time-cycle without causing 'bottlenecks' at the computing stage.

With the development of desk computers, some of a Computer Manager's work has been decentralised. In this respect he would be responsible for advising on the choice of desk models, assisting in the programming and providing training for the users.

5.7   The Safety Officer

The services of a Safety Officer would be required in any but the smallest factory, but they are also often required in other establishments where there is a large staff (as in warehouses).

He is generally responsible for the safety of personnel. He must ensure that all dangerous machinery is provided with safety guards and that they are always in position; that machines and equipment are regularly inspected; that prescribed protective clothing is worn; that staff are trained in safety pre-cautions and adequately supervised.

Any accident must be reported and investigated.

He will consult with unions and advise management on safety matters.

5.8 The Board of Directors

At the top of the executive structure of a company are the directors. Effectively, a Board of Directors is a committee. As such, it acts under authority from the shareholders to manage the affairs of the company and to make policy decisions. Because of this power it is very necessary that the Board be so constituted as to be an effective management team. To this end the following principles are generally applicable:

(*a*) There should be a mixture of **executive** directors (those holding executive positions in the company) and **non-executive** directors ('outside' directors).

Each executive director can bring his particular type of expertise into board deliberations. Such directors are actively engaged in the day-to-day work of the business and therefore have intimate knowledge of all the circumstances. The expertise must be balanced, however. For example, it would be very unwise if an engineering company had a Board consisting entirely of engineers. At the least, it should include an accountant or a finance expert. It may be advisable to have someone well experienced in, say, marketing or labour relations.

There should also be non-executive directors. Those directors who are on the staff may tend to be introspective and be too much involved in internal affairs. Also, in Board discussions they may speak from biased positions and favour only the interests of their own departments and not those of the company as a whole. Non-executive directors, however, would not speak from such entrenched positions and could therefore contribute a more balanced viewpoint. Non-executive directors can also bring expertise and knowledge which is external to the company, such as wide experience of a particular overseas market. They may have a wider commercial experience outside the company than the other directors and be more aware of such matters as the economic outlook, the availability of finance, political prospects, etc.

(*b*) Some senior executives should be appointed to the Board. If they have proved their efficiency and loyalty they could bring with those qualities an understanding of the philosophy and internal politics of the company they have grown up with.

(*c*) A Board should be large enough to provide the necessary range of expertise and to make it difficult for any faction to dominate it. Too large a Board, however, can lose dynamic impetus.

(*d*) Because the functions of the Chairman and the Managing Director are essentially different, it is generally accepted that one person should not hold both posts.

The **Chairman of the Board** (it is incorrect to refer to 'the chairman of the *company*') occupies a somewhat detached position. He chairs all meetings of directors and shareholders and acts as spokesman for the company in making public statements. He should, therefore, appear as a 'figurehead'.

The **Managing Director**, on the other hand, is the chief administrative officer. Although he helps to formulate policy as a director, his responsibility as an executive is to implement it. He must provide the motive power and he is therefore deeply involved in administration of the company. Frequently, he is the 'driving force' and exercises a dominating influence. His essential qualities must be those of leadership and organisational ability. He need not necessarily be an expert in the company's activities; many successful managing directors have been in charge of companies in widely differing industries.

The duties of a Board include the following.

(a) To determine major policies.

(b) To comply with relevant legislation and, in the case of 'listed' companies, the regulations of the Stock Exchange.

(c) To decide the methods of raising and spending capital.

(d) To divide profits between reserves and dividends.

(e) To appoint senior staff.

(f) To aim to produce high staff morale.

5.9 The Company Secretary

There is a legal requirement for every company to have a secretary. He is responsible for submitting such returns to the Registrar of Companies as are prescribed by law. On behalf of the directors, he issues notices of shareholders' meetings and has the responsibility of organising such meetings. He also acts as secretary to the Board and its meetings. He is regarded as being the link between the members and the directors, and handles correspondence with shareholders.

He is responsible for all matters relevant to transfer of the company's shares and maintains the Register of Members and supporting records. These duties are sometimes delegated to a **Registrar** who, in a large company, would have his own staff.

A Company Secretary frequently has other responsibilities additional to the statutory ones. In a small company he may also be the Office Manager. In larger companies his duties may be combined with those of the Chief Accountant. Often, he is a specialist in other areas and may be responsible for, say, legal matters or staff pensions.

The structure of a Company Secretary's department may be similar to that shown in Fig. 2.3 (page 15).

5.10 The Qualities of Managership

A functional area can only be as efficient as its leader. In this connection, 'efficiency' is not confined to expertise but includes the ability to organise and lead. A particularly proficient accountant, for example, would be ineffectual if he was unable so to organise the work of his staff as to facilitate completion of set work within stipulated periods. If he could not supply another department with certain figures on time he would be a failure as an executive, no matter how brilliant he was as an accountant. Similarly, if he was the sort of person who upset his subordinates or who was constantly in conflict with his equals and superiors, he would have an inefficient department.

The twin requirements of effective management, therefore, are as follows:

(a) Work must be *planned*. This requires not only devising the most effective methods but also choosing the right persons when sharing the work.

(b) His personal attitude to his staff must be such as to elicit their co-operation. A manager should *lead* and not *drive*. There is a requirement to *explain* what is to be done, to acknowledge good work and to reprimand fairly when necessary, and to encourage initiative.

5.11 Executives' Terms of Reference

In discussing the inadequacies of organisation charts in Chapter 2 it was noted that charts cannot particularise the duties and responsibilities of executives. If this information is not detailed somewhere there is the danger that an executive will unwittingly exceed his authority or fail to appreciate he has a particular responsibility. Such misconceptions could have serious consequences. It is therefore necessary, as part of an efficient system of organisation and in fairness to the executive, to detail specific information. This is documented and is known as an executive's 'terms of reference'. It could then be referred to as evidence in the event of there being a dispute as to whether or not an executive had exceeded his powers or failed in his responsibilities.

The document would be headed with the executive's name and official title. It would then give the name of the superior to whom he is directly accountable. His broad functions as leader of a group would be listed.

The document would then go into considerable detail as to what he is responsible for and any limitation on those responsibilities. Similarly, the spheres and extent of his authority would be fully specified. For example, it may be prescribed that he has authority to sign cheques but only in respect of certain matters and up to specified amounts; the personal expenses he could claim may be set out; any limitation on his power to give orders to a subordinate may be stated.

There would be a list of his immediate subordinates and his relationships with associated executives would be specified.

There would also be a list of committees to which he belongs because of his position.

(Such a document must not be confused with a **service contract**. This specifies the conditions of employment, e.g. salary, pension rights, length of notice required for either side, etc.)

Key Points

1. **Financial accounting** is concerned with *current and historical recording*.
   Management accounting (cost accounting) facilitates *forecasting*, *planning* and *control*.

2. Every company must have an **auditor**. He is not on the staff although he is paid by the company. He reports to the *shareholders*.
   Internal auditors are staff members.

3. The **Personnel Department** is responsible for:
   (*a*) recruitment;
   (*b*) training;
   (*c*) staff records;
   (*d*) welfare;
   (*e*) implementing the personnel policy.

   The **Labour Relations Department** is concerned with non-managerial and non-clerical staff, mainly in connection with trade union negotiations.

4. An **Office Services Department** may

    (*a*) advise (e.g. on improved methods of working);
    (*b*) control (e.g. purchase of equipment);
    (*c*) provide general services (e.g. telephones).

5. A **Board of Directors** is a *committee*, appointed by the *shareholders*. It should be balanced, between types of expertise and between executive and non-executive directors.

    The **chairman** should be a 'figurehead'; the **managing director** is the chief administrative officer.

6. A **company secretary** is also *secretary to the directors* and provides the link between them and the shareholders. The law requires a company to have a secretary and imposes sundry legal obligations on him.

7. A **manager** must:

    (*a*) *organise* in order to achieve the objectives for which he is responsible;
    (*b*) have the *technical expertise* relevant to his work;
    (*c*) be a true *leader*.

8. An **executive's terms of reference** specify:

    (*a*) his duties and responsibilities;
    (*b*) the extent of his authority;
    (*c*) to whom he is accountable and for what;
    (*d*) his relationships with subordinates and other executives.
    (Not to be confused with a **service contract**)

6

METHODS AND PRINCIPLES OF WORK-SHARING

6.1 The Reasons for Sharing Responsibilities

The most obvious reason for sharing responsibilities is to reduce the burden on one person. This will take place at the earliest stage when the owner of a small business transfers some of his work to someone else, but it subsequently becomes a continuous process as the extent and complexity of the work increases.

Areas of responsibility can also be altered in circumstances where it is advisable to do so in the interests of management efficiency. For example, a small exporting department may grow to a size where it would be sensible to give it more control of its own work. The reverse can also apply where a section of work is common to two functions and is transferred to a new area to serve both functions, e.g. the new department could provide statistical services to the original pair.

The principle can also relate to decision-making whereby courses of action are decided by groups of people instead of by individuals.

Any restructuring aiming at sharing work must be a form of **decentralisation** in that part of the responsibility is transferred from a central point. The process is that of **delegation** because responsibility and authority are bestowed on the new holders.

6.2 Forms of Decentralisation

(a) Decentralisation of Management

This relates to the moving of responsibility and authority to lower tiers in the management structure. It includes the classic example of delegation whereby one person transfers some of his work to subordinates. This process applies throughout the management structure, reaching down to the lowest level. It therefore follows that *absolute* decentralisation of management is impossible because all authority and responsibility stems from the top. Centralisation continues to exist because the source of all obligations and powers is at the highest level of the structure.

Absolute *centralisation* is also not practical because even in the most autocratic of structures day-to-day decisions must be made at all levels.

(b) Decentralisation by Functions

As business units are always divided into functional areas one may say that every business is decentralised to that extent. There are dangers in applying this practice with too much rigidity, however. For example, if the manager of a major function is given extensive authority, he may, in furtherance of his own objectives, issue directives to managers of other functions. This may be done in ignorance of its effect elsewhere so that the senior manager's achievement of his sectarian aims may be at the expense of the other departments and may even upset global plans. Thus, a Finance Officer's refusal to authorise some expenditure may prevent the carrying out of one stage of a plan involving several departments which had already been partly completed.

Earlier, the necessity has been noted for understanding and coordination between such major functions as production and marketing. This serves to illustrate the dangers of functional decentralisation carried to extremes.

(*c*) Decentralisation by Products

A company may have large sections, each of them manufacturing or dealing in separate products or services. For example, it may produce motorcars and commercial vehicles. In such instances it may be more efficient to separate the two types of production into what are often called 'divisions'. Where this is done the result is that each division effectively becomes almost a separate business. Each would have an allocation of capital and a management team (including, often, a 'local board of directors') entirely responsible for its activities.

In spite of the clear-cut separation, however, decentralisation could not be absolute. The production of both types of vehicles would be subject to an overall marketing policy, because there may be, for example, the necessity to cut back production of cars to allow the commercial vehicle division to take advantage of a 'boom' in the sale of lorries. The financial resources of each would depend upon the total resources; components used in both types of vehicles may be purchased centrally for reasons of economy, etc.

Such a system does, however (as in any form of delegation), increase the personal involvement of those concerned. The smaller a unit the more a person identifies with it.

The method is sometimes referred to as **federal decentralisation.**

(*d*) Geographical Decentralisation

Where a company's products or services are available nationwide and in some strength, authority and responsibility can be granted to the managers in those areas. This carries with it the major advantage of allowing a manager to operate in a manner which is suitable to local conditions that may not apply throughout the country. Buying-patterns vary between districts and a local officer is in a better position to recognise and react to them than someone in the head office. A sales policy decided at a central point can fail in some districts because of ignorance of local prejudices.

As in all cases, geographical decentralisation cannot be absolute. Global policies must be adhered to; branch targets must be set within total targets; financial strategy can be devised only at the centre.

6.3   Centralisation v. Decentralisation

It can be seen from the above that absolute decentralisation is impossible. It is also the case that even in the most centrally controlled of organisations degrees of decentralisation must exist.

Advantages can accrue following decentralisation but there are many instances where centralisation gives more favourable results. The degree to which a business should go in either direction is not easy to determine. Often the deciding factor is the stage of development reached by the company. With increasing size and perhaps more areas of activity, it is often wise to split the structure into more manageable units. Often, however, complexity can be reduced by *combining* parts into a more rational framework.

In making the choice, some of the following factors may be relevant.

(*a*) Where centralisation is extreme there is the possibility of creating a bureaucratic and authoritarian structure. In such conditions everyone feels he is a cog in an ever-growing wheel. Rules and procedures proliferate. Personal commitment diminishes as the feeling of impersonality increases.

(*b*) Generally, decentralisation in any form promotes initiative, because people are given more responsibility and are more deeply involved in a smaller area. This can, however, lead to a parochial attitude whereby people identify too closely with their own sections and regard other sections as being 'foreign'. The objectives and philosophy of the total may be lost sight of in their sectarian involvement.

(*c*) Centralisation is beneficial to the extent it can exploit the advantages of size. Buying materials, components, equipment, etc., in bulk obviously provides advantages of economy. The centralisation of services, such as those applicable to office work, training, advertising, etc., means that they will cost less to supply.

(*d*) Centralisation makes increased standardisation of procedures possible. This could be beneficial to the extent that returns from all areas to the head office are uniform, but those *within* a decentralised area should not be designed at the centre. The possible danger of standardisation leading to an excess of 'red tape' always exists, however. Standardisation of procedures which is kept within reasonable bounds will make central control easier.

(*e*) Decision-making will generally be slower in conditions of centralisation. If problems from various levels and sections have to be referred to a central body, delays are inevitable. On-the-spot decisions can be more successful because of their immediacy and the fact that the decision-makers would be more aware of the directly relevant factors. Against this, one must recognise that locally-made decisions may have consequences which unwittingly run counter to centrally-made plans.

6.4 Delegation of Authority and Responsibility

The act of delegating means that a person is given the duty of carrying out a specified activity. This has two implications:

(*a*) The delegate is *responsible* for performance of the duties, but only to the *delegator*. The person delegating retains ultimate responsibility. The scope of his total responsibility would have been determined when he was given it and the fact that he passes some of that responsibility to someone else does not absolve him from responsibility for the whole to *his* superior. A failure on the part of the subordinate implies a failure in managership by his superior in not delegating efficiently.

(*b*) The extent of the *authority* which is delegated must be clearly understood by both parties. Decisions made by the subordinate within his sphere of authority become the decisions of the superior, because, as shown above, the latter has full responsibility.

The Principles of Delegation

A person cannot give what he does not already possess. Any responsibility or authority delegated must be within the delegator's range of duties. Further, a person may not delegate at all unless he has the authority to do so.

Delegation having been effected, the superior must protect himself and act fairly towards his subordinate. Consequently, a degree of supervision will be necessary. This must be the optimum amount of supervision because either of the extremes can have unfortunate consequences. If the subordinate is *under*-supervised the superior runs the risk of being held responsible for his delegate's errors. All supervision contains an element of training and the subordinate is unfairly treated if he is not given sufficient guidance or is denied advice when he asks for it. On the other hand, *excessive* supervision can have unfortunate psychological effects. One of the benefits of delegation is that the bestowing of responsibility increases initiative and this in turn promotes more interest in the work. This advantage is lost if the superior is constantly 'breathing down the neck' of his subordinate. This stifling effect may be due to the superior's lack of confidence in his subordinate, but one of the duties of a manager is to assess the potential of people and to choose delegates accordingly.

The Justification for Delegating

Obviously, some delegating is inevitable in that work must be divided into areas because of its extent and complexity. The process also brings with it certain advantages:

(*a*) It allows for the exploitation of specialist knowledge and natural aptitude. The process of continually narrowing the range of function areas allows for greater degrees of specialisation. There are therefore places for those with particular abilities. For example, part of the work of the Chief Accountant may be to produce extensive and complicated mathematical analyses. This could be undertaken by a staff member who has a particular aptitude for that type of work—which probably the department head has not.

(*b*) It enables a manager to concentrate on managing. It gives him more time to plan and control work in his department, consult with those outside it and attend meetings. An example of this has been produced by the increased size of State schools in which headmasters are almost entirely occupied with managerial duties.

(*c*) The carrying down of the opportunity to use initiative to lower levels incidentally results in a form of training. Some organisation of work and decision-making is necessary where even the smallest degree of responsibility is held. The ability to manage thereby becomes apparent at an early stage and, with the confidence and experience gained, can be an elementary factor in a scheme for management succession.

The Human Element in Delegation

As with so many management principles, concepts can be upset by the characteristics of people and their reactions to each other. This fact is particularly relevant to the process of delegating.

One must first consider the possible attitude of the person called upon to delegate. Some people regard delegation as an erosion of their responsibility. They are the kind of executives who like to have everything under their immediate control, jealously guarding their 'little empires'. Such a person often considers that no one could do the work as well as he and as a consequence resents the 'intrusion' of a helper. In such circumstances one must expect an uncomfortable relationship between the officer and those working under him.

It must also be admitted that a manager may be so situated that delegating will 'expose' him. A person can inflate the extent and importance of his job, either by exaggerating or being so inefficient he never 'gets on top' of it. If his work is shared, his deceit or inefficiency is revealed. (The irony is that the delegating would have been decided upon *because* of the apparent demands of the job!)

Other managers welcome delegation by acting as though it releases them from responsibility. They are then 'carried' by their staff until something goes wrong and some form of reckoning becomes necessary.

The attitude of the subordinate must also be taken into account. Some people welcome responsibility; others would prefer to avoid it. Effective delegation includes the ability to choose those persons who not only have or could have the necessary expertise but who also have the personal qualities which are essential.

Span of Control

There is a limit to the extent one person may delegate efficiently. The number of persons involved with a delegator is known as the 'span of control'. If that span is too *wide*, an excessive amount of the superior's time will be spent in supervising and he will have insufficient time for his other managerial duties. It may be that in spite of this he will still be unable to supervise adequately. Because of the demands on his time his subordinates would too infrequently have direct access to him for guidance. Training would thereby suffer, as would the morale of the staff. Where the span is too *narrow* the dangers of over-supervision may exist, again adversely affecting morale.

The optimum span of control depends upon *the characteristics of those concerned* and *the nature of the work*.

A good manager with organising ability and the aptitude for handling people could cope with a comparatively wide span. In practice, a superior's span of control has sometimes to be deliberately restricted because of his obvious lack of the necessary qualities. The span will also be influenced by those to whom the work is to be delegated. If supervision is to include a larger than usual amount of training, or the ability or intelligence of the staff is below average, then, obviously, the span must be narrower than it would otherwise be.

The type of work is also an influencing factor. It is possible to control a comparatively large number of people if the work is repetitive, such as card-punching and copy-typing. The span must be narrower where the work is individual and close control is necessary. This would be the case, for example, with a department containing people engaged in analytical work or non-routine accounting.

Where the work process consists of successive stages, each being dependent upon others, fewer people can be effectually controlled. This would be the case where, for example, customers' orders have to go through a number of consecutive processes, one person or group dealing with each process. If such a system does not apply (e.g. a typing pool in which each girl works independently) the span can be much wider.

6.5 Work-sharing by Committee

Work can be shared by allocating it to committees. The general principles previously stated apply—that is, the scope of the delegated work must be within the scope of the appointing body and that body must have the power to delegate.

Committees have two main functions: they may carry out investigations and report on their findings, leaving the appointing body to make the decisions; or they may have executive power to implement their own decisions. In both cases the advantages of specialisation exist, because one of the principles of the committee system is that it allows for experts to be chosen to deal with matters about which they are particularly knowledgeable.

In recent years there has been a considerable increase in the use of committees. This is expressive of an emerging philosophy that people should at least be consulted on matters which may affect them. This can extend to situations where people at comparatively low levels can partake in the making of management decisions.

Effectiveness of the Committee System

The committee system can be said to be acceptable in that it aims to increase the democratic content of business management. There were undoubtedly abuses whereby remote 'bosses' made decisions with little consideration for or consultation with those to be affected by them. The system also puts into effect the principle which is now generally accepted by both sides of industry, that cooperation and mutual understanding are essential if management is to be successful.

The increase has not, however, been confined to areas of *vertical* consultation and negotiation. Committees also allow for more consultation between different groups so that each is more aware of the other's attitude and more people can contribute to attainment of main objectives. There has therefore been a large increase in committees on *horizontal* lines, allowing for more to partake in management.

A study of the working of the system allows for some evaluation of its effectiveness.

(*a*) It has practical advantages in that experts can be appointed to committees to advise those who are not experts. For example, directors who know little about computers may have to decide if the accounts are to be computerised. That decision must be based on the views of those who can provide the requisite expertise and that advice may come from a committee of experts.

(*b*) Frequently, a small group can reach a decision more quickly than a large one. Certainly an investigation can be more competently made by a small number of people.

(*c*) In contradiction of the above statement, it must be admitted that group discussions can be unduly prolonged. Committee members must be permitted adequately to express their views and procedures must be complied with, but the result is that meetings often take up a considerable amount of time. Added to this is the fact that a lot of time can be spent attending meetings and preparing for them. Where a meeting is ineffectual, this represents time wasted.

(*d*) In a large organisation, the committee system can get out of hand. Committees tend to spawn subcommittees and working parties. Committees can proliferate because of the view that 'everyone must be consulted about everything' and 'when in doubt, form a committee'. In addition to an increased amount of time being spent on committees, this can also result in a complex and often confusing structure of committees.

(*e*) An extensive committee system must require the establishing of a large secretariat to organise and service the system. This can result in a bureaucratic framework, leading to a negation of the principles of good management.

(*f*) The committee method lends itself to 'political' manipulation. 'Committeemanship' is an art which can defeat democratic aims; fair decision-making can be prevented by lobbying and by 'trading' between factions; advantages can accrue from being elected to powerful committees and to 'blocking' committees.

Key Points

1. **Work sharing** is synonomous with *decentralisation* and *delegation*.
   Decentralisation of management relates to *delegation of responsibility and authority*.
   Decentralisation by function relates to the establishing of *functional areas*.
   Decentralisation by products results in almost autonomous *divisions according to products*.
   Geographical decentralisation makes it possible to *allow for local conditions*.
   In no instance can there be *absolute* centralisation or decentralisation.
   Decentralisation promotes initiative; *centralisation* gives firm control but may result in rigidity.

2. A delegator retains *ultimate* responsibility.
   A delegate is responsible *only* to his delegator.
   Delegation must be within the *delegator's* responsibility.

3. The **span of control** relates to the number of delegates to one delegator. Its width depends on

   (*a*) the character of the delegator;
   (*b*) the character and intelligence of the delegates;
   (*c*) whether the work is routine or non-routine.

   In delegating, the twin dangers are *over*-delegation and *under*-delegation.

4. **Committees** can have the following
   advantages: wide participation; pooling of views; advice of experts; sharing of work;
   disadvantages: time-consuming; 'politicising'; 'talking shops'; complicated structure and bureaucracy; inconclusiveness.

SECTION 2

ADMINISTRATIVE SYSTEMS AND PROCEDURES

7

INFORMATION TECHNOLOGY

7.1 The Necessity for Information

Business feeds on information. There must be a continuous flow of information into, within and out of a business.

Information must be received from customers and other business associates. It provides the source of all the activities of a business in the form of orders, enquiries, etc.

Information must be sought from market surveys, official statistics, etc.

Information must be converted so as to be in a form capable of being processed within a business.

Information must be responded to within the procedures of a business, such as by fulfilling orders, etc.

Information must be classified into records, such as by the keeping of accounts.

Information must be analysed to aid management, such as by providing statistics, forecasts, budgets, etc.

Information must be published in the form of final accounts, official returns, etc.

7.2 The Internal Demand for Information

Within itself, a company requires to have information for the following purposes:

(a) To Provide Current and Historical Records

The daily recording of transactions serves to show current positions. For example, the amount owed by one customer and the total owed by all customers at any one time can be ascertained. Similar information is available concerning debts of the business, the cash in hand, etc. The periodic assembling of the accumulation of such items results in the production of historical records.

(b) To Facilitate Analysis

The grouping of transactions enables figures to be produced for analytical purposes. For example, total sales can be broken down into sales of each product; areas where expenditure is particularly high can be identified.

(c) To Facilitate the Making of Short-Term Decisions

Analysed information can be used as a basis for decisions which have to be made for the immediate or near future. For example, it should be possible to estimate the amount of cash which should be available in a month's time and, possibly, up to six months ahead and thereby be forewarned of any cash flow problems; the amount and types of sales last month would influence the current plans for purchasing, producing (where relevant) and storing; the identifying of a rising cost may enable corrective action to be taken.

(d) To Facilitate the Making of Long-Term Decisions

Policy-making in respect of quantifiable aspects has the general aims of increasing income by increasing either prices or turnover, and of reducing unit costs and overheads.

Before increasing prices it would be necessary to ensure that demand is sufficiently strong to make the increase acceptable. If turnover is to be increased there must be the assurance that the market potential exists and that the business could cope with the increased supplies required. The basis of any forecasting must be past and current records, supported by research.

To reduce costs it would be necessary to analyse past figures and decide the feasibility of any proposed new measures.

(e) To Provide Controls

Business activities are planned. Consequently, the information system must allow for the making of forecasts, the measuring of performance and the comparing of it with forecasts, and the making of any adjustments necessary in the event of deviations from forecasts.

7.3 The External Demands for Information

A business must also provide information:

(a) To Business Associates

Customers require invoices and statements; orders must be sent to suppliers. These would be produced as part of the *internal* information system of the business—that is, records for use in the business would be designed in such a way as to produce simultaneously records required externally. Other information (such as replying to enquiries) could not be automatically provided as part of an extensive internal system.

(b) To Official Bodies

Information in prescribed forms must be provided for Government agencies. For example, the Department of Trade requires company accounts to be filed; returns must be made to the Inland Revenue concerning corporation tax, employees' income tax and National Insurance contributions; value added tax returns must be made to the Excise authorities. Various Government departments will also require statistical information to be provided from time to time.

(c) To the Investing Community

Information must be provided in such a form as to permit analyses to be made of the company's activities by the financial world. Information must be available to shareholders and creditors of the company. Returns must be made to any concern involved in the financing of the company, such as bankers, associated companies, etc.

7.4 The Necessity to Convert Information

The receipt of information is the first link in what may be a long procedural chain. The initial document produced within a business must be so designed as to make all subsequent actions as simple as possible. The complete process will depend upon the form and content of that first document and, as will be shown later, it is often possible for copies of the initial document to serve as all the subsequent documents. The planning of procedures and the designing of the relevant documents must therefore be done jointly as part of a complete system.

As some information *comes into* a business and some is provided *from within* the firm, it is first necessary to study the problems of ensuring that it is in a form compatible with internal procedures.

7.5 Information from Internal Sources

As a business has control of information derived internally it can frequently dictate the style in which it is first provided. For example, the first document used to obtain goods from a supplier would usually be an order form designed by the business as part of its purchasing system and would therefore not require to be converted. In such instances, the initial form can be a 'master' which will be designed so that copies of it provide the further documents required.

This is not always possible, however. For example, an order may have to be made on a form provided by the supplier. In that case the initiating document of the ordering procedure would be a conversion of the order form. In other instances, it may be necessary to design the firm's first form in such a way that it can be easily converted into the initiating document. For example, returns of hours worked would be designed so as to be capable of being completed by a foreman in factory conditions. It must then be possible to convert the information so that it would provide the first stage of a procedure within that office which has to calculate and pay the wages due.

Reducing the Compiler's Work

In designing forms to be completed internally account must sometimes be taken of the circumstances in which the forms are to be completed. One must also allow for the fact that clerical work is not always part of the compiler's main duties. A van driver, for example, would not take kindly to having to do more than the absolute minimum of writing, particularly as it would probably be done in his cab. He would have to provide some information, however, and therefore his task must be made as easy as possible. He would normally be required to log his milometer readings for his daily journeys and to detail any expenses (supported by vouchers) for which he required reimbursement. Provision should also be made for him to report any incidents which are not required to appear on special forms (such as accidents and breakdowns). A specimen of such a form is given in Fig. 7.1.

Forms which are required to give more information must also be designed to allow for the conditions under which they are completed. For example, a travelling salesman dealing in a fairly limited number of items could be provided with forms listing all the products. An order given by a customer could

DAILY LOG					
Driver....................................... Vehicle.........					
Date ... Time: Start.......... Finish........... Route..........					

From	To	Milo Rdg		Miles run
		Start	Finish	

Driver's report

...... (Signed)

	Ex Depot			On journey			FOR OFFICE USE	
	Qty	Price	Cost	Qty	Price	Cost	Petrol	
Petrol Oil * Other supplies							Oil	
							Others	
*Expenses								
*Details:				(Vouchers attached)			Reimbursement of on journey costs: £ Received.......	

Fig. 7.1. Driver's log sheet.

be indicated by merely entering the number sold against the title and code of each product. This could make the salesman's task easier and would simplify the work of those to whom the form is sent for processing. An example of such a form is given in Fig. 7.2. The top copy would be sent to the Sales Department, the part above the perforation serving as the order form and the bottom part providing marketing information. The first undercopy would not include the bottom part and would be handed to the customer as confirmation of the order. The salesman would retain a bottom copy.

It is sometimes possible to eliminate writing almost entirely. Fig. 7.3 shows another form designed to be completed by a visiting salesman. The company has been conducting a sales promotion scheme and the form is intended to indicate the responses to it by the retailers involved. Following discussion with a retailer, the salesman would mark the relevant answers to each question. Forms from all retailers would be analysed by the Marketing Department as part of its monitoring procedure. The results could be analysed by a computer 'reading' the answers if they are written by a pencil which the computer will accept. This is known as **marksensing** (see page 155).

BISCUITS LTD

Corner Stores
21 High Street Blanktown

Date 11/2/19--

Biscuits	A/24	6 x 24
	A/25	
	A/26	10 x 24
Shortcake	B/1	12 x 12
	B/2	

Wafers

- -

(Perforation)

Customer responses:

    Any quick or slow sellers?   Little demand for wafers
    Competitive rating?   Too upmarket for this district
    Suggestions or complaints

                          Representative

Fig. 7.2. Salesman's sale form.

7.6 Information from External Sources

Where the motivating information comes from outside the business it is usually not possible to prescribe the manner in which it is presented. A business cannot dictate to a customer, for instance, the form he should use when placing orders. One reason would be that the customer's system of ordering would be part of *his* internal procedures.

There are, however, some cases where information received from outside the business can be formalised as required by the recipient. For example, a coupon in a magazine advertisement may appear somewhat as shown in Fig. 7.4. This would simplify the despatching of literature and any follow-up procedure. Similarly, a member of a book club could be required to indicate his choice of books by marking a suitably worded form.

In general, however, it must be accepted that information received from outside the business will have to be converted to fit into the business's own systems.

7.7 Examples of Converting Sales Orders

The most frequent event which provides information from outside a business would be orders received from customers. In using this as an example it will be seen that the aim is to show how information received in various forms can be converted into a standard document. That document will be the start of the firm's system for processing orders. (If a salesman used the system mentioned

---

Retail Survey
Promotion of Apex Tissues

Retailer: *Jackson Ltd. Market Square Lawtown.*

1. Is the special display used?   YES/~~NO~~
   1a. If YES, was it prominent?   ~~YES~~/NO
2. His special offer target was *200*. What was the performance? *100*
3. Do you consider that Stage 2 of the promotion would be justified here?

   ~~YES~~/NO

4. Was the retailer satisfied with the offer bonus?   YES/~~NO~~
5. Does the retailer consider there should be an improvement in

   ~~Advertising~~   Display   Price

(Indicate answers by deletions)

Sales Area/Rep. *3/5*   Signed *T. W. Binns*

1/5/19--

Fig. 7.3. Promotion survey form.

earlier in the chapter or telephoned his orders, the procedure in the office would be the same as that for dealing with customers. All those methods of receiving orders can therefore be included in this example.)

Various methods of converting can be used and include those listed below. The aim is to produce all the documents required to process a sale in one operation. As will be seen, some methods allow this to be done automatically; others produce a master which, as explained in Section 7.9, must be duplicated to provide further copies.

To Warmfloors Ltd., Tower House, Mill Road, Lecton, Bucks.

Please send me   □ 'How to have a comfortable home'
                 □ Pattern book and samples
                 □ List of local stockists
(Tick appropriate box)

Name .... Address ....

....   (In block letters please)

Fig. 7.4. Advertisement coupon.

(*a*) The sales order clerk writes a preliminary draft of a telephoned order and then types it out on a standard form. This would be the master document.

(*b*) A more direct way of dealing with telephoned orders is to type out a master document as the information is received. Details of written orders would also be transferred directly on to a master.

(*c*) An electro-mechanical accounting machine can be used. Received information is typed and the calculations are done mechanically. Additional documents can be produced by means of carbons or a two-register machine which will produce specified information on separate forms.

(*d*) Writing-boards can be used for recording by hand. The forms are so arranged that one writing operation produces all the documents required.

(*e*) A more sophisticated method is by the use of a computer. A sales order clerk receiving an order keys the account code of the customer. A visual display unit (similar to a television screen) immediately shows details of the customer's account, including his present balance, any credit limitation, etc. Items ordered are keyed in and for each item the panel indicates the amount in stock. In the case of telephoned orders the clerk is thereby able to tell the customer if any item is out of stock and when it will be available, and he may be able to suggest alternatives. Instructions about delivery would also be keyed in.

The result is that the invoice is produced immediately and may either be sent with the goods or held back for invoicing on a weekly or monthly basis. At the same time, stock levels are adjusted for the goods sold and despatch notes are made out. The sales information is stored until required for updating the customer's account and for updating and analysing sales records.

(*f*) Another method is to use a computerised electronic typewriter. Basically, this is a typewriter linked to microprogrammes specially designed to provide the processes required by the user. The operator needs to type in only the variable information (such as details of the goods ordered) and the machine will then automatically calculate, tabulate and print the relevant figures. Fig. 7.5 illustrates an invoice produced by this method. The shaded areas indicate those which the machine prints automatically, including an analysis of the cost into price, discount and VAT. On completion of a batch of invoices the machine will produce totals, analyses of sales and the amount to be accounted for in respect of VAT. The system can also automatically provide for subsequent postings to ledger accounts and daybooks. Additionally, such a machine may provide word-processing facilities (see page 145).

7.8 Integration of Systems

As explained above, a procedure consisting of several operations and involving a number of departments can be made more effective by using a master document at the first stage and allowing copies of that document to provide the forms required at the subsequent stages. This practice sets the following requirements:

(*a*) The **master document** must provide the total of the information required *for the system as a whole*.

(*b*) Each **copy document** must provide only the information required *by the department using it*.

(*c*) The copy documents must be distributed so that they become operative at the required times.

It follows that any procedure in which each section plays its own part must be planned as a composite whole. Expertise is therefore required for the designing both of the forms and of the integrated system.

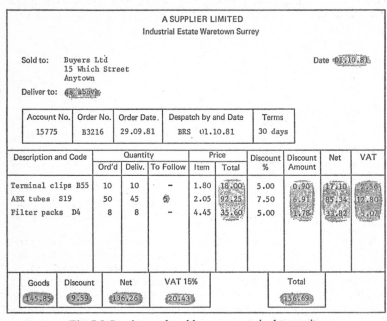

Fig. 7.5. Invoice produced by a computerised typewriter.

7.9 Producing Copies for an Integrated System

Systems integration requires a method of producing copies from the master form. As already shown, some systems provide these automatically. In other cases the choice of method may be summarised as follows:

(*a*) The master can be handwritten so that copies are produced by inserting **carbon paper** in a set of sheets. The number of legible copies possible is not more than three and the risk of poorly written forms exists. An example of this method is an invoice produced for a sales-counter transaction as illustrated in Fig. 8.1 (page 75). More legible copies can be produced by a typewriter, particularly if it is an electric one.

(*b*) The copies in a set of documents can be already interleaved with thin **'one-time' carbon paper** to save the time spent in inserting sheets by hand. The carbon paper is removed and thrown away after the set has been typed.

(*c*) An integrated system usually requires that only certain information has to appear on some of the forms. For example, an invoice sent to a customer must show the price of each item and the total cost. One copy of the invoice may be an authorisation for the goods to be drawn from stock. Obviously, it is unnecessary (and perhaps unwise) to notify the storekeeper of the price and, accordingly, that information should be omitted. This can be done by having forms made in one of the following ways:

(*i*) Each form has carbon fixed to its back only beneath the data required to be shown on the next form. A simple example of this method is given in Fig. 7.6. The shaded areas are those **carbon-backed.** Item 1 would appear on each

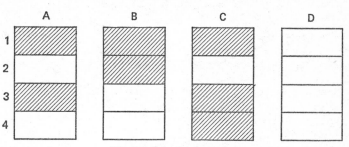

Fig. 7.6. Selective carbons.

document. Item 2 would be reproduced only on documents A and C. Item 3 would appear on documents A, B and D. Item 4 would be shown on documents A and D.

(*ii*) A more effective method is to use **chemical carbonless paper.** One sheet has a coating of colourless dye capsules which break under pen or typewriter pressure and react with a clay coating on the top of the sheet below, forming an image in (not on) that sheet. This is shown in Fig. 7.7. Up to 12 legible, smudge-free copies can be made at one time with a typewriter, although this figure can vary depending on the typewriter used. To produce copies which will show only selected information, the paper can have desensitised areas. Fig. 7.8 shows a specimen delivery note as one copy in a set of documents produced by typing the invoice, which forms the top sheet of the set. The specimen delivery note omits details of the prices because the relevant area is desensitised (and is at free disposal to hold specific printed matter). This is a more effective method of selective reproduction than printing a 'scramble pattern' on the copy.

(*iii*) Probably the most sophisticated method is the **Automatic Overlay Device** which is marketed by Rank Xerox Ltd. This unit is linked to a Rank Xerox duplicator and a sorter. Up to 20 individual overlays (one for each type of form in a set) are mounted on a transparent web which travels under the platen. These have the effect of 'blanking off' areas of data which are not required on any one form. The operation is programmed by using a peg-board so that a copy of each type of document is produced, containing only the information specific to a document. Where necessary, one or more documents can be omitted and more than one copy of any one document can be produced. A unique advantage of the system is that stocks of pre-printed forms are not required because all the copies are printed on blank sheets. Only the master has to be pre-printed.

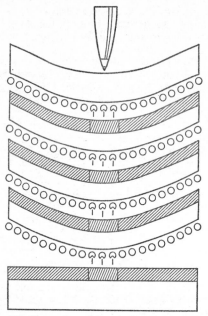

Fig. 7.7. The action of chemical carbonless paper.
(By courtesy of Wiggins Teape Ltd.)

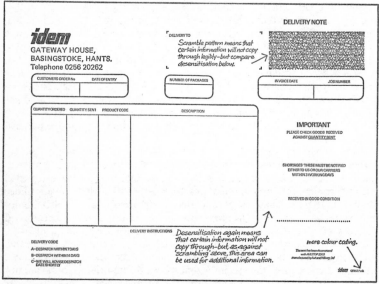

Fig. 7.8. Specimen of a delivery note on chemical carbonless paper.
(By courtesy of Wiggins Teape Ltd.)

7.10 Distribution of the Documents

The practice of distributing copies of a master form may be demonstrated by showing an example of its application following receipt of an order from a customer. The requirement would be to provide the following documents:

(a) An **invoice** to the customer, giving details of the goods to be supplied, the price of each item, the discount allowable and the relevant conditions, the amount of VAT, the total cost and where the goods are to be sent (as was demonstrated in Fig. 7.5).

(b) A **copy invoice** to be retained by the Sales Order Department.

(c) A **posting slip** to the Accounts Department to charge the customer's account.

(d) A **requisition** for Stores to supply the goods ordered.

(e) An **instruction** to the Despatch Department to pack and deliver the goods.

(f) A **delivery note** to be sent with the goods to the customer.

(g) An **acknowledgment** of receipt of the goods by the customer.

The operational stages would be as follows.

1. The invoice would be typed, each copy document providing only the information required by its user.

2. The copy invoice would be used to check the customer's credit. Approval of the credit is marked on the copy invoice and retained by the Sales Order Department as its record.

3. The invoice would be sent to the customer or held for despatch later.

4. The posting slip would be sent to the Accounts Department and used to write up the customer's account.

5. The remaining four documents would exclude any information about prices. They would be sent together to the Stores.

6. Stores would draw the required goods, using the requisition to adjust its stock records.

7. The goods and the remaining three documents would be sent to the Despatch Department.

8. The goods would be packed and delivered to the customer with the delivery note and the acknowledgment. The Despatch Department would retain the instruction.

9. The customer would sign the acknowledgment which would then be returned to the Despatch Department and filed with the advice note.

A flow chart depicting this distribution is illustrated in Fig. 7.9. The procedure provides the following advantages.

(a) Only one typing is necessary to cover all the systems. Provided the master is typed accurately, all copies will have a similar accuracy.

(b) Each copy is specifically designed for use by the department concerned. Each has its own title and contains only the information required by the department.

(c) Each department is provided with instructions and retains a document as evidence that they have been complied with.

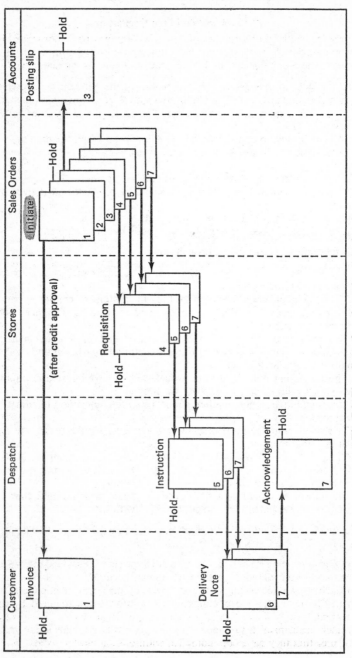

Fig. 7.9. Flowchart of a sales order procedure.

7.11 Control of Data Flows

The above example is of an extensive and continuously used procedure. It would therefore be designed by experts because it would constitute one of the fundamental procedures. However, there would be many other information flows which, although important, would not be so firmly established. In a large business the feeding in of information and the consequent flow of directives, analyses and proposals results in an extensive pattern of information channels. Examples of how these come into being include the following:

(*a*) The passing between departments of information mutually required.
(*b*) The commissioning and submitting of reports.
(*c*) The setting of targets and the recording of performances.
(*d*) Notices, supporting documents and minutes of meetings.
(*e*) Notes of conversations passed to interested parties.

In every case there must be an established pattern of distribution. Designing such a pattern should be the responsibility of an expert. This is not always possible because some procedures do not have a long life. For example, people may be brought together to tackle a problem and then disperse when a solution has been found. In any scheme, however, the following principles should apply:

(*a*) *All* the information required should be distributed but *not more.*
(*b*) Distribution must be to *all* those requiring the information and to *no one else.* The tendency to send copies to all and sundry without regard to their interest in the matter must be discouraged.
(*c*) Information should be passed with the minimum delay.
(*d*) Executives must be prevented from devising their own distribution networks. Failure to observe this precept can lead to a proliferation of paperwork and a confusing of communication lines.
(*e*) Systems must be reviewed frequently. In most large concerns one can find statistics, forms and reports being submitted which serve no useful purpose. They may have been required in the past but no one has noticed (or pointed out) that they have become unnecessary because of changed circumstances.

7.12 The Designing of Forms

The efficient functioning of procedures depends upon the practicability of the forms used. Business forms provide the very foundation of information flows and unless they are well designed and objective the efficiency of the business will suffer. The designing of forms and their routing through procedures must be the responsibility of experts. Staff should not be allowed to design their own forms, because the result could be a confused mass of wasteful documents. There is always the tendency for some managers to devise their own systems and forms—often evidence of an 'empire-building' attitude—and this must be curbed. This does not apply, of course, to forms which are completely within a department; the danger exists when internally-generated forms get into interdepartmental exchanges.

Before instituting a form, the following questions should be asked:

(*a*) Is the form really required at all? It is surprising how often, after honest study, the answer must be 'no'.

(*b*) Could an existing form serve the same purpose?

(*c*) Could the new form be designed so as also to achieve the objectives of one or more existing forms, thereby reducing the paperwork?

The following principles apply in designing a form.

(*a*) Its layout and content must take account of any procedure of which it is to be part. It must contribute to the procedure objectives and not contradict or duplicate the function of another form.

(*b*) It must have an indicative title and, where necessary, a code reference.

(*c*) The name of the company should not appear on forms used internally.

(*d*) The items should appear in a logical sequence.

(*e*) If the form is to be completed by typing, the line-spacing must be appropriate.

(*f*) Adequate space must be provided for entering information.

(*g*) As much as possible of the form must be pre-printed to reduce the amount of written work.

(*h*) Where relevant, the surface must be suitable for handwritten entries.

(*i*) The quality of the paper will be determined by the amount of handling required. Top-quality paper should not be used except where necessary for 'prestige' purposes.

(*j*) For filing purposes the paper must be of a standard size. Margin widths must be relevant if the form is to be punched or spine-bound.

(*k*) The layout should be such as to facilitate the extracting of information.

(*l*) The layout must be balanced, providing a neat appearance. A variety of print-faces should not be used.

(*m*) Where necessary, instructions for completing the form should be included.

(*n*) Where possible, answers should be called for in the form of markings instead of words. For example, a person assessing something (or someone) as 'fair' could be required to so indicate in one of the following ways.

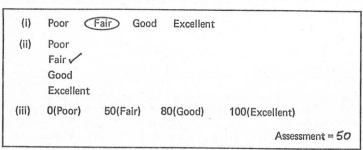

7.13   Reducing the Paper Mountain

Because of the constant necessity to obtain and process information, even the smallest business acquires an extensive amount of paper. In larger organisations it reaches vast proportions. One of the major objectives of administration is to reduce the quantity so far as it is safe to do so without damaging efficiency or security. To this end, various principles are generally accepted.

(*a*) Some paperwork can sometimes be eliminated completely. As an example one may quote a well-known multiple store which in the past had the practice of requiring counter-assistants to make a written requisition on the Stores for whatever stock they needed to replenish their counters. It was eventually realised that such a practice served no useful purpose. Assistants now simply draw supplies as they require them and the storekeepers note the consequent reductions in their stocks. (Other examples of this principle are given on page 179.)

(*b*) Information should not be retained merely 'in case it is needed'. A manager who dare not distinguish between useful and useless information will become encumbered with files which are never referred to. His problem can be eased by ensuring that information is distributed only to those who require it.

(*c*) Filing can be very expensive. The cost of floor-space used for filing is a major factor and wasted space means unnecessary cost. This cost can be reduced by a judicious 'weeding out' of records which are too old to serve any useful purpose. The space occupied by records which must be kept can be considerably reduced by microfilming them.

(*d*) Efficient layout of documents can increase the ratio of data to paper space. A form can be designed so as to serve more than one purpose and thereby reduce the number of forms.

Key Points

1. Information *coming into* a business must be converted into a form suitable for processing.

    Information *from within* a business may or may not have to be converted.

    Information *going out of* a business may or may not have to be converted into a form acceptable to the addressee.

2. An **integrated information system** requires a master copy which will automatically provide copies to serve as subsequent documents. This has the advantages of:

    (*a*) requiring completion of only the master;
    (*b*) allowing for selected information to appear on the copies.

    Copies may be produced

    (*a*) automatically;
    (*b*) by carbons; one-time carbons or carbon-backed paper;
    (*c*) by carbonless paper.

3. A **flow chart** shows the distribution of copies in an integrated system.

4. **Data flows** are essential but must be controlled to prevent proliferation.

5. The **designing of forms** is a specialist function and should be controlled.

    A form should

    (*a*) be logically arranged and with a balanced layout;
    (*b*) make it easy to write/type on and to file;
    (*c*) have a title and a coding;
    (*d*) be directly relevant to its purpose.

8

BASIC PROCEDURES AND FORMS

8.1 Introduction

The previous chapter provides a summary of the principles and practices relevant to the receiving and processing of information. Any business will have procedures specific to itself because of the nature of its activities, but there are some fundamental procedures which are common to many businesses. This chapter aims to provide examples of such procedures and the relevant documents. In so doing it must be explained that no matter what method is used for any one procedure the basic pattern will be the same, because the main objectives of a procedure in one business will also be those of another business. Techniques used in processing and recording information therefore differ, although a general principle is that as many documents as possible will be produced from a master document.

A number of procedures have a direct link with accounting records and, as a consequence, they must be designed accordingly. Any procedure relevant to accounting, however complex it is, must be based on the principles of double-entry book-keeping. Therefore, the observations made in this chapter about sales accounting and the available methods of posting accounts are also applicable to procedures relevant to purchasing and cash transactions.

8.2 Counter Sales

Fig. 8.1 refers to an across-the-counter sale by a supplier of electrical goods to a firm of electrical contractors.

Any sales on credit would be based on an agreement between buyer and seller. Following trade enquiries by the merchant, there would be an agreement to supply goods on credit up to a certain value. The length of the credit and any discounts allowable for early payment would also be specified. There would be a condition as to which employees could obtain supplies on credit by signing on behalf of the contractor.

The illustration is of a **sales ticket** issued when goods are ordered at the premises of the supplier. It may be analysed as follows:

(*a*) As this is a credit sale, the identification of the customer by name and account number allows a retained copy to be used to debit his account. His agreement to this is evidenced by the signature of his representative.

(*b*) Had it been a cash sale the ticket would have been marked accordingly. The supplier would have signed the top copy and handed it to the buyer as his receipt. The total of the ticket as shown on the retained copy would have been added to those of all other cash sales for that day (probably on an adding-listing machine), so that a reconciliation could be made with the cash in hand at the end of the day. This in turn would be related to the amount then banked and any cash retained as a 'float'.

(*c*) A third copy may be retained in order to relate it to stock records, but it is more probable the supplier would rely only on visual stock checks.

(*d*) The amount of Value Added Tax would be extracted to VAT records, eventually to be accounted for to the authorities. The purchaser is also provided with evidence of tax suffered.

SPARKS LTD Electrical goods merchants 59 Blake Road, Billton, Surrey						Counter Sales	
Name and address: ABEL ELECTRICS LTD, 15, BAKER STREET, HOMETOWN.						Date 3/8/19..	
Collected/deliver to..							
Sold by . 5. ..... Cash/cheque Charge account no. .2291.........							
Quantity	Description		Price		Amount		
12	Tumbler switch XB/29/1		1	50	18		
5	Break Safe Unit A21		4	10	20	50	
6 - box	Pins JS/455/A2		1	20	7	20	
					45	70	
	VAT @ 15%				6	85	
					52	55	
C9987	Ordered by ... J.S. Mills .... Paid						

Fig. 8.1. Sales ticket.

(*e*) Had it been required that the goods be delivered, the information is available for compiling loading and delivery schedules.

(*f*) The person effecting the sale is identified in case there is a subsequent query about the transaction. (In some businesses such an identification may be necessary for assessing salesmen's commission.)

(*g*) The ticket number serves as a control on sales tickets.

(*h*) The top copy provides the contractor with a record of his purchases and may be used in costing the job(s) in which the supplies are used.

8.3   Sales Accounting

A procedure for *processing* sales is given in the previous chapter. It was shown that a copy of the invoice was used to debit the customer's account, but it is now necessary to consider the subsequent procedures in order that the following records are produced:

(*a*) The amounts and dates of each customer's purchases, identified by the invoice numbers.

(*b*) The amounts and dates of each customer's payments, referenced to Cash Book entries.

(c) The amounts allowed to any customer for returned goods, identified by **credit notes.**

(d) The amount owing by each customer.

(e) The total amount of sales, analysed as required into products, areas, etc.

(f) The total owed by all customers.

(g) Statements of Account to be sent to customers.

Traditional and Other Methods

Whatever system is used to produce the above records, it can only be based on the traditional hand-kept book-keeping method. Fig. 8.2 outlines the traditional method and compares it with the basic operations in other systems. (In the interests of simplicity, the example deals only with procedures relevant to sales. Similar principles apply in recording payments by and allowances to customers.)

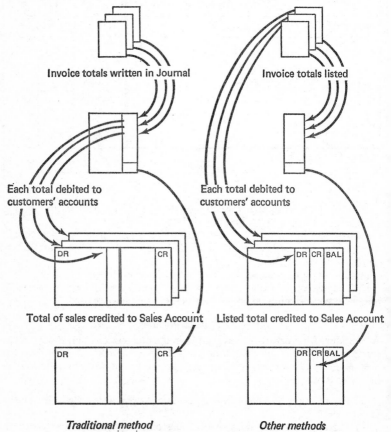

Fig. 8.2. Sales accounting processes.

In both cases the initial posting media are copy invoices. In the traditional method the amounts are written in a Sales Journal (which may be analysed) and totalled for the day. In other methods the totals of all invoices are listed and totalled by machine. At the simplest this would be an adding machine.

The traditional method then requires that each item is transferred from the Journal to the debit of the appropriate customer's account. In other methods, however, the invoices are used. As compared with the traditional method, accounts are kept on loose-leaf cards which are usually housed in binders. Invariably, they display the figures so that each entry produces a new balance, instead of the traditional 'two-sided' book method

The total sales for the day are credited to the Sales Account, either from the total of the Sales Journal or the tally list of invoices.

As a Statement of Account is merely a copy of a customer's account, entries on it and the account can be made in one operation if the accounts are in loose-leaf form.

Posting Methods

These may be broadly divided between manual and mechanical. (Because the processes and techniques of computerisation are unique they are considered in Chapter 14.)

The most efficient method of posting by hand is the **manifold posting system.** Various forms of equipment are available but the basic principle is that several documents can be written at the same time. This, obviously, reduces the amount of labour involved and ensures there is no inaccuracy in transferring a figure from one document to another. The bottom document is the Sales Journal. This is overlaid by two copies of the customer's account, one being the Statement of Account. They are so placed that the next entry on them is duplicated on to the next vacant line of the Journal. The method is made easier if non-carbon paper is used (see page 67).

The documents may be aligned on a writing board or they may be positioned in a loose-leaf binder as shown in Fig. 8.3.

Accounting (or **ledger-posting**) **machines** are tending to be superseded by computers but they continue to be useful where there is insufficient work to justify computerisation. The machine not only posts but also makes the required calculations. To post an account it is necessary first to key in the existing balance. Entry of the debit or credit then produces the new balance. Duplication provides the Statement of Account. Interchangeable control bars can be fitted to provide all such additional data as is required.

8.4 Purchasing

The functions of the Purchasing Department and its relationships with other departments are discussed in Chapter 3.

The Order

This must be a standard form, printed with the buyer's name and address. Fig. 16.1 (page 186) demonstrates how this may be a master document, copies of which provide the other documents required for the complete process. It must contain the following:

(*a*) The name and address of the supplier.
(*b*) The date of the order.
(*c*) The reference number of the order.
(*d*) Exact details of the goods ordered, including the *supplier's* description and code, and the quantity.

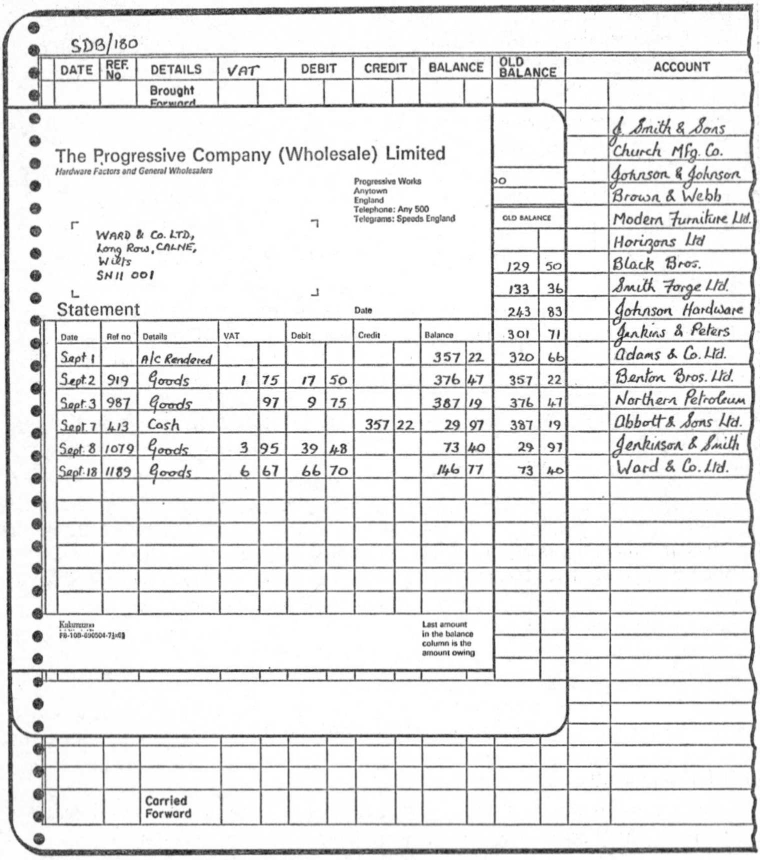
SDB/180

DATE	REF. No	DETAILS	VAT	DEBIT	CREDIT	BALANCE	OLD BALANCE	ACCOUNT
		Brought Forward						
								J. Smith & Sons
								Church Mfg. Co.
								Johnson & Johnson
								Brown & Webb
								Modern Furniture Ltd.
								Horizons Ltd
							129 50	Black Bros.
							133 36	Smith Forge Ltd.
							243 83	Johnson Hardware
							301 71	Jenkins & Peters
							320 66	Adams & Co. Ltd.
							357 22	Benton Bros. Ltd.
							376 47	Northern Petroleum
							387 19	Abbott & Sons Ltd.
							29 97	Jenkinson & Smith
							73 40	Ward & Co. Ltd.
		Carried Forward						

The Progressive Company (Wholesale) Limited
Hardware Factors and General Wholesalers

Progressive Works
Anytown
England
Telephone: Any 500
Telegrams: Speeds England

WARD & Co. LTD,
Long Row, CALNE,
Wilts
SN11 001

Statement

Date

Date	Ref no	Details	VAT	Debit	Credit	Balance
Sept 1		A/c Rendered				357 22
Sept. 2	919	Goods	1 75	17 50		376 47
Sept. 3	987	Goods	97	9 75		387 19
Sept. 7	413	Cash			357 22	29 97
Sept. 8	1079	Goods	3 95	39 48		73 40
Sept. 18	1189	Goods	6 67	66 70		146 77

Kalamazoo
FB-100-690504-7½×6¾

Last amount in the balance column is the amount owing

Fig. 8.3. A manifold posting system.
(By courtesy of Kalamazoo Ltd.)

(*e*) The price (if previously agreed).
(*f*) The place of delivery.
(*g*) Any conditions as to packing, etc., and any imposed by statutory regulations, custom of the industry, etc.
(*h*) The delivery date required.
(*i*) The signature of an authorised person.

A specimen order form is given in Fig. 8.4.

```
                        ORDER FORM
                 COMMERCIAL PRODUCTS LTD
                      Abercorn Place
                  Milton Road  Blanktown

┌                           ┐
  Abel Baker Ltd                      Order No. 1597/5
    Driad Works
      Industrial Estate              Date 5/9/19..
        Billington                   Ref AB/JS
└                           ┘
Please supply the following goods:
```

Quantity	Description	Unit price	Price
6 carboys	Stripping fluid BL9	12.50	75.—
50 litres	Refining liquid RG22/XP	5.60	280.—

```
Deliver to: Motor Division    Delivery          Conditions
            Baker Street      required     Packing to comply with
            Billington        1.10.19..    trade conditions S/155


 A. Brown.
 ............... Buyer
```

------------------------------perforation------------------------------

Please complete this slip and return it within 7 days.
To Commercial Products Ltd: Your purchase order 1597/5 is accepted
                                  in accordance with the conditions stated.

                          Signed . . . .

Fig. 8.4. Purchase order form.

Other Documents

Titles and functions of the other documents used by the purchaser are quoted in the description of the procedure on page 186. The supplier would send a **delivery note** with the goods, detailing the consignment. The note must be checked against the unopened packages and, if they agree and there is no apparent damage, a copy will be signed and handed back to the delivery driver (see Fig. 7.8, page 68).

Order Follow-up

Having given an order, it is the responsibility of the Purchasing Department to 'chase' the supplier if the goods are not received on time. Fig. 8.5 shows the record kept of the order illustrated in Fig. 8.4. Motor Division requisitioned the goods on 4th September. A quotation was agreed with the supplier on 5th September and the order was sent the same day. As the goods had not been delivered by 1st October, the supplier was telephoned the following day. The goods arrived on 4th October and the Motor Division was notified immediately. The invoice was received on 1st November and vouched for payment the following day.

Supplier Albert Baker Ltd. Order No. 1597/5								
Requ. received	Quote agreed	Order sent	Due	Follow-up	Goods received	Dept advised	Invoice received	Invoice vouched
4/9 Motor div	5/9 Telephone	5/9	1/10	2/10 Telephone	4/10	4/10	1/11	2/11

Fig. 8.5. Order record.

8.5   The Stores

Stock Records

A card is maintained for each item in stock, giving the title of the article and its code. An article and another almost similar one must have separate cards and codes. For example, two metal plates, each serving the same purpose but being of different thicknesses, may be coded as ABX/25/1 and ABX/25/2, the suffixes indicating the size differences.

Cards may be maintained in a visible index system (see page 116). Sometimes they are kept in or on the containers holding the goods (and are then known as **bin cards**)

A stock card is used like a ledger, whereby amounts are debited and credited, each entry producing a new balance figure. The document for recording incoming stock is the **goods received note** (see page 185), made out when goods are received. Outgoing stock is entered from **requisitions**, signed by those withdrawing stock (see below). Both documents are filed after the requisite entries have been made. A stock card is illustrated in Fig. 8.6.

The significance of the 'minimum' and 'maximum' figures on the card is its control function. There must always be sufficient stock in hand to meet requirements, but the amount held must not be so large as to incur unnecessarily high storage costs. It is therefore necessary to decide the amount below which stock should not fall and the amount above which it would be uneconomic to store. To determine this it is first necessary to assess the average rate of consumption of stock—that is, the amount normally issued over set periods. Obviously, there must always be sufficient available to meet foreseeable demand but this is complicated by the length of time it will require to obtain more stock. It may be safe to hold stock sufficient for, say, two weeks' consumption,

but it would not be so if it took four weeks to get additional supplies. Therefore, the time required for delivery (known as **lead time**) must be taken account
of. The minimum figure therefore includes this factor. It is sometimes referred
to as the 'reorder' figure.

Mixer taps – chrome – ogee MX/25/A/4				Minimum 200 Maximum 500
Date	Source ref.	Inward	Outward	Balance
				220
4/10	29554	200		420
6/10	15782		20	400
7/11	20044		150	250
15/11	32221	200		450
1/12	20277		50	400

Fig. 8.6. Stock record card.

Every item should be listed in a **stock manual,** giving detailed specifications
and possible suppliers.

Requisitions

Drawings of stock are made on standard serially-numbered forms and
must be signed only by authorised persons. Where appropriate, a requisition
should be referenced to the job for which the stock is required as a form of
production control. If the price of the issued stock is entered, a copy of the
document would thereby provide information for costing a job or calculating
departmental expenses.

A specimen requisition is shown in Fig. 8.7.

STORES REQUISITION				
Store	Department	Cost ref. or job no.	Date	No.
3	Drawing Office	6/255	1/12/19--	74559
10 Packs of 100, Tracing Paper WPX 6077/4.				£69-50
Authorised signature or stamp *J. Wallis*		Storekeeper's stamp (STORE 3)		

Fig. 8.7. Stores requisition.

Stock-taking

This is sometimes known as **stock check** or **inventory.** It is an essential process for the following reasons:

(*a*) *Records must be checked for inaccuracies.* It is not always possible to rely on the accuracy of stock records. This is particularly so when small items are issued in bulk, such as nails. Where the count discloses a difference the record should be adjusted accordingly. It may sometimes be found that the effective level of stock is less than that shown because some of it has deteriorated or been damaged. There may even be losses due to pilferage. In any such cases the amount of the loss must be written off in the accounts. It should also lead to a tightening of control.

(*b*) *The value of stock must be shown in the final accounts.* In general, auditors accept the figures of the stock-takers if those figures are certified by the directors. The auditors may supplement this by spot checks.

There are two main methods of stock-taking.

(*a*) **Annual stock count.** Every item is counted once a year under this method. This gives a positive year-end figure and in that respect it is the preferred method. The disadvantage is the disruption it causes. Staff, most of whom have no experience of the work, have to be organised to carry out the count. While it is on, goods received and issued have to be allowed for, thereby complicating the process. This would not apply, of course, if the exercise could be carried out when the business was closed, but this is frequently not possible.

(*b*) **Perpetual inventory.** This means that the count goes on throughout the year. A staff of specialists works to a programme so that every item is counted during the year. The disadvantage that the year-end figure will not be exactly correct can be reduced by arranging for fast-moving items to be counted more than once. The system allows for the job to be incorporated into the normal work process, with no interruption of daily activities. It also allows for the operation to be undertaken more thoroughly and it enables discrepancies to be identified at an earlier stage.

8.6 Wages and Salaries

There are three major stages involved in the payment of wages and salaries. As shown in Fig. 8.8, the basic information is passed to the Pay Office, which then makes further calculations and the cashier pays the net amounts due.

Calculating Gross Wages

Wages are usually calculated at hourly rates. There would be a rate for the agreed 'standard' working week and another rate for overtime. It is therefore necessary to have a record of the number of hours worked by each hourly-paid employee. This could be in a form similar to that in Fig. 8.9 and could be completed by the employee writing in the relevant figures or it could be done automatically by using time cards in conjunction with time-recording clocks.

If the employee is working under a bonus scheme, methods must be devised to calculate his entitlement. The methods will differ according to the circumstances and the practice of the firm. If the bonus is based on a standard time for completing a task his entitlement will be related to 'time saved'—that is, the standard time allowed for the task less the time he spent on it. This may be calculated on a **job card**, which relates to a particular process and records the relevant figures. Alternatively, the bonus may be based on output which, again, would be related to a standard.

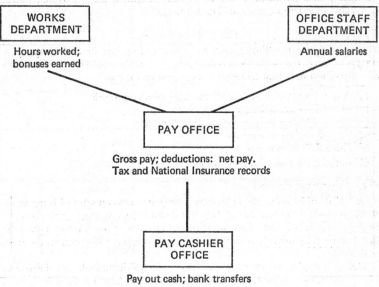

Fig. 8.8. Wages and salaries data flow.

Calculating Net Pay

Details of each hourly-paid employee's work as calculated above are sent to the Pay Office. Information about fixed salaries would be given to the Office only when appointments are made or changes in pay are effected.

A **payroll** lists all the employees and shows, in respect of each, the gross pay, deductions for income tax, National Insurance, staff pension contributions, etc., and the resulting net pay. There would also be shown the *employer's* contributions to National Insurance in respect of each employee. The totals of the relevant columns therefore provide the following information:

(*a*) The cost of wages and salaries.

(*b*) The amount to be paid to each employee.

(*c*) The amounts accountable for income tax deductions and National Insurance contributions by employees and employer.

(*d*) The amounts to be transferred to staff pension funds, etc.

Taxation Documents

It is necessary to have a pay record for each employee in order to record the cumulative wage and tax figures over the fiscal year. This can appear on the

| Name .... | | | | Works No. .... | |
| Department .... | | | | Week ending .... | |

Day		Start	Finish	Total hours	Ord. hours	Overtime
M	am	0800	1230	9	8	1
	pm	1330	1800			
TU	am	0800	1230	8	8	—
	pm	1330	1700			

Weekly Totals			48	40	8

Foreman's signature	Bonus　£
....	Job card

FOR OFFICE USE.	Ordinary hours @		
Pay clerk	Overtime hours @		
....	Bonus		
	GROSS PAY		

Fig. 8.9. Time card.

Government **tax deduction card (form P11)** but an internal system can be used if it is approved by the Inland Revenue.

Each employee must have a **pay advice slip** each time he is paid, showing how his net pay has been calculated (see Fig. 8.10).

Various methods are used to produce the required documents. If it is done by hand, probably the best method is the copy-writer method. The system enables the payroll and the two documents mentioned above to be completed simultaneously by overlaying them on a writing board. Duplication is simplified if non-carbon paper is used.

Whatever method is employed, the requirements are to do the work quickly and accurately, to provide the necessary totals and facilitate their transfer within the accounting system, and to comply with Inland Revenue regulations.

At the end of the fiscal year the employer submits form P35 to the Inland Revenue, detailing, in respect of each employee, the amount of pay for the year and the deductions which had been made for tax and National Insurance. At the same time form P60 is given to each employee, showing his gross wages, the tax deducted and his wages after tax. Upon an employee changing his employment he is given form P45, showing his tax position at that time,

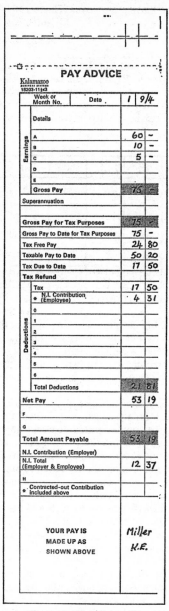

Fig. 8.10. Pay advice slip.
(By courtesy of Kalamazoo Ltd.)

so that he may hand it to his new employer. The top copy is sent to the Inland Revenue.

Paying Out

The proportion of wages and salaries which is paid in cash has declined considerably in recent years. Paying cash causes additional work and has obvious security risks. Accordingly, employers encourage staff to accept payment by transfers to their bank accounts. If both methods are used, the total net amount due must be divided between cash payments and transfer payments.

	£10	£5	£1	50p	10p	5p	Net pay
Mr. A	40	5		.50	.10	.05	45.65
Mr. B	60		1			.05	61.05
Mr. C	40		2	.50	.10		42.60
Mr. D	30	5	3	.50		.05	38.55
	170	10	6	1.50	.20	.15	187.85

Fig. 8.11. Payroll cash analysis.

The amount to be paid in cash must be drawn from the bank in a mixture of notes and coins such as will allow the exact amount to be placed in each envelope. Fig. 8.11 provides a simple example of a cash analysis, indicating the multiples of notes and coins to be drawn. Many companies 'round up' any pennies to 5p to avoid the inconvenience and extra work of dealing in bronze coins.

In making up pay packets, each sheet of the payroll should be dealt with separately. The total cash (analysed as to its makeup) required to pay those on one page should first be counted out. One clerk should then call the name or number of the first employee and the amount due according to the payroll sheet. A second clerk should check this figure against the amount shown on the pay advice. He should count out the money required and hand it and the pay-slip to the first clerk or another for checking. The cash and the slip should then be placed in the envelope, which should be left unsealed. When the name of the last employee is reached the remaining cash should equal the amount due to him. The only possibility of error would be a compensating one. Reducing the number of operations necessary before exhausting the cash makes such a mistake unlikely. The accuracy of the cash insertions may then be assumed to be proved and the envelopes can be sealed.

The actual handing out of pay packets differs between organisations. It is usual to do it by departments or sections so that packets must be sorted into 'pay stations'. Shop-floor workers collecting packets may be identified by their foremen or they may produce their clock cards. The amount of the net pay will be shown on or through the envelope and there are often perforations enabling the employee to see the amount of cash inside. The employee may acknowledge receipt by signing a register or a tear-off portion of the pay advice slip or envelope, or he may sign his clock card when he produces it.

There may be unclaimed pay packets. The pay clerk will return these to the cashier, together with whatever record is kept of acknowledgments of pay packets. The cashier will check that all packets are accounted for, either collected or returned, and will sign to indicate he has custody of the unclaimed ones. Arrangements must be made for any absent employee to receive his wages—unless, of course, he is away for only that day. The usual cause of absence is illness, in which case the money may be sent to him by money order or given to someone else on the employee's authority.

Where payment is by bank transfer, Bank Giro slips and Giro schedules are handed to the bank with a cheque for the total. The amounts are then distributed through the Bank Clearing House system. Each such employee must receive from the employer a pay advice slip.

8.7   Cash Transactions

At the centre of all recording relevant to cash transactions is the **Cash Book**. In designing and maintaining the Cash Book the following principles apply:

(*a*) *The sources of all incoming money must be identifiable.*

(*i*) Money received by post must first be entered in a **Mail Book,** with an identification of the sender. The book and the remittances must be handed to the cashier who will then sign the book as evidence of receipt (see page 138).

(*ii*) Items received as bank transfers must be linked to the related transfer advices.

(*iii*) Money received direct from salesmen and collectors must be accompanied by identification of the payers in the case of transactions which were on credit, so that the amounts may be posted to the debtors' accounts.

(*iv*) Amounts received by bank transfer which had been paid into bank branches by salesmen must be reconciled with lists of the payers submitted by the salesmen. These could be in the form of duplicate bank paying-in slips, itemising the payers.

(*b*) *All money received by salesmen and collectors, whether for cash or credit transactions, must be reconciled with a cash register tally roll or duplicates of issued receipts.*

(*c*) *The total of money received, as shown in the Cash Book, must be reconciled with a bank paying-in list.* As a general rule, every day's banking should equal the amount of the previous day's income.

(*d*) *Where possible, suitable methods should be used so that duplicating of documents provides posting media to other records as well as the Cash Book.* For example, duplication of particulars of cheques drawn can serve as posting media.

Petty Cash

It is usual to make provision for payments to be made for small items and 'emergencies'. Essential features of such a system are as follows:

(*a*) Written directives must be given as to the items for which petty cash may be used and the amount which may be expended on any one item. For example, small stationery supplies which the company cannot immediately provide may be bought from a local stationer; an employee may require a bus or taxi fare to go on company business.

(*b*) Authorisation of expenditure may be given only by specified people.

(*c*) Details of the expenditure must be entered on a **petty cash slip**, signed by the authorising person and the person drawing the money (see Fig. 8.12). Where possible, a sales ticket should be attached.

```
┌─────────────────────────────────────────────────────────┐
│ PETTY CASH SLIP          Date . . . . . . . .      1552   │
│                                                           │
│ Dept. . . . . . . . . . . . . . . . . Authorised by . . . . . . . . . . . . . . . . . │
│                                                           │
│ PCB Ref . . . . . . . . . . . . . Drawn by . . . . . . . . . . . . . . . . . . . . . . │
├─────────────────────────────────────────────┬──────┬─────┤
│                                             │      │     │
│                                             │      │     │
│                                             │      │     │
│                                             │      │     │
│                                             │      │     │
│                                             │      │     │
│                                             │      │     │
└─────────────────────────────────────────────┴──────┴─────┘
```

Fig. 8.12. Petty cash slip.

(*d*) A person must be responsible for keeping the **petty cash book** and the cash float. Both must be reconciled and checked by the cashier at intervals.

(*e*) Petty cash slips should be serially numbered and the relevant number must be entered against each item in the petty cash book. The slips must be produced when the cash balance is reconciled.

(*f*) The petty cash book should allow for analysis of the expenditure items so that the totals may be incorporated in the main accounting system.

(*g*) The book should be kept on the **imprest system,** whereby money spent is reimbursed to restore the cash in hand to the agreed amount of the float.

8.8 Production Control

A considerable number of documents are used in controlling production, each of them specifically designed to meet the requirements of the particular manufacturer. However, it is possible to itemise those used by most producers and outline their functions.

Certain plans and calculations must be made before a production process commences. The amount and types of goods to be produced having been decided, it will be necessary to compile **materials schedules,** giving the amounts and specifications of materials to be obtained by the Purchasing Department. The production process will be analysed into stages so that the time each machine will be occupied on the work can be calculated. These will be entered on **machine-loading records** so that there is no undue 'idle time' or 'queueing'. The sequence of operations will be planned and the time allowed for each will be determined. These will appear on a **sequence schedule.**

From these and other calculations a **master planning schedule** would be compiled. Within that schedule the following documents would be operative:

Route sheet or card. This indicates the sequence of operations and travels with the job.

Operation sheet or job card. This lists all the details relevant to one operation or job, detailing the processes, objective criteria and the time allowed for its completion. It is issued to the person responsible for that particular job or operation.

Progress sheet. This provides an overall record of performance. The completion of each stage is marked on the sheet and related to the relevant target. It thereby indicates any deviation so that, if possible, corrective action can be taken.

Inspection sheets. These indicate the points of inspection and the checks to be made at each point. The inspector's report at each stage is made on the sheet and returned to the Production Control Department.

(The functions of the production area and its relationships with other areas are considered in Chapter 3.)

8.9 Export Documentation

By the very nature of international trade, documents used in exporting travel to every country. There is, therefore, a degree of uniformity, which must, however, take account of the local controls exercised by governments in respect of goods and payment for them. Standardisation in respect of European trade has been increased because of the necessity to comply with the complicated systems of subsidies and duties which are part of EEC regulations.

The principles of simultaneous copying already discussed in this book have been officially accepted by a body known as the Simplification of International Trade Procedures Board (SITPRO). Its recommendation is that a master document be prepared so that all the required documents are automatically produced as copies. This is demonstrated in Fig. 8.13. It is estimated that 90 per cent of export documentation is now done by simultaneous copying methods.

The main documents may be briefly described as follows:

(*a*) **Documents of Title.** In former times the first of the documents of title named below (the Bill of Lading) was made out for every overseas consignment. It represented ownership of the goods while they were on the high seas, and could be used to transfer ownership of the goods by selling the document which represented them. Today, exports travel by such a variety of methods that a whole range of documents with similar properties to the Bill of Lading has been developed. Not all of them are used to transfer *ownership*, however, since in some cases the goods move so fast there is no time to sell them before they reach their destination.

(*i*) **The Bill of Lading.** This represents title to the goods, so that its transfer has the effect of changing ownership of the goods. It will normally be used for general cargo sent by sea (as distinct from containerised cargo) and attached to it will be the **invoice**, and the **certificate of insurance,** which provides indemnity in the event of damage or loss at sea.

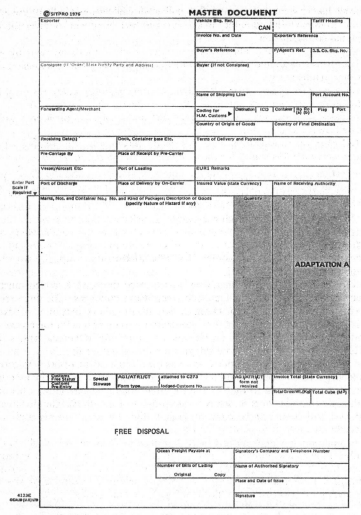

Fig. 8.13. Simultaneous copying of export documents.

(ii) *The Short Form Bill of Lading*. Where goods are carried by container by a responsible combined-transport operator it is usual to use this document. Because it does not specify a particular ship, or a particular port of loading or discharge, it gives the transporter greater flexibility in the use of ships, lorries, etc. Since the carrier usually assumes full responsibility for the whole transport operation the old restrictions placed upon him to use ports convenient to the exporter and the importer do not apply.

(iii) *The Freight Forwarder's Certificate of Shipment*. Where a freight forwarder has a 'groupage' system (i.e. one where he groups several consignments to make a full container load) he issues this document to cover the individual consignments.

(*iv*) *The Air Waybill.* This document is used when goods are sent by air. It conforms to an international agreement and places specific responsibilities on the various parties.

(*v*) *The CMR Consignment Note.* This document (which is the result of an international agreement) is used for goods travelling by road, using the short-run cross-Channel routes. CMR stands for the Convention on Merchandise carried by Road Hauliers.

(*vi*) *The CIM Consignment Note.* All goods travelling by rail are covered by this document. CIM stands for the Convention on International Merchandise.

(*b*) **The Customs Declaration Form.** This is used by the UK Government to provide statistics of exports, etc. It provides facilities for claiming 'process inwards relief' for exporters whose goods were made from imported materials on which duty was paid when they were imported.

(*c*) **The National Standard Shipping Note.** This lists the goods which are being passed to a Port Authority, the ship they are to be loaded on to and the identification marks of the goods. It is submitted to the Authority with the goods.

(*d*) **The Certificate of Origin.** This is used when there is a free-trade agreement between the exporting and the importing countries. The importing country must be assured that the goods actually originated in a country which is party to the agreement and that they were not sent by a circuitous route in order to claim a concession which was not valid. The document states the origin of the goods and is certified by a competent authority.

(*e*) **EEC Documents.** Special documents are required in respect of goods which are subject to EEC regulations. A **Movement Certificate** can be used for a consignment which is to be within the Community because no Customs duties are payable when it passes between member-countries. The document will certify that the goods freely circulate in the exporting country and that accordingly there is an entitlement to the concession.

A more sophisticated document is the **T Form.** This not only declares the status of the goods but also allows them to go through Customs posts without inspection. The goods are inspected by Customs at the Office of Departure and the vehicle is sealed. At all subsequent Customs posts the seals are inspected and if they are intact the vehicle is passed unopened.

Key Points

1. Any **accounting procedure** must be based on traditional book-keeping methods. **Posting methods** include:
   (*a*) manifold posting by hand;
   (*b*) accounting (ledger posting) machines;
   (*c*) computers.

2. A **purchasing procedure** requires:
   (*a*) an order form, possibly with copies for further documentation;
   (*b*) records of orders made;
   (*c*) 'follow-up' of late deliveries.

3. **Stock records** include:

    (a) *stock cards* for every item (filed or bin cards), showing minimum, maximum and reorder levels (allowing for 'lead time');

    (b) *requisitions* (signed by authorised person) for posting to stock cards;

    (c) *goods inward forms* (possibly as copies of orders) for posting to stock cards;

    (d) *stock manual*, containing details of stock items and suppliers.

4. **Annual stock count**

    (a) causes disruption to normal working;

    (b) may be hurried and involves non-specialists;

    (c) gives true year-end figures.

Perpetual inventory

    (a) is continuous and non-disruptive;

    (b) involves specialist staff;

    (c) quickly identifies discrepancies;

    (d) can give a fairly accurate year-end figure.

5. **Paying wages** requires a system which will provide:

    (a) *in respect of each employee*—gross entitlement, deductions, net pay, pay advice, cash or bank transfer;

    (b) *in total*—cost, cash analysis and bank transfers, National Insurance and tax deductions, other deductions, Inland Revenue returns.

6. **Handling cash** requires:

    (a) Identification and vouching of all incoming and outgoing items.

    (b) Reconciliation of net intake with banked amounts.

    (c) Control of petty cash.

9

PRESENTATION OF INFORMATION

9.1 Introduction

In previous chapters it was shown that data often have to be compiled in such a manner as to enable subsequent documentation easily and logically to become part of the overall procedure. However, information has also to flow *outside* the confines of those procedures which serve fundamental functions. The following points have relevance to the presentation of information:

(*a*) It must be provided as a basis for *decision-making*.

(*b*) It must be part of *planning and control*.

(*c*) It can take the form of *expressing opinions and proposals*.

(*d*) It can *inform* those who do not take decisions but who will be affected by them.

(*e*) It can be in the form of *directives*.

(*f*) It can pass *outside the business*.

The effectiveness of such information is largely dependent upon the manner of its presentation.

9.2 The Sources of Reports

In any sizeable organisation a considerable number of reports will be used as vehicles for passing information. They will exist for various reasons.

(*a*) *As part of an established pattern.* Programmes are often established which call for regular reports. In the normal process of work, financial statements and summaries of various sorts will be made, formalised returns will be submitted, etc.

(*b*) *In response to a request.* A person or body may make a report on the instructions of another person or body. Such a report should identify its source by having a preamble similar to the following:

As requested by the Finance Committee at its meeting on . . . I submit my report herewith.

(*c*) *Following an occurrence for which a report is prescribed.* Regulations will frequently stipulate that on the happening of a specified event a named person or body must report to others on the circumstances. For example, departmental managers are usually required to report if any member of their staff is absent beyond a certain number of days without permission; rules will provide that any accident must be reported.

(*d*) *By nature of a person's responsibilities.* The responsibilities of a person often carry with them the requirement to make reports. For example, a representative of the staff on a joint consultative committee would have as part of his duties the requirement to give to his members accounts of meetings he had held with the management side.

(*e*) *As part of committee procedures.* A structure of committees will have an inbuilt pattern of reports from one committee to another.

9.3   Effective Report-writing

Reports must make positive contributions. To achieve this it is necessary they be framed to accord with certain principles.

(*a*) *They must convey information clearly and adequately.* The person(s) to whom a report is addressed often has to make decisions based on facts stated

```
From Staff Amenities Committee

To Staff Council

    We have looked at the problems of erecting
a new pavilion and studied various estimates
for building it.

    We recommend we accept the tender from Briggs
& Co. on the understanding they complete it in
time for the opening of the cricket season.
We don't agree, however, that the veranda floor
be in tiles.   To reduce cost it should be in
wood.

1st October, 19..
```

Fig. 9.1. An ineffective report.

in the report. A report which is ambiguous and which fails to provide positive information is useless. An example of such a report is given in Fig. 9.1. It will be seen that it gives no detail about the contract, so it would be impossible for the Staff Council to decide whether or not to bind itself to meet the cost. The Council could not make an informed decision if it had no information about the other tenders. No mention is made of the comparative costs of the two types of flooring.

(*b*) *They should not contain slang or jargon.* Reports need not necessarily be 'stuffy' but they must not go to the other extreme.

(*c*) *Account must be taken of the recipients' understanding of the subject matter.* Directors will often commission reports from experts because the Board does not include those knowledgeable in the relevant areas. Any committee so appointed then has the often difficult task of wording a technical report in a manner understandable by the directors. The directors must appreciate that in their interests the report will not go into such detail as to make it unintelligible to them. In turn, this places a responsibility on the experts to not hide certain facts on the ground that 'it would only confuse them'. The directors must therefore make a decision based on their faith in the accuracy and honesty of the report.

(*d*) *They must not be couched in terms likely to arouse resentment*. Fig. 9.2 gives an example of a bad communication and one which would certainly

---

From the Chief Personnel Officer

To All Office Staff

My attention has been drawn to the unhappy fact that there appears to be a lamentable failure to duly process through the offices of the Staff Association such matters as are provided for under the agreement made in 1976.

By reason of my office and the attendant responsibilities imposed upon me I am required to remind you of the stipulated procedures and the imperative necessity to adhere to them in every respect. It is contrary to such requisites to proffer complaints other than through the freely determined channels. Recently I have had the disturbing and exasperating experience of having complaints from individual staff members deposited on my desk and which patently had not progressed through the defined lines of communication.

I must therefore take this opportunity to state that in the event of further un-authorised submissions reaching me by unrecognised methods I will be forced to take such action as I deem to be called for in the particular circumstances.

Fig. 9.2. A badly worded memorandum.

cause ill-feeling. It is long-winded, the language is pretentious and the tone abrasive.

(*e*) *Information must be presented logically*. So far as possible, one item should lead directly to the next. For example, if a report aims to propose changes it should open by outlining the *present* position.

(*f*) *Reports must be formalised in layout* (see below).

From the Safety Officer

To the Establishment Officer

Copies: House Committee Secretary
Mr J Bundy
Mr T Lipsey, House Manager   13th February, 19..

Investigation of accident to Mr J Bundy and subsequent events

As requested in your memorandum dated 6th February, 19.., I have
investigated the above circumstances and report as follows.

1. The accident

1.1 Sources of information. I interviewed Mr J Bundy, porter,
at my request on 9th February, 19.. I also interviewed his
colleague, Mr S Owen, at the same time.

1.2 The incident. Both parties informed me that the accident
occurred as they were leaving work at 5 p.m. on 1st February,
19.. They stated that Mr Bundy slipped on the second step
from the bottom of stairway C, falling sideways so that his
wrist struck the left-hand wall. Mr Bundy complained of pain
in the wrist but did not consider it to be sufficient to
warrant medical examination.

2. Subsequent events

2.1 Evidence by Mr Bundy. Mr Bundy informed me that his wrist
became swollen and was very painful during the night. He saw
his doctor first thing the next morning and was sent to St
Mildred's Hospital. The Casualty Department diagnosed
fracture of a small bone in the wrist and treated him.
(Hospital report attached.)

2.2 Evidence by Head Porter. Mr T Lewis, Head Porter,
informed me that he received a telephone message from Mr
Bundy at about noon on 2nd February, explaining why he was
not in for work. Mr Lewis asked him if he had reported the
accident when it happened and Mr Bundy replied that he didn't
think he had harmed himself and that it wasn't worth reporting.

3. Subsequent investigations

3.1 The accident area. I found that the leading edge of the
stone step had been damaged. An area extending 8" in length
and 1½" in width was missing.

My opinion is that the bottom of the stairway is inadequately
lit.

3.2 Earlier report of damage. On referring to the House
Office records I found that the damage to the step had been
reported by Mr A Sexton, clerk, on 11th November last. An
entry had been made in the Report Book but obviously no
action had been taken as a result. I asked Mr T Lipsey,
House Manager, why no action had been taken following the
report. He said the work had been scheduled to be done but
was not regarded as being urgent. I have my doubts as to
whether Mr Lipsey did, in fact, see the report.

4. Recommendations

    4.1 Repairs and improvements. I recommend that the step be repaired immediately.

    As early as possible, an additional light, permanently in the 'on' position, should be fixed immediately over the bottom of stairway C.

    4.2 Report Book. All incidents appearing in the Report Book should be acted upon with such urgency as the circumstances indicate. This step remained in a dangerous condition for over two months after the damage was reported. Stairway C takes a lot of traffic and the damage should have been attended to immediately or the stairway closed until repairs had been effected. I recommend that the House Manager submits to me a monthly account of all incidents in the Report Book which have not been attended to.

    4.3 Accident reporting. Mr Bundy should have ensured that details of his accident were entered in the Accident Book before he left the building, particularly as he noticed the damaged step. Failure to report accidents can lead to complications in the event of claims for compensation. I recommend that a reminder of this rule be issued to all staff. I agree that in view of all the circumstances it was not unreasonable for Mr Bundy not to have sought medical attention immediately after the accident.

J Bowers

Fig. 9.3. Report of an accident investigation.

9.4 Report Format

Certain established principles must be observed in the layout of a report. The following points should be considered in conjunction with the specimen report in Fig. 9.3:

    (*a*) *Address*. It must be headed by the name and/or office of the person making it, and the person or body to whom it is addressed must also be identified. It is usual to place them in that order, although the addressee is sometimes placed first. Those who are to receive copies are then named.

    (*b*) *The date*. This may appear at the top or the bottom. As a point of reference it is preferable for it to appear at the top, particularly if the report is one of a series and carries an identifying number.

    (*c*) *The title*. Every report must have a title. It should be as short as possible but must be clearly indicative of the subject matter. If there are several reports on the same matter they must all have the same title so that they may be filed together to form a 'history'.

    (*d*) *The preamble*. The specimen illustrates the point made in Section 9.2(b).

    (*e*) *The body*. All the information must be set out in a logical manner in the form of paragraphs. Each paragraph should deal with one point and have an indicative title. The numbering of the paragraphs makes it easier to refer to a point in the report when it is being discussed in meetings or referred to in other documents.

(*f*) *Supporting documents.* These must be attached to the report and either mentioned in the report or itemised at the end.

(*g*) *Recommendations.* These should be made *only* if asked for or if to do so is part of the compiler's duty.

(*h*) *Signature.* It should be signed by the person making the report. If it is made by a body it must be signed by a member authorised to do so and be made in his representative capacity.

(*i*) *Salutations.* A report contains no conventional correspondence openings or closures. 'Dear sir' or 'Yours faithfully', for example, do not appear.

9.5 Other Aspects of Reports

(*a*) If a report is extensive it should open with a contents page. This should list the contents by paragraph number and, where appropriate, by sections.

(*b*) An *agreed* system of abbreviations may be used in addresses. For example, 'From GM to FD CA cc Inv' could be interpreted as 'From the General Manager to the Finance Director and the Chief Accountant, with a copy to the Investments Manager'.

(*c*) Where there is an extensive series of reports and other documents referring to one matter, there may be a point at which a summary of the history is called for. This first requires a thorough reading of all the literature to discern a pattern. If this discloses irrelevant material it should be detached so as not to interfere with the central theme when the summary is made.

If the literature includes a lot of correspondence it may be useful to identify the letters by using a uniform code in the summary. For example, letters between the Registrar of Companies and the Company Secretary may be referenced as Reg/S 1.9.19 . . .; Reg/S 2.10.19 . . ., etc.

(*d*) Any assumptions, conjectures or forecasts must be clearly stated to be such, e.g. 'It is assumed that . . .'; 'the probable rate of return would be . . .'

9.6 Statistical Presentation

A considerable amount of information is presented in statistical form. To be effective, certain principles must be observed.

(*a*) A series of statistics must consist of presentations in the same style. If presentation is in tabular form, for example, it must not suddenly change to being presented in graphic form.

(*b*) The reader should not be required to make his own calculations. The data required must be given and be supported by such calculations as are necessary to indicate the derivation of the data.

(*c*) There must be a clearly indicative title.

(*d*) The unit of measurement must be clearly indicated, e.g. £m, tonnes. Only *agreed* abbreviations should be used, e.g. m/h (miles per hour); d/wt (deadweight).

(*e*) The sources of data used must be identified.

Specific rules apply to certain forms of presentation, as indicated below.

Tabular presentation

(*a*) The period covered by the table must be shown at the top.

(*b*) Comparable figures must be immediately adjacent. Any consequent ratio should be close to the derivative figures:

1979 £	1980 £	Change %
15,500	15,887	2½+

(*c*) Large numbers may be 'rounded up', 'rounded down' or quoted to the nearest whole number. Whichever method is used must be clearly indicated. For example, £29,587,211 could be quoted as £29.6m; £29.5m; or £30m.

Ratios

Any ratios quoted must be meaningful. For example, the following figures would not be fully informative:

	Firm A	*Firm B*
Growth (this year's sales/ last year's sales)	10%	30%

For the figures to be useful would require more positive information. Firm A may be a market leader and therefore much more growth may not be possible. If Firm B had a very small share of the market last year, its growth rate is not so spectacular as it may at first seem. A more illustrative presentation would be as follows:

	Firm A %	*Firm B* %
Share of the market:		
This year	55	13
Last year	50	10
Increase	10	30

Charts and Diagrams

These have the general aims of making recognition of trends and comparisons more readily discernible. Such presentations take numerous forms but whichever method is used it must be appropriate to its purpose and take account of those who are expected to read them. Sophisticated methods can be used for specialists such as production planners and financial analysts. At the other end of the scale, simple forms such as pie charts and pictograms would be suitable for those unversed in advanced interpretations.

Graphs

In constructing graphs the following rules are applicable:

(*a*) A key to the coordinate lines must be given.

(*b*) Lettering should be displayed horizontally.

(*c*) If the effective scale commences well above zero, the vertical reading can be shown thus:

(*d*) Confusion can result from attempting to show too much information.

Index Numbers

Current numbers can be related to those prevailing on a certain date. A 'base time' is chosen and the figure then prevailing is, for the purpose of the exercise, regarded as being 100. For example, assume that the base year is 1979. Actual sales in that year amounted to £210,000 and are given an index number of 100. If sales for the year 1980 amounted to £231,000 its index number would be 110 (a rise of 10%).

9.7 Presentation by Correspondence

Principles concerning the handling of correspondence must be laid down in the interests of efficiency, customer relations, business relations and public relations.

(*a*) Much business activity stems from correspondence. It is therefore necessary that any action arising from correspondence be taken correctly and without delay. Requests by and promises to customers must be actioned immediately. Where it is impossible to provide the correspondent immediately with what he wants he should be so informed in order that, at least, he knows the matter is in hand.

(*b*) The content of letters must indicate efficiency. For example, *all* the information required by the addressee must be given; *all* the questions asked must be answered.

(*c*) Moderation in expression is essential. It is very easy to become impatient with a troublesome customer but the tendency to be brusque must be resisted. A balance between extreme formality and familiarity must be struck.

(*d*) There should be a uniform style of letter-writing and rules should be set out in a manual. Such matters as how to address customers (Dear Sir, Dear Mr, etc.) and the terminations to be used (Yours faithfully; Yours sincerely, etc.) must be prescribed.

(*e*) 'Commercialese' should never be used. 'Assuring you of our best attention at all times' is surely an unnecessary assurance to give! Such phrases as 'We beg to remain', 'thanking you in anticipation', 'trusting to have your continued custom' are completely out of place in modern business.

(*f*) Rules should be laid down so as to ensure uniformity of layout, e.g. size of margins, indented or non-indented paragraphs, line spacings, etc. There must also be agreement on the methods of quoting dates, the titles of officers, etc.

9.8 Accounts of Meetings

Information may be required concerning events at meetings. An account may be called for (in which case it would be a **report**) or it may be produced as an integral part of committee procedure (and would then be in the form of **minutes**). The differences between the two accounts are important—not the least being the legal significance.

A **report** consists of the observations of the person making it and is similar to that appearing in a newspaper. In addition to recording decisions made at the meeting, it may include an account of the proceedings—what was said, the 'atmosphere' at the meeting, any 'incidents', etc. It may be selective by reporting only certain of the events which took place. It has no legal significance as a record of the meeting.

Minutes should record only decisions made and business completed at the meeting. They should not include an account of the discussions which led up to the decisions. (They may include such words as 'After a lengthy discussion it was decided that . . .' but this would be beyond the strictly defined purpose of minutes.) They must record *all* decisions made and without any qualification. For example, if a resolution was passed by nine votes to eight the inference would be that the meeting was almost evenly divided, but if a simple majority decision (i.e. over 50 per cent) is binding then the resolution is that of the meeting *as a whole*. Accordingly, it would not be essential to record the votes for and against, although it may be the practice to do so.

Subject to any contrary regulation, the majority required to pass a resolution is of the votes *cast*. If in the above example three members abstained from voting the resolution would still be passed even though only nine of the 20 votes available were in favour.

Minutes signed by a chairman constitute legal evidence of the proceedings and validate all decisions made at the meeting. This evidence is *prima facie*—that is, they are accepted as a true account unless someone can prove they are not. Thus, the onus of proof rests with the person challenging their accuracy.

9.9 The Form of Minutes

The following comments may be made on the minutes shown in Fig. 9.4:

(*a*) If minutes of the last meeting were sent with the agenda and notice, as is common practice, there is no need to read them at the meeting unless a member insists, because those attending would be assumed to have studied them.

(*b*) It is incorrect to 'approve' or 'confirm' minutes. Once a decision is made it cannot be reversed or even qualified unless a contrary resolution is passed at a subsequent meeting.

(*c*) Items must be enumerated. The prefix allows an index of the titles to identify these items as having been dealt with at the tenth meeting. The subject-matter of item 10.3 would obviously be indexed to a number of meetings and therefore the same title must appear in every set of minutes which contain a reference to it.

(*d*) Item 10.4 is a 'minute of narration'. Item 10.5 contains a formally worded resolution and is known as a 'minute of resolution'.

```
Office Staff Joint Consultative Committee
```

MINUTES of the 10th meeting held in the Board Room on
Monday 6th February, 19.. ·

Present: Mr A Thomas (in the chair)

> Management representatives: Mr A Walters, Mr K L
> Jones, Miss P Bayne, Mr O Lockyer.
> Staff representatives: Mr J Abrahams (Accounts),
> Miss O Williams (Personnel), Miss T White (Typists
> and Secretaries), Mr L Gray (Sales), Mr V Lomas
> (others).

In attendance: Miss B Miles, Secretary

10.1 Minutes. Minutes of the last meeting were taken as
     read and signed as a true record.

10.2 Election of new member. The chairman announced that
     following resignation from the company's employ of
     Mr C Baker, a valid nomination of Mr L Gray to
     represent the Sales Department had been received.
     It was agreed that Mr Gray be appointed as a member
     of the committee with immediate effect.

10.3 Pension Fund – proposed alteration. Following an
     earlier enquiry by staff representatives concerning
     the possibility of male staff qualifying for pensions
     at the age of 60, Mr Jones announced that figures had
     now been received from the insurance company and would
     be distributed to the members immediately following
     the meeting.
     It was agreed to discuss the matter at the next
     meeting after the members and those they represented
     had studied the figures.

10.4 Beverage Vending Machines. It was agreed that the
     tender dated 4th January, 19.., from Truetaste Ltd
     to instal 10 beverage vending machines be accepted
     and that on installation the contract with Cheers
     Ltd be terminated.

10.5 Constitution. It was resolved:

> THAT the membership be increased to 12 by the addition
> of one management representative and one staff member
> representing Office Services Department, Mr Lomas
> continuing to represent staff with no departmental
> representation. Nominations are to be received and
> elections made at the next meeting.

10.6 Next meeting. It was agreed to call the next meeting for
     8th March, 19.., and that the chairman would be Miss
     O Williams.

Fig. 9.4. Minutes of a meeting.

(*e*) The tender mentioned in Item 10.4 is firmly identified (there may have been other tenders) and the members would have copies of it.

(*f*) Item 10.6 refers to the common practice of chairmen of these types of meeting alternating between the two 'sides'.

9.10 Inter-office Memoranda

Typed memoranda between one department or person and another will, in general, conform to the rules relevant to report-writing, but there are fre-

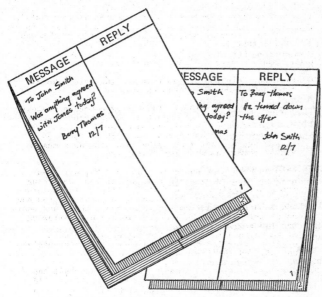

Fig. 9.5. An inter-office memo set.

quently occasions when short 'notes' have to pass between people. These are usually handwritten but being somewhat informal there is often a lack of control. This can be overcome by using **memo sets** in the form of three-page pads of non-carbon paper. As shown in Fig. 9.5, the originator writes his message, retains part 3 and sends the other two parts to the addressee. The recipient replies by writing on part 1, which copies through to part 2. The latter part is returned to the originator who thereby has a full record and can then destroy his retained copy. The other party has a similar record on part 1.

Key Points

1. **Reports** may be:

   (*a*) *called for* (e.g. by General Manager or Sales Manager);

   (*b*) part of a *routine* or by *prescribed circumstances* (e.g. by an engineer about a machine breakdown);

   (*c*) as part of *a person's responsibility* (e.g. by a manager giving staff reports);

   (*d*) within a *committee procedure* (e.g. a delegate reporting to his appointing body).

2 **Reports** should:

(*a*) state facts and opinions clearly and adequately;
(*b*) be sufficiently brief as is necessary to serve its purpose;
(*c*) take account of the addressee's understanding of the subject;
(*d*) be formalised in layout;
(*e*) not contain slang or loose wording;
(*f*) contain no salutations.

The *sequence* of a report should be as follows:

(*a*) Address and date.
(*b*) Title.
(*c*) Preamble.
(*d*) The body.
(*e*) Recommendations (if asked for).
(*f*) Signature.

3. Rules concerning **statistical presentations** include the following:

(*a*) A series must all be in the same style.
(*b*) They must present all the required information without confusion being caused by too much detail.
(*c*) They must have titles.
(*d*) Units of measurement must be stated.

4. **Effective correspondence** requires:

(*a*) uniformity of layout between correspondents;
(*b*) diplomatic and clear expression;
(*c*) absence of 'commercialese'.

5. **Minutes** constitute a *legally recognised* record of all the business completed at a meeting.

Reports may be *selective* in their content, may include *comments* of the compilers and have *no legal significance*.

10

MAINTAINING RECORDS

10.1 Record-keeping

A major part of office work is concerned with record-keeping for the following reasons:

(a) Any written work necessary to carry out a clerical operation must result in the creation of a record. The writing of a letter, the completion of forms and the entering of items in a ledger are all functional activities which automatically produce records.

(b) Any form of categorising, such as listing overdue accounts, analysing expenses and classifying, constitutes record-keeping.

(c) It includes the operations of storing information which is no longer current.

10.2 Filing

The maintaining of records must involve the assembling of them in some sort of order. All documents of one type would be together and within each grouping the documents would be arranged in a logical sequence. This classifying and orderly arranging constitutes filing, which may first be broadly divided as follows:

(a) *Current filing.* This refers to records of events of a contemporary nature, compiled in day-to-day work. It therefore includes 'live' accounts, correspondence on matters still being dealt with, etc.

(b) *Archival filing.* This refers to historical records, kept in case they are needed again. Certain documents are retained for legal reasons, either because they may be required as evidence or because the law requires them to be preserved.

Material for which provision for filing must be made include the following:

(a) Accounts and statistical records.
(b) Legal documents and agreements.
(c) Original letters and copies of replies.
(d) Microfilmed documents.
(e) Computerised records.
(f) Minutes and other records of meetings.

10.3 Storage and Retrieval

Although filing relates to the assembling of records in some logical order, the storing of documents is, in itself, pointless. The purpose of a filing system is to ensure that stored documents can be referred to without difficulty. 'Filing', therefore, refers not only to *storage* of information but its possible *retrieval* as well. A filing system is required to store documents safely and in such a manner as will allow any of them to be found and extracted quickly.

To achieve these objectives the equipment and procedures used will differ according to the types of material to be filed, but the following factors are relevant to any filing system:

(*a*) *Simplicity.* The system must be easily understandable and as simple to operate as possible. Simplicity contributes to the reduction of errors.

(*b*) *Economy.* Any form of filing is expensive. Measures must be adopted to ensure that the equipment used gives the required efficiency at the lowest possible cost. Planning must aim to reduce to a safe minimum the floor space to be used.

(*c*) *Accessibility.* Any information required from *archival* records must be readily available. Information in *current* filing must be close to those who require it most frequently.

10.4 The Cost of Archival Filing

Obviously, the space which is required for archival filing will initially depend upon the total of documents to be stored. This immediately identifies a major consideration: *the high cost of floor space devoted to filing.* In the normal processes of work documents are continuously produced, with the result that more and more past records have to be filed. Unchecked, this must result in ever-increasing costs for storing material, much of which will never be referred to. Methods have therefore to be devised to reduce the cost of filing so far as it is safe to do so.

Choice of Equipment

Accessibility is not a dominating requirement in filing historical records; the vital consideration is to reduce space. Unlike current filing there is no requirement to provide adequate working space at the filing point; all that is needed is sufficient space to extract files. Retained files are therefore usually stored on shelves or racks, arranged in closely aligned rows. These rows can be very close if the shelving units are mounted on runners so that one can approach a back row by moving those in front.

Reducing Document Space

The space occupied by some documents can be reduced very considerably by **microfilming** them (see page 114).

An examination may show that some documents have been filed unnecessarily. It may be found that two or more types of documents used in a procedure have been separately filed, whereas all the information required is available in one type of document. Careful consideration of the implications of so reducing archival filing is necessary before devising a new filing procedure.

Retained files must be periodically 'weeded out'. This carries with it the obvious danger that a document may be destroyed and then be urgently required. To guard against this there must be a **retention policy**. This will classify the different types of records and stipulate at what age each type should be destroyed. The policy must be agreed by various senior officials and in some cases it would be necessary to take legal advice. A **destruction programme** would be drawn up and records kept of the batches of documents which have been disposed of. The operation is made easier if much of the filing is done in date order—that is, if standard documents such as invoices are filed in annual 'runs'.

'Two-stage Filing'

Before the stage when destruction of a file has to be considered it may be possible to divide the filing between recently current documents and those over a certain age. Because the former are more likely to be referred to than the latter they could be filed in a more accessible manner. There would have to be an agreed programme for such a division.

10.5 Protection of Files

Files require to be protected against fire, dust, damp and theft.

Atmospheric conditions have little or no effect on 'active' files because their storage life is not long and they are constantly in use. Precautions are necessary in respect of retained files, however. The storeroom should be cool and well ventilated. As the files will usually be on open shelves they should be protected by being placed in special containers made of Kraft board, polythene, etc. Some protection can be provided by plastic sheets covering the shelves.

Concerning security of current files, it must be recognised that elaborate precautions are not always necessary. Some filing equipment cannot be locked and those that can are unlikely to deter a determined thief. Special protection is, however, necessary for files containing truly confidential material. Personnel records should be given particular attention and any secret material should be kept in a safe.

Generally, complete protection against fire is not provided for. Even heat will buckle ordinary cabinets and most more secure methods are only 'heatproof'. Secret material must, obviously, be filed in fire-proof safes.

Valuable documents can be stored away from the office, either in other buildings or in places specially provided to give protection, such as vaults. Copies of the documents could be kept in more accessible places.

10.6 Equipment for Current Filing

The choice of equipment to hold documents in current and recent use will be influenced by the following considerations:

(a) How frequently is a file normally referred to?
(b) In what ways and for what purposes are the files used?
(c) What degree of security is required?
(d) How much floor space is occupied by the equipment?
(e) What are the capital and running costs?

There is a considerable variety of filing equipment on the market. It is not part of the purpose of this book to detail them but it is helpful to specify the following categories:

(a) *For holding loose papers.* Leaflets, catalogues, etc., can be filed in **box**

files in which spring clips hold the papers in position. They should not be used for holding administration documents because the papers are disarranged every time one has to be removed. If a box is full of papers the contents become muddled; if it is not full it occupies an undue amount of space.

Concertina files can be used for temporary storage. The method is rather clumsy but can be used to hold documents which are under constant scrutiny. It can also be used to pre-sort documents before filing.

(*b*) *For holding standard documents.* Standardised documents are best filed in book form so that they may be held in numerical or alphabetical order. This requires the use of one of the many forms of loose-leaf containers. These can be in true book form with the papers held in a **loose-leaf binder**, or **lever-arch** or **ring binder** files may be used. A common requirement of all methods is that the documents must be designed to conform with the binding method. Holes in the document must fit prongs or posts in the binders; slots must agree with thongs in other binders, etc. The advantages are considerable:

(*i*) Documents can be inserted in any position, so that there is no interference with the set order of the documents.

(*ii*) 'Dead' documents can be removed without disturbing the rest.

(*iii*) Reference is easy.

(*iv*) Loose-leaf binders can be used as active records (i.e. they can be written in) as well as for filing as such.

(*v*) The contents can be easily transferred to cheaper binders when they are no longer current.

(*c*) *For filing correspondence.* Correspondence is usually held in folders, the differences in the systems being the methods by which the folders are housed.

In **horizontal filing** the files are placed behind each other, spines lowermost, in drawers. **Suspended horizontal filing** refers to a system whereby the files hang in pockets within the drawers. It has the advantage that the files are always upright, even when the drawer is partly filled. It is usual to have labelled slips on the tops of the pockets so that the indexing is immediately apparent. Such cabinets cannot hold more than four drawers. A taller cabinet would topple over if the top drawer was opened. Also, it would be impossible to see into a fifth drawer. This means that space above a height of 52 inches is wasted. A greater disadvantage is the waste of floor space. The floor space effectively occupied is twice the area of a cabinet because room has to be allowed for a fully-opened drawer.

Lateral filing solves this problem of space-wasting. The files hang in cupboard-type structures with no drawers. Not only is the open-drawer space not needed but it is also possible to have a cabinet 6 feet high and yet have every file immediately accessible. Fig. 10.1 demonstrates the saving in floor space. The drawer cabinet effectively occupies 6 square feet and has a capacity of 13 cubic feet. A lateral cabinet occupying 6 square feet has a capacity of 36 cubic feet.

(*d*) *Filing combined with recording.* Any system whereby documents are maintained in a set order while they are being worked on (such as a loose-leaf ledger) is a method of filing in that the information is arranged so as to be immediately accessible. Methods of recording information in indexed form are considered later in this chapter.

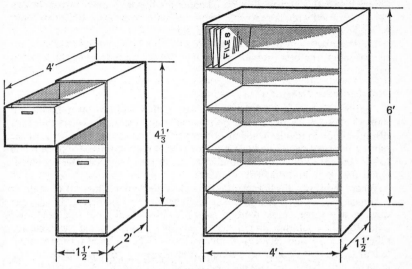

Fig. 10.1. Space-saving by lateral filing.

10.7 Classification of Files

Efficient classification often requires extensive subdividing. Documents will first be placed in broad categories, such as correspondence, invoices, orders, etc. All those in one category will be filed together, but within that group there must be subsidiary classification. Invoices, for example, may first be divided into years and then filed according to invoice numbers.

Classifying correspondence, however, is more difficult. It may, for example, be filed according to the name of the correspondents, perhaps divided into customers and other categories of business associates. In many cases, however, it may be more logical to file according to the **subject-matter** of the correspondence. For example, a large contract would have entailed correspondence with a considerable number of people and it would obviously be more sensible to have the whole history of the contract in one file. As such a file would contain letters from and to various people it will be seen that a particular document may be found under one of several possible headings.

Accordingly, the principle must be first to allocate documents to the most obvious categories and, secondly, it must be possible to trace a document if it is not found in what seems to be its most logical location.

It may therefore be necessary to have a method of **cross-referencing.** This can be contained within the files themselves. For example, Smith may be a consultant who has worked with the company on a number of contracts. In the file for each of those contracts there would be correspondence with Smith. There would also be a *personal* file for Smith to hold correspondence which is not specific to any one contract. To solve the obvious problems, each contract file could contain a list of all those involved in the contract so that, if necessary, a personal file could be referred to to find a particular letter.

Similarly, Smith's personal file could contain a list of all the contracts he has been concerned with. As shown later in the chapter, the same objective could be achieved by using a **cross-indexing system**.

If a letter was sent to or received from Smith which referred to more than one contract, the best practice would be to place a duplicate of the letter in each of the relevant files.

Alphabetical or Numerical?

Standard documents will be numbered, so they will obviously be filed in numerical order. As an example one may envisage a situation where there is a dispute about an invoice which is now several months old. As the name of the party concerned would be known it would only require reference to be made to his account to identify the number of the disputed invoice. The document could then be found under its number.

Where, however, documents are referenced to by name instead of number a choice has to be made between alphabetical and numerical filing. The obvious and most simple method is to file aphabetically but this can cause difficulties in planning filing space. If one has a certain area available for filing, how does one decide how much space will be required for each initial letter? One could decide, for example, that shelves 1 to 4 would be for the letter A and that letter B would occupy shelves 5 to 10. As more files are added there may be insufficient room in the allocated space for A filing. To extend the end of the A files into the beginning of the B area will probably mean moving along the whole of the system. If one guards against this by an over-generous allowance of room there would be a waste of storage space.

Filing in numerical order avoids this problem. A new file is given the number following that of the last file which was opened and placed next to it. To find a file under such a system does mean, however, that an index must be maintained. This should be in some form of self-indexing so that the names are always in strict alphabetical order (see page 116). The cross-indexing system mentioned below could be incorporated in such an index.

A combination of the two systems is the **alpha-numerical** system. The total of files is first divided into alphabetical sections so that all files beginning with the same letter are stored together. But within each alphabetical section the files are numbered and stored in numerical order. Each alphabetical section would have a guide card, identifying numerically the files in that section as shown in Fig. 10.2. A disadvantage is that such a card cannot be self-indexing.

B		
Baines J 13	Blackstone J S 14	Bucknall R 10
Baynes A 6	Blenkinsop V 11	Byers O T M 4
Baynes A L 3	Bowers J 5	Bolton J S 15
Bennett K K 2	Bowers J S 7	
Bignall O 9	Brewer M M 8	
Billington Bros 1	Brighton Corp 12	

Fig. 10.2. Alpha-numerical guide card.

The illustration shows that the newest file could not be entered in alphabetical order and must wait until a new card is compiled.

Cross-indexing Cards

The problem of filing Smith's correspondence discussed above can also be dealt with by using cross-indexing cards. There would be a card for each contract, listing the files of all those concerned. Similarly, individuals would be indexed and referenced to contracts.

The system can also be used for 'problem' files. For example, a firm may refer to itself on the telephone as 'Southern Growers Ltd', whereas its full title is 'United Southern Growers Ltd'. Confusion is sometimes caused by the similarity of, say, 'Johnston' and 'Johnstone'. As such variations become obvious a diligent clerk would make out suitable cards as a guide to himself and his colleagues.

10.8 The Filing Department

If a major proportion of the filing takes place in a central position, the office concerned must be efficiently organised. Such an office provides a vital service to the business and if there is failure to do so competently one of the fundamentals of administration would be impaired. The efficiency of any business largely depends upon the efficiency of its information storage and retrieval systems. Filing must therefore be acknowledged as a specialist operation and must receive the particular attention of management at a high level. The tendency to give the responsibility to low-grade staff because the work is largely routine is a dangerous one.

Efficient filing first requires careful planning of the room and the procedures to be adopted, and the provision of suitable equipment. Filing operations must be under the control of a supervisor with an orderly mind.

The Layout

In designing the layout the objectives are to:

(a) reduce as much as possible the space occupied by cabinets;
(b) make provision for possible expansion;
(c) make ancillary equipment accessible;
(d) provide adequate working areas;
(e) facilitate issue and reception of filing material.

It will be seen from Fig. 10.3 that as many files as possible are housed in lateral cabinets. The back row is against one wall and the other rows are double-banked so as to face in opposing directions. The gangways are narrow but adequate for passage and working.

For some documents a row of drawer cabinets is provided, facing into the room.

The index cabinets are positioned to give adequate working space.

Shelving is provided for box files and other containers.

A large work-table provides space for pre-sorting correspondence and for holding files before and after storage.

There is a reception area for receiving and issuing files.

Filing Control

The basis of successful filing is an efficient routine, firmly applied.

Loose correspondence for filing must be sorted and filed as soon as possible after it has been received.

The issuing of files must be controlled so that it is always possible to locate a file which is absent from the system. All staff must be made aware of the

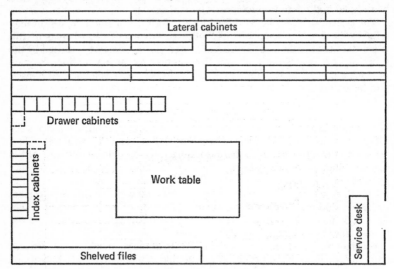

Fig. 10.3. Filing room layout.

rules and no matter how senior the officer demanding a file may be he must be subject to those rules. The filing supervisor must receive support from the highest levels if there is an attempt by any officer to transgress.

Requests for files must be made on standard forms, signed by those drawing the files. There must be a set limit to the length of time a file may be retained, subject to an extension being granted for a justifiable reason. There is always the tendency for people to hold files longer than necessary and this must be curbed.

When a file is withdrawn it must be replaced by an 'out' card. This is the same size as a file but with a projecting tab. It contains details of the person to whom the file was issued. The **file requisition** may be kept in a special container or binder, in which case the 'out' card should contain a reference to it. Alternatively, the requisition may be placed in a pocket of the 'out' card or attached to it (see Fig. 10.4).

10.9 Centralised Filing

Absolute centralisation of filing is not possible because documents continually used in daily work must be immediately available to those engaged on them. Also, confidential records should *never* be filed centrally. Centralised filing, therefore, can apply in respect of documents which are not in constant use

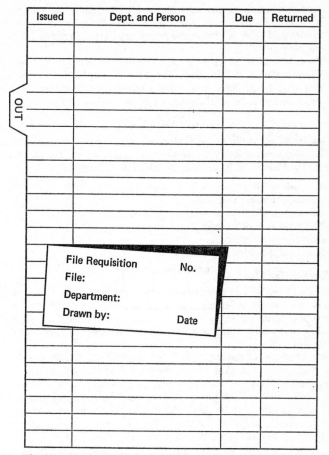

Issued	Dept. and Person	Due	Returned

OUT

File Requisition   No.
File:
Department:
Drawn by: Date

Fig. 10.4. 'Out' card for lateral filing and file requisition card.

and those which are not specific to any one department. Archival filing must *always* be centralised.

(*a*) Centralisation provides all the advantages of specialisation. Those engaged in it would be experts and the result should be a maximisation of efficiency. Specialisation also means that the filing room can be designed for the purpose so that a high level of protection would be possible.

(*b*) Centralisation is a more economical method of filing. Less equipment is required than would be the total of equipment used in decentralised filing.

(*c*) There is uniformity of classification and procedures if files are kept centrally.

(*d*) Centralisation ensures that all data relevant to one subject are in one file. It could otherwise be the case that some information would appear in several files and that some would not be in all files.

(e) Decentralisation means that files are immediately available to those requiring them. Delays result when documents have to be drawn from a central point and there is always the possibility that the required file may be out to someone else.

(f) Those who have an intimate knowledge of a matter can more accurately file relevant material. A filing department would not be in this position and there may thus be misfiling unless filing instructions were provided by the department concerned with the subject-matter.

10.10 Microfilming

The *process* of microfilming is that of duplicating but its *application* is in respect of filing. Accordingly, it is dealt with in this chapter. The characteristics of the method may first be broadly classified as follows:

(a) A considerable reduction in the bulk of filed records.
(b) Ease of reference and retrieval.
(c) Efficient duplicating of originals and copies.
(d) The provision of security.
(e) Durability of records.
(f) Standardisation of document size.

The Space-saving Element

One of its most remarkable aspects is the enormous amount of filing space which is saved by microfilming, because it can reduce storage space by up to 98 per cent. The difference in the space occupied by paper-filing cabinets and that taken up by microfilm cabinets obviously considerably reduces the rent-cost of filing.

This will apply, of course, only if the original documents are destroyed. Legal strictures require that certain documents are kept for long periods. If they are removed to 'safe custody' areas, microfilmed copies of them can be retained in more accessible positions. It is usual for some documents, such as recent past accounts, to be retained for a certain time. Such 'intermediate' filing—between 'current' and 'archival' filing—can be microfilmed and stored so as to be readily available, the originals being destroyed.

In general, it would be too expensive to microfilm every document in a correspondence file. The usual practice is to store the original file in 'intermediate' storage and later to extract any papers which are regarded as being essential to retain. These are microfilmed and the rest destroyed.

Making the Record

The first recording stage is on microfilm in **roll form**. Each roll of 16 mm film will hold several thousand images. It may be filed in this form but because it is not possible to update it it is suitable only for certain records. Where rapid retrieval is required the film is made into a flat format (or **unitized microfilm**). This can be in one of the following forms:

(a) **Microfilm jackets.** These consist of two thin polyester films welded together to form channels into which strips of film are inserted. This constitutes a microfilm 'file'. One or more jackets are used as a file for, say, one customer. The file can be kept up to date by inserting new microfilmed information and removing the outdated information. Jackets are identified by number and colour codes.

(b) **Microfilm aperture cards.** These also house film in channels but have the advantage that the cards can be written on. They can therefore be used as conventional record cards. Again, it is possible to update the microfilmed information by inserting new images.

(c) **Microfiche.** This consists of a sheet of film containing more than 200 images, equivalent to a very full folder. It is used mainly in recording a complete set of material, such as a book or a series of legal or technical documents where no change in the information is anticipated.

A development of the system is **computer output on microfilm**—generally referred to as COM. Computer data recorded on magnetic tape can be converted to microfilm which, when enlarged, has the same appearance as normal line printout.

Cassettes can be used where appropriate. For example, manufacturers can provide customers with catalogues on cassettes, together with updating facilities.

Retrieval

Of almost equal importance to space-saving is the ability of microfilming immediately to produce any required extract from information filed in an appropriate manner. The system allows for a vast amount of information to be instantly available to the person requiring it. There is no necessity to fetch papers—a saving in time and labour—because the data can be displayed at the desk of the person concerned. The advantage of being able to conduct a telephone conversation, for example, with all the required information immediately to hand is obvious.

If film is used, the appropriate roll is loaded into a microfilm reader. The film is run through, showing the series of images in enlarged form on a reader screen, and the operator stops the machine at the required document. A more efficient method is **image-indexing**. There are various methods but the basic principle is rapid identification of the required record and its projection on to a screen.

All systems use a filmed reference and cross-reference list of all recorded material so that the required roll, jacket, card or fiche can be immediately located.

Other Aspects

Access is widened because the ability to produce duplicates of microfilm images enables copies to be kept by more than one department or branch.

Security is improved by using duplicates, with the originals stored in a safe place. This not only ensures their safety but also avoids the risk of documents being tampered with or removed.

Standardisation is achieved by reducing all documents to the same size, thereby facilitating handling and storing.

Printed copies of the original documents can be obtained in any required number.

10.11 Card Records

Every business uses a variety of card records, ranging from the simple to the comparatively complex. The general objectives are to:

(*a*) record information on a continuous basis; and
(*b*) assemble the cards in indexed order.

The cards therefore usually require to be designed so as to allow them to be written on and for them to be retained in the required order. Where the cards are required for reference only they can be housed in drawers (such as those used in libraries). Such a system is unsuitable if information has to be written on the cards because access is difficult and continual removal of the cards damages them.

Blind-Indexed Cards

These are cards stacked one behind the other with identification showing only on the first card. The difficulty of finding the required card is obvious, although it can be made easier by inserting guide cards at intervals. The system is unsatisfactory because if the cards are used often they soon become dog-eared.

Visible Index Cards

These cards have a self-evident index by positioning each card slightly offset from its immediate neighbours. The identity of a card can be shown on its bottom edge or on a diagonal edge across the top right-hand corner (see Fig. 10.5).

Such cards may be housed in book-style folders, with each card held in the required position. Coloured signals fixed in appropriate positions can highlight specific information, such as overdue accounts.

Where the cards are not written on by hand, as would be the case with ledgers where accounting machines are employed, they are housed loosely in containers during use. On completion of an operation they are usually bound in loose-leaf binders.

10.12 Indexing

Record cards can also be used as indexes—that is, they facilitate the location of other records. An essential is that the identifying media can be moved so that the whole is always in alphabetical order. The insertion of cards must not disturb the order and blank spaces resulting from cards being removed must be filled. Various systems achieve this objective, including the **strip index**. This consists of a frame holding card strips which can be inserted in the correct order and removed as required.

Indexing Conventions

Alphabetical indexing should be 'strict' alphabetical—that is, the alphabetical sequence should apply to the first letter and then to each succeeding letter in order.

Certain principles are generally accepted but there can occasionally be

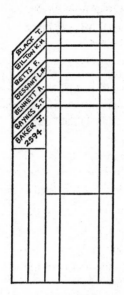

Fig. 10.5. Visible index cards.

more than one way of indexing names. To avoid misfiling, the manner in which certain names are to be indexed must be clearly laid down. The usual practice is to adopt the methods shown in the Post Office Telephone Directories:

(*a*) M', Mc and Mac are all treated as 'Mac' and the next letter in the name determines the position of entry, e.g.

> McNutt, J.
> Macon Ltd
> Macpake, T.

(*b*) The names of firms consisting wholly or partially of initials are listed at the beginning of surnames with the same initial letter, e.g.

> C.T.S. Ltd
> C.V. Computers Ltd
> Cable, A.

(*c*) Names with apostrophes and hyphens are listed as though they did not exist, e.g.

> Deacon, J.
> De'Ath, A. M.
> Deavin-Smith, D.

(*d*) Names beginning with 'St.' are listed after 'Saint'.

(*e*) Names with a separate prefix (such as 'De', 'La', 'Le') are listed so that all those with the same prefix come together, e.g.

> Valter, K.
> Van Allen, T.
> Van Loon, D. D.
> Vance, G. R.

(*f*) Numerical entries appear before the alphabetical list, e.g.

> 1001 Ideas Ltd
> AA Fire Alarms Ltd

Key Points

1. **Filing** is divided into *current* filing and *archival* filing, the latter usually having a subdivision of *recently current* filing.
   Filing is pointless without the facility of *retrieval*.

2. **Filing space economy** is facilitated by:
   (*a*) *choice of cabinets* (lateral filing is the most effective);
   (*b*) adopting a *destruction and retention policy*;
   (*c*) *microfilming*.

3. **Filing equipment** may be broadly divided into:
   (*a*) *Box files*—leaflets, catalogues, etc.;
   (*b*) *Concertina files*—temporary or transitional filing;
   (*c*) *Loose-leaf, lever-arch and ring binders*—standard forms; always in strict order. For storage and/or active use.

(d) *Horizontal and suspended horizontal*—drawer cabinets holding individual files;

(e) *Lateral filing*—individual files suspended in cupboards.

4. **Alphabetical filing** provides the quickest access.
   Numerical filing is the easiest to install; requires an alphabetical reference.
   Alpha-numerical filing—numerical filing within alphabetical sections.
   Cross-indexing is usually required for

   (a) 'problem' files;
   (b) where a file qualifies for more than one position.

5. **Centralised filing:**

   (a) provides specialisation of staff, equipment and accommodation;
   (b) is economical;
   (c) does not give immediate access.

6. **Microfilming** provides the following advantages:

   (a) Saving of filing space.
   (b) Instant retrieval to diversified stations.
   (c) Duplication of copies and originals.
   (d) Security for originals stored elsewhere.

7. **Card records** can be used

   (a) for holding information, e.g. personal details of customers;
   (b) for holding and recording information, e.g. ledger cards;
   (c) solely as indexes, e.g. in libraries.

11

REPROGRAPHY

11.1 The Choice of Methods

The increasing use and complexity of forms results in the necessity for sophisticated methods of producing copies of them. The choice is wide but the main deciding factors are the characteristics and functions of the forms to be duplicated. The purpose for which a form is created will largely determine the best method of reproducing it. Consequently, an office will use more than one method of duplicating because of the differing objectives of the forms used. Within such distinctions other factors are relevant in making a choice, such as the following:

(a) *The number of copies required.* If a master has to be produced from an original the life of the master will differ between systems. Some of the other systems produce only a limited number of copies direct from an original document. A prior assessment must therefore be made of the expected number of copies required for different categories of documents.

(b) *The production cost per copy.* This has some relevance to the above factor. Costs must include the expense of any master which has to be made. With some equipment the cost becomes constant only after a certain number of copies have been produced—that is, beyond a certain output the only cost is that of the paper and below that level unit costs are higher. The lengths of the 'runs' may therefore be an important factor.

(c) *Any capital cost of equipment.* There will be no capital cost if the only machine used is a typewriter producing carbon copies, because the machine would already be employed for other purposes. The true cost of necessary equipment is the initial outlay and any maintenance costs, spread over its anticipated life. This must be related to the cost of producing copies because the high cost of one may be offset against the low cost of the other.

(d) *How quickly copies are produced.* One factor to be considered is: how quickly are copies required? Obviously, one would require a long run to be completed as quickly as possible, but if only a few copies are required speed can rarely be a matter of great importance. Some machines will duplicate faster than others but a more important consideration is whether or not a master must first be made. Any time which must be spent on producing a master must be added to the time used in running off copies of it.

(e) *The quality of the material to be produced.* Generally, literature to be circulated outside the business will be of a fairly high standard. Material used internally can be of a lower quality but it must be capable of withstanding normal usage by the recipients. For example, an office copy of a document sent to the factory can be quite flimsy if it is to merely be filed. The factory copy, however, may be subjected to continuous handling and needs to be more robust.

(*f*) *Whether colour is required.* For some documents, particularly diagrams, it may be essential to reproduce in two or more colours. Some equipment is capable of doing so; with others, the method is lengthy; many cannot produce in colour at all. It is therefore necessary to consider where and to what extent colour reproduction must be catered for.

(*g*) *Any limitations on the matter to be duplicated.* Some systems will copy only matter which has a specified ink makeup. There are often limitations on the acceptable size of original matter.

11.2 Categories of Methods

Reprographic methods may be divided into the following very broad categories:

(*a*) The term **copying** relates to the automatic production of copies as the original is being written and, consequently, can be described as 'simultaneous copying'. The number of copies obtainable by such methods is limited.

(*b*) **Duplicating** relates to the producing of copies from a master which must be previously prepared (such as a stencil) or the original document. In other words, copies are not made at the same time as the document is produced.

The distinction made above must not be interpreted too rigidly because, in practice, both terms are used to refer to reprography generally.

11.3 Simultaneous Copying

In Chapter 7 reference was made to the methods of producing multi-copies of standard documents, but simultaneous copying also relates to other documents (as in typing letters, for example). A more detailed study of the methods is now necessary.

Multi-use carbon paper consists of a plastic film coated with carbon dope. An ordinary typewriter will produce four good copies but the number is increased if an electric typewriter is used. The method is time-consuming in that carbon paper has to be interleaved with the copy paper and the whole has to be lined up each time it is used. The life of a sheet of carbon paper varies according to the quality. No more than three good carbon copies of handwritten material are possible.

One-time carbon papers come already interleaved in pre-collated sets. They consist of carbon-coated tissue papers which are removed and thrown away after one typing. They provide a considerable saving of typists' time, and in view of the cost of that time and the lower cost of the carbon paper, this method is more economical than the one above. A standard grade will produce up to six copies in a set, while more copies are possible if 'hard'-grade paper is used.

Carbon-backed paper can be used for selective duplicating and is described on page 67.

Carbonless paper can use the 'mechanical transfer' or the 'chemical transfer' method. The former transfers a colour coating from the back of a sheet by pressure on to the sheet beneath. The most common method, however, is that of using coatings of colourless chemicals, the major product being

IDEM* paper manufactured by Wiggins Teape Limited. The process is described on page 67. The use of such paper is not restricted to typed sets of documents, however. It is used for hand-kept manifold posting systems, accounting machines, computer print-outs, telex rolls, etc. In each case, selectivity of duplication is possible by desensitisation of appropriate areas. A further advantage is that space otherwise used for storing carbon paper is saved. (The average mini-computer can use seven miles of carbon paper in a year!)

11.4 Spirit Duplicating

This is a long-established method which is still widely used.

A master is produced by placing a sheet of art paper (i.e. one with a smooth shiny surface) into contact with a hectographic carbon. The matter to be reproduced is typed or drawn with a ballpoint pen on to the white sheet, imparting on its reverse a mirror image. The master sheet is then fitted on to the drum of a spirit duplicator. Copy paper is fed in and is first damped with spirit from a roller. It then passes under the roller containing the master so that a deposit of carbon is dissolved by the spirit, thereby transferring the image.

The system has the major advantage of being capable of producing several colours in one run. This is done by changing the hectographic carbon sheet to the required colour during the writing process.

It is one of the most economical methods but as a master will not produce more than 300 copies it is not suitable for very long runs. As against this is the fact that because the master costs little to produce it is particularly suitable for shorter runs.

11.5 Stencil Duplicating

This is probably the cheapest form of duplicating as several thousand copies can be produced from one master. The master is prepared by writing on a wax stencil with a typewriter (with the ribbon out of action so that the key heads strike directly into the wax) or with a stylus. It is therefore a suitable method for reproducing drawings as well as typing.

Stencils may also be produced electronically. An **electronic stencil scanner** will automatically produce stencils of almost any matter, such as typescript, illustrations, photographs and print. The material to be copied and an electronically conductive stencil are rotated side by side on cylinders. As a photoelectric cell reflects a beam of light from the scanner a hole is cut in the stencil corresponding to every dark spot on the original. Once started, the whole process is automatic.

Another method of producing stencils is to use a **thermal copier** (see below). The image is transferred from the original by the action of heat melting the relevant areas of a special type of stencil.

The stencil having been made, it is placed on a drum which rotates in contact with a pressure roller. There are variations of the basic principle of ink then being forced through the stencil cuts to produce copies.

Previously, the copy paper had to be absorbent, which meant that high-

*IDEM is a registered trademark of Wiggins Teape Limited.

class duplicates could not be produced, but equipment is now available capable of producing on all classes of paper.

Coloured inks can be used but if more than one colour is required separate stencils must be made, with a run for each stencil.

11.6 Dry Copiers

This is a convenient term to cover a number of copiers as distinct from the outmoded photographic methods which produced 'wet' copies. A common factor is that they duplicate direct from originals, without the necessity to produce masters.

Thermal Copiers

Here the process is to use infra-red heat to produce copies. The original and the copy paper are placed on top of each other and exposed to the heat, which in turn produces an image through chemical change. A condition is that the print of the original must have a carbon-based ink. This means that it cannot reproduce colours because coloured printing inks have vegetable-based dyes.

An advantage is the simplicity of the copier's construction so that there are few working parts which can become faulty. The machines are compact and occupy little desk space. The operation is simple and clean.

They can produce masters for spirit and stencil duplicating and transparencies for use in projectors.

This method is also known as **heat-transfer copying**.

Dual-spectrum Copiers

These are similar to thermal copiers but use ultraviolet light rays (the other end of the spectrum) as well as infra-red heat. The result is that it is not restricted to carbon-based originals and consequently can reproduce colour.

Dyeline (Diazo) Copiers

A feature of this system is that the originals must be on transparent or translucent paper. This is fed into a rotary machine with copy paper coated with diazo salts. The original is exposed to ultraviolet light which can pass through only those parts containing no image so that those areas are bleached on the copy paper. The copy paper is then passed through a developer to produce the duplicate.

The method is very economical because diazo paper is not expensive. It is not the best choice for long runs because the cost is directly proportional to the number of copies. The main disadvantage is the limitation on the type of paper for the original. Opaque papers and those printed on both sides are unsuitable. There is also a tendency for copies to fade if exposed to strong light. A limited number of colours can be produced but to do so requires the use of different coatings and developers.

Because of the fumes generated by such equipment it is usual to provide for special ventilation.

Xerographic Copiers

These use a form of **electrostatic** copying. 'Xerography' derives from the Greek words for 'dry writing' and the system may be regarded as the supreme example of dry copying.

The unique process is based on the principles of static electricity. The image of the original is projected on to a selenium drum which has been given a positive electrical charge. The effect of the selenium is that where the original is shaded the electric charge remains and where the light falls the charge is lost. The result is that the drum receives an invisible image made up of positive electrical charges. Ink powder toner which is negatively charged is applied to the drum and is attracted to the pattern of positive charges. The powder pattern is then automatically transferred to the copy paper and bonded by heat.

The system is the most commonly used method of office duplicating because the advantages are so apparent. The operating process is very simple, requiring no more than the inserting of the original and the pressing of one or more buttons. No chemicals have to be handled. Copies are always perfect and may be produced at a very rapid rate.

The equipment is capable of producing translucent dyeline masters and plates for offset litho machines (see below).

Some machines provide automatic document feeding, capable of accepting a variety of paper sizes and producing different sizes of copies. Some models will print on both sides of the paper.

Plain-paper copiers, as they are also known, do not use coated paper, which reduces the average cost per copy from 2p to 0·4p. Capital costs are high, however, averaging £3,000 and up to more than £18,000 and it is reckoned that such equipment is economic only for volumes exceeding 4,000 copies per month.

11.7   Offset Lithography

This system will produce the highest quality of duplicating at high speeds. It is therefore useful for producing not only internal forms but also literature which is sent out of the office.

It requires the preparation of a master copy on thin metal sheets or specially surfaced paper. These can be typed on with the use of a special ribbon, or offset pens may be used. One reason for the increased popularity of offset lithography is the ability to use masters which have been produced by electrostatic duplication.

The process is based on the incompatibility of oil and water. The master is fixed to a drum which first contacts damping rollers and then inking rollers. The unprinted parts of the master become wet and therefore do not pick up any ink. The printed parts of the master being greasy, however, reject the water and accept the ink. The inked image is transferred to a 'blanket' roller which picks up the image in reverse. This is then again reversed on to the copy paper.

A paper master will produce up to 2,000 copies and up to 100,000 can be produced from a metal master.

The cost of the equipment is high in comparison with most others, but because masters can be produced so easily it is economical to produce other than a very small number of copies. The prime advantage is the high quality of the copies.

11.8 Addressing Machines

Strictly, an addressing machine is not a duplicator but it is included in this chapter because it performs the function of duplicating. It is used when standard information has to be reproduced repeatedly and at different times. The obvious example is that a statement has to be headed with each customer's name and address every month. The names and addresses will change infrequently and therefore it is reasonable to prepare masters which can be used over and over again. The stock of masters can be adjusted to include new customers and exclude those who are no longer customers.

The name of the equipment is something of a misnomer because it is capable of doing far more than print names and addresses on envelopes and labels. It can, for example, list the names on payrolls and dividend lists, head up time cards and pay envelopes, produce analysed lists of customers, etc.

The masters can be in the form of embossed metal plates, wax stencils or hectographic masters. The operating principle with any system is that the masters are automatically fed into the machine in their set order. As each master reaches the printing point a carbon-impregnated ribbon comes between it and the copy paper. Pressure is applied and the image is transferred to the paper.

Additional features usually include the following:

(*a*) Parts of the masters can be 'masked' so that only part is reproduced. For example, one plate could selectively print on the payroll, time card, pay envelope and pay advice by producing in each case only the required data.

(*b*) The machine will 'skip' any master not required to be duplicated. Thus, a circulation could be limited to a certain class of customer.

(*c*) Each master can be programmed to produce more than one copy.

(*d*) Masters required for printing can, where necessary, be selected mechanically by tabs on the plates or electrically embossed 'pips'.

(*e*) The date or any other common information can be automatically added to each print.

(*f*) There is automatic feed of envelopes, lists, documents and continuous stationery.

11.9 Control of Duplicating

The accessibility of duplicating equipment which is easy to use can encourage its over-employment. If a document has to be circulated there is a common tendency to produce more copies than there are addressees 'in case we need them'. It also intensifies the ever-present inclination to send copies to those who do not really require them. Easy access to duplicating facilities can therefore contribute to the unnecessary proliferation of paper. Not only is more paper produced but more of it has to be read and more finds its way into files which are rarely (if ever) referred to again. The bureaucrats who exist in most sizeable businesses regard the duplicator as a heaven-sent gift.

It must be admitted that prevention of abuse is difficult and this is particularly so if staff have unrestricted access to equipment. Some monetary control is possible where a department has exclusive use of a machine because the cost of the material supplied would be known, but firmer control is possible only if there is a degree of centralisation. Xeroxing machines are metered so that the number of copies made is known. It is possible to give each department sharing the use of such a machine a key which has to be inserted to operate it. This provides separate metering of the utilisation by each department. Offset duplicating machines would almost certainly be centralised, even if only because of their high cost. It therefore becomes a simple matter for the Reprographic Department to monitor all work sent to it and to 'debit' each department accordingly.

The problem puts a responsibility on middle management. A departmental head should ensure that his staff does not use equipment unnecessarily and that the most suitable method is always employed. In most cases, however, he is unlikely to do this unless some form of budgeting is imposed by a superior level of management.

The major cost of some methods is for the preparation of masters. Training and supervision must ensure there is not a high rate of spoilage in preparing stencils, offset plates, etc.

Key Points

1. The **choice of duplication methods** is influenced by:

   (a) capital and maintenance costs;
   (b) cost per copy (is it constant or does it reduce?);
   (c) cost of paper (is special paper required?);
   (d) whether a master has to be made (cost and time factors);
   (e) speed (is it essential?);
   (f) the standard of material required;
   (g) any necessity to produce in colour;
   (h) any limitation on the matter which can be duplicated.

2. The **methods of duplicating** are broadly as follows:

   (a) *Spirit*—requires a master; economical; produces colour in one run; limited to 300 copies.
   (b) *Stencil*—very long runs; requires a master; separate stencils for different colours; stencils on wax sheets, by electronic scanner or by thermal copying.
   (c) *Thermal*—direct image transfer; cannot produce colours. (Also known as *heat-transfer copiers.*)
   (d) *Dual spectrum*—direct image transfer; can produce colours.
   (e) *Dyeline (diazo)*—original must be transparent or translucent; direct image copy must be developed; inexpensive paper; tendency to fading.
   (f) *Xerographic*—direct image transfer; simple to operate and clean; rapid production; can produce dyeline masters and offset litho plates; high capital cost; low copy cost. (Also known as *plain-paper copiers.*)
   (g) *Offset lithography*—high quality; high speed; requires a master; high capital cost; economical for long runs.

3. **Addressing machines**

   (a) do not duplicate *documents* but reproduce *standard information*;
   (b) are used for circularising, listing, etc.;
   (c) can be automatically selective;
   (d) use metal plates, wax stencils or hectographic masters.

12

COMMUNICATION SYSTEMS

12.1 Selecting the Methods

Having considered the importance of efficient recording and presenting of information it is now necessary to know something of the available systems for transferring information. This will entail a study of communication equipment and associated procedures. These may be broadly classified as follows:

(a) **Data transmission,** i.e. sending information in recorded form but excluding mailing.

(b) **Oral.** This includes all telephonic and radio methods.

(c) **Document transfer,** i.e. the physical movement of documents.

(d) **Visual.** This includes methods of displaying information on screens.

(e) **Mailing.** This is dealt with in the next chapter.

The choice of method will be largely determined by the operation concerned, so that, obviously, several systems will exist in an office. With a variety of methods available, however, it is possible for a member of the staff to use one which is not the best for the particular purpose. For example, there may be a choice between sending a letter and sending a telegram; a telephone call may be more effective than either. In the interests of efficiency and economy it is therefore necessary that some guidance be given as to which method should be used in a particular circumstance. This can be in the form of a directive to supervisors to ensure that their subordinates act sensibly or it can be addressed to those exclusively engaged in communication functions. For example, the telephoning practices of junior staff should be controlled by their superiors; mailing clerks should be instructed as to when first-class mail can be used.

The decision as to the method to be used in any particular circumstance will be influenced by the following considerations:

(a) *Speed.* To what extent is quickness of delivery a vital factor? In some cases, such as the despatch of price lists and advertising material, speed is not essential and the prime consideration will be cost. In other instances speed will be a prime factor.

(b) *Record.* Is it essential that the information be given in some permanent form? Obviously, a document with a legal content must be in writing but there are many other cases where it is necessary to provide the addressor and the addressee with a record. In other instances the message may be given by telephone or displayed on a screen. Where appropriate, this may be supplemented later by a message in recorded form.

(c) *Accuracy.* Will the method used ensure that the information is transmitted accurately? There is an obvious possibility that a communication by telephone may be misunderstood or that the brevity of a cable may lead to misinterpretation.

(*d*) *Safety*. How essential is it that there is no danger of loss in transit? Ensuring safety can be expensive (such as using registered post) and the extra cost may not be justified in many circumstances.

(*e*) *Data storage*. Must the information be filed? Is it retrievable from storage, either as the original or a copy?

(*f*) *Time difference*. If the message has to be sent a considerable distance, will the difference in time zones have to be considered?

(*g*) *Cost*. In conjunction with any of the above considerations, the comparative costs of the available methods will be the deciding factor. This must include not only the easily determined costs (e.g. that of a stamp) but also the incidental costs, such as for stationery, the usage of equipment and labour.

12.2 Information Retrieval Systems

These are those methods which make stored information immediately available to those requiring it at remote points. An example is the ability to produce full-size copies of microfilmed information which is filed elsewhere, as explained on page 115.

Its most common use, however, is in conjunction with computerised systems. Page 65 illustrates how information about stock levels, customer status, etc., can be made immediately available. Other systems provide an intelligence service whereby computer input is directly related to computer output. For example, when a production line reaches a certain stage a punched card can be inserted in a unit on the factory floor so that the necessary information is immediately passed to a computer display screen in the production controller's office.

Viewdata

This term has general application to processes whereby information stored in a computer which is external to the business can be called up by telephone and displayed on a screen. For many years City offices have used desk-top screens which display the latest financial and commodity prices, and Reuters also transmits news items. Establishments such as the Stock Exchange and Lloyds use public screens for broadcasting information to their members.

A public system has been developed by the Post Office and a number of manufacturers to provide a selective information service called **Prestel**. A viewdata-equipped television set can be plugged into the telephone circuit. Operation of a remote control unit then produces a general index on the screen from which specific information can be received by keying the relevant index code.

Over 150 organisations provide the data, such as newspapers, the Central Statistical Office, the Department of Prices and Consumer Protection, the British Library, the Automobile Association, etc. Welfare information will later be provided by local authorities and Citizens' Advice Bureaux. The receiver can also call up Ceefax and Oracle, the information services provided by the BBC and IBA respectively, known generically as **Teletext**. The system also allows a subscriber to communicate with the computer, with the answers appearing on the screen. By a system of programmed learning, problems such as those to do with income tax can be dealt with.

The system is still in the development stage but it is expected to be in widespread use in the near future.

An outline of the system is given in Fig. 12.1.

12.3 Telegrams and Cables

The use of these methods is comparatively expensive but is justified in the following circumstances:

(*a*) When speed is essential.

(*b*) When information must be recorded—that is, the recipient must have written evidence—or when misinterpretation of complex information is possible if sent by telephone.

(*c*) When the time difference between the parties means that telephoning is impracticable.

Costs can be reduced by sending messages by one of the established code systems. A further reduction is possible by using the telegraphic addresses registered and published by the Post Office. Both methods result in fewer words being used, thereby reducing the cost. It is also possible to send at reduced rates when the speed of transmission is not a vital consideration.

12.4 Teleprinters

The teleprinter enables a message to be typed on a machine which has a normal typewriter keyboard and for the message to be reproduced almost simultaneously on a similar machine at a distant point.

The **Telex system** allows for teleprinters to be hired from the Post Office and for them to be connected, through the telecommunications network, with other teleprinters in many countries. In an increasing number of cases, connection with other countries is possible by direct dialling—that is, not via the Post Office exchange operators. The cost depends upon the length of the call. This can be reduced by using punched tape so that coded messages can be transmitted at very high speeds. Reading facilities enable such messages to be automatically decoded into printed form at the receiving station.

The system is particularly useful for passing information between distant countries, because the time difference problem is reduced. A message sent from England in office hours would be received in, say, Australia during that country's night hours. The incoming message would be recorded on the receiving teleprinter during the night and would await the arrival in his office of the addressee.

Those who are not Telex subscribers can have telegrams sent by the Post Office to Telex subscribers. The Post Office will also deliver to non-subscribers messages sent by Telex subscribers.

Teleprinters can also be used *within* an organisation to enable printed messages to pass between sections through an internally wired circuit.

12.5 Facsimile Telegraphy

This method allows for rapid transfer of images (such as drawings, statements and reports, charts, etc.) between stations. The sending unit consists of a

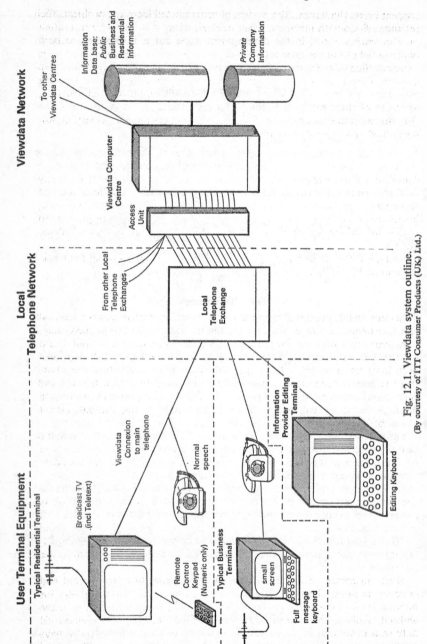

Fig. 12.1. Viewdata system outline.
(By courtesy of ITT Consumer Products (UK) Ltd.)

reading head which scans the document as it revolves on a metal drum. The pressing of a button activates the receiving unit and starts the transmitting process, so that the message is almost simultaneously recorded on sensitised paper at the receiving station. If a long message has to be sent this method is more effective than the teleprinter process. Instead of typing at the same time as transmission, the whole document is typed previously, thereby avoiding transmission errors. It is also possible to transmit tabulated information, which Telex cannot do.

If the addressee cannot receive direct, the Post Office will deliver 'photo-telegrams' in an overseas country by express post.

12.6 Datel Services

The Post Office provides facilities for transmitting digital data. It is mainly used for sending information from a remote source to a computer and for subsequent feedback. Data may be transmitted over the Telex network, leased telegraph circuits or public telephone lines. It is therefore possible to obtain immediate access to a computer from any part of the telephone system.

Various Datel services are offered, the fastest of them allowing for transmission of 48,000 'bits' per second, using punched tape.

12.7 Telephones

This most widely known of systems may be broadly divided between internal and external installations, but it is common to combine the two in one system.

A system which is **completely internal** consists of a private circuit, purchased or rented from a manufacturer or hired from the Post Office. A high proportion of telephone calls in most businesses is internal, particularly where there is extensive decentralisation or departmentalisation. If a lot of those calls would otherwise go by Post Office lines (such as to branches or outlying departments) there will be a point where the cost of hiring a private circuit would be less than the cost of metered calls.

The system has the advantage of being completely separate from the external system. This means that an incoming call on the external system can be put through to the called person even if he is engaged on an internal call, because he would be using a different circuit.

Such internal systems may have an **intercom system** facility. This can be designed so that instead of talking into the mouthpiece of a handset, speech is picked up by microphone from any point in the room and incoming speech is broadcast by loudspeaker. Connections are made by push-buttons instead of by dialling. It is possible for one person to talk to several others simultaneously so that a 'meeting' may be held without the parties coming together physically.

Most businesses have a system which gives access to both internal and external networks. **PABX (Private Automatic Branch Exchange)** allows for internal connections to be made and for outgoing external calls to be made without involving the switchboard operator. Thus, the operator is concerned only with dealing with incoming calls. Modern versions of the system have electronic switching, the consoles are more compact than the switchboards of older models and the same volume of traffic can be handled by fewer Post Office lines.

Telephone economy

(*a*) Even for the smallest firm, the cost of telephone bills is a major item of expense. To a large extent such high costs are often unnecessary. One reason could be that a telephone is immediately accessible to most office employees and as a consequence is frequently used thoughtlessly. Costs then rise because:

(*i*) the telephone is used when it is not essential to do so; and
(*ii*) when it *is* used justifiably it is not done so economically.

Most businesses from time to time exhort their staff to take measures to reduce telephone costs. They will tell them not to telephone in the mornings, when costs are higher; 'don't hang on, get them to ring back'; not to telephone at all if possible. The experience of most firms, however, is that such operations have a limited success in the long term and many resort to other methods of control.

(*b*) Various systems are available for **monitoring the length of calls**. The Post Office can provide a cyclometer which will record the length of individual calls. Systems purchased from private suppliers will log all traffic and produce statements of the usage by each extension, including the numbers called, their duration and cost. Such equipment has been reckoned to reduce telephone bills by up to 20 per cent.

(*c*) A lot of time can be wasted, not on the call but on the dialling of it. This is particularly so when calling abroad, or a wrong number is obtained, or the person called has to be redialled later because he is not available. Speedier dialling is possible by using one of the **automatic dialling** devices available. One system allows for up to 400 numbers to be stored on tapes. To operate, a button is pressed until the required number appears in a 'window'. It takes only 12 seconds to run through all 400 numbers. Lifting the handset automatically dials the number. Smaller units will hold 32 numbers on a visible panel and automatic dialling is achieved by pressing the appropriate nameplate. Punched cards in another system provide an unlimited capacity of numbers.

(*d*) Much time is also wasted while the telephone line is open. Little can be done about time wasted in 'chatting' but certainly time wasted because nothing is being said can be prevented. For example, in order to deal with an enquiry on the telephone it may be necessary to put down the handset to look up documents in a filing cabinet. Such a waste of telephone time can be avoided by the use of a **loudspeaker telephone**, similar to the intercom system mentioned above. This is more generally known as the **direct speech** system. As shown in Fig. 12.2, it enables a conversation to continue from any part of the room, allowing, in this case, for the speaker to read direct from his file. It also leaves both hands free. A further advantage is that it reduces the number of call-backs; instead of telling the caller one will look up the file and telephone him again, the information can be given immediately. Thus, efficiency as well as economy is increased.

(*e*) Other savings can be made by using facilities available on the **PABX** system, such as the following:

Trunk offering. If an important call comes in for someone already engaged on an internal call the operator can interrupt to offer the incoming call. If the outside call is then accepted, the time and cost of calling back is saved. It also, of course, provides a better service to the caller.

Fig. 12.2. A loudspeaker telephone.

'Ring when free.' A less important call received in the above circumstances can be put on to a 'waiting' circuit. When the person called is free the outside call is automatically put through immediately he replaces the handset. The danger of the operator forgetting the waiting caller is avoided.

Trunk-call barring. A circuit can be arranged so that only local calls can be made from certain extensions. Thus, juniors can be prevented from making expensive calls, unless they ask the operator and provide a justification.

(*f*) As mentioned above, economies can often be effected by the choice of systems or of combinations of them.

Telephone Answering Equipment

These machines record incoming calls made in the absence of the person called, with the facility to play back the messages. A taped message placed in the machine will tell any caller that the called person is not available and ask that a message be left. A person absent from his office can thereby accept telephone calls and listen to them when he returns.

The user can be connected to his machine by telephone from any part of the world and listen to messages received in his absence. Instructions can also be left for him in the same way. He can also leave messages by telephone. For example, an executive who is in Los Angeles at 6 p.m. local time may require to send a report to his office in London—where it is 2 a.m.

A considerable saving can be effected by having sales representatives telephone in orders after 6 p.m. when calls are cheapest. These would be ready for processing first thing the next morning. It has been shown that this can reduce the cost of representatives' telephone calls by up to 75 per cent.

12.8   Staff Location

Radio-telephony. The nature of some people's work is such that they are frequently away from a telephone or are so mobile that it is difficult to locate them at any one time. The use of short-wave radio enables immediate contact to be made with those with receiving apparatus. These could be in mobile units such as cars or vans, or the person called could carry a small 'walky-talky' set.

Paging systems. Another method of contacting staff is to equip them with small 'bleepers', which are about the size of a pocket pen. A signal can be sent from a central station which will produce a note only in the receiver of the person called. That person would then go to the nearest telephone in order to receive his message.

Public address systems. Loudspeakers can be used to contact staff. This would be done only where not all the staff can be reached directly by telephone, as in workshops or yards. It is therefore rarely used in offices, particularly as it has the disadvantage of disturbing the work of other staff.

12.9   Document Transmission

Where large bundles of documents have to be moved frequently it is possible to use horizontal or vertical conveyors similar to those employed in factories and warehouses. An office is, however, more likely to require the movement of single documents. Where there is a frequent flow, such as to and from a drawing office, the introduction of **pneumatic tubes** may be justified. Transferring documents by messenger between widely separated offices is time-consuming and has security risks. (Sent by tube, they travel safely and at 20 miles per hour.) Where there are a number of stations to be served the system can be very sophisticated. One method is the continuous-loop system whereby a complete circuit embraces all the delivery points. The document is placed in a cylinder around which is an electrical control band. This is set with the code number of the destination station so that it is automatically routed to the receiving point.

Documents can also be distributed within an office by **belt conveyors.** A document is placed in a flexible transparent wallet and its destination indicated by a slide tab on the wallet. After being placed on the moving belt the wallet travels automatically to the selected desk.

Key Points

1. The **choice of communication method** will be influenced by
    (*a*) how important is *speed of delivery*;
    (*b*) the *cost*;
    (*c*) any necessity to produce a *record* of the message;
    (*d*) whether the *time zones* of the two parties differ;
    (*e*) the importance of *accuracy*.

2. **Information retrieval** means accessibility to stored information. The most vital factor is *speed*.

3. **Information methods** are broadly as follows:
    (*a*) *Mail.*
    (*b*) *Telephones* (see 4 below).
    (*c*) *Telegrams and cables*—fast; provide copies; useful when time zones differ; economy by use of codes and telegraphic addresses.
    (*d*) *Teleprinters*—simultaneous transmission and reception by typing; useful when time zones differ; private internal system or Telex for external systems; speed increased by use of punched tape.
    (*e*) *Facsimile telegraphy*—simultaneous transmission and reception of *images*; cheaper than teleprinters for long texts (must be previously typed).
    (*f*) *Datel services*—transmission of data to and from computers by Telex, telegraph or telephone.

4. The efficiency of **telephones** can be increased by the following:
    (*a*) *Call monitoring*—to reduce wasteful calls.
    (*b*) *Automatic dialling*—to save time and money.
    (*c*) *Direct speech* (*or loudspeaker*)—enabling conversations to be made from any point in a room. Can also be used as a form of '*intercom*'.
    (*d*) *Trunk offering* and '*ring when free*'—used for incoming calls when the called person is engaged on a telephone.
    (*e*) *Trunk-call barring*—prevents unauthorised trunk calling.
    (*f*) *Telephone answering equipment*—accepts and records calls in the absence of the person called.

5. **Staff location** systems include:
    (*a*) *radio telephones*—called person must have a receiving and sending station;
    (*b*) *paging system*—electronic 'bleepers' using individual wavelengths; called person cannot reply direct;
    (*c*) *public address systems.*

6. **Document transmission** refers to methods of physically transferring documents. Compared with messenger services, automatic transmission increases *speed* and *security*.

13

DEALING WITH CORRESPONDENCE

13.1 An Integration of Processes

Correspondence plays a major part in any business and a business which handles it in an inefficient manner will be weak in a fundamental area. Slackness in dealing with correspondence will have repercussions throughout the organisation. To achieve efficiency it is necessary to accept two principles:

(a) The Mailing Department is a specialist area which must operate with competence and economy.

(b) All departments concerned with correspondence must feed into and out of the Mailing Department, so that cooperation is essential.

In other words, people in all sections of the business and at all levels of seniority deal with correspondence, but the focal point of receiving and despatching that correspondence is one department. Consequently, the whole of the correspondence activity depends not only upon the efficiency of the Mailing Department but, also, the effectiveness with which other departments cooperate with it. There must therefore be efficient organisation within the Mailing Department and in all the procedures which relate to it. These relationships may be summarised as shown in Fig. 13.1.

Total efficiency in dealing with correspondence demands the following:

(a) Handling incoming and outgoing mail must be recognised as being a specialist function.

(b) The Mailing Department must be supplied with suitable equipment and trained staff.

(c) Mailing costs must be kept as low as possible.

(d) Incoming mail must be distributed by a set procedure and with the minimum of delay.

(e) Timetables must be established so that outgoing letters are signed and made available to the Mailing Department by prescribed times.

(f) Letters must be produced by the most efficient and economical methods possible.

13.2 The Importance of the Mailing Department

It is a regrettable fact that in many businesses the mailroom is an area which is largely ignored by management. Mailroom supervisors are often regarded as not being part of middle management and their department is frequently overlooked by those responsible for efficient administration. Unless the business handles a very large volume of post (as, for example, a mail order business does) it is rare for exercises to be carried out to improve the efficiency of mailing. Usually, the department does not require to be fully manned all day, so the normal practice is to use junior staff at peak periods. This may be

FROM MAILING DEPARTMENT	Executives	Department Heads	Clerical Officers	Personal Secretaries	Typists
Inward mail					
Distributed to	X	X	X	X	
Outward mail					
Originated by	X	X	X		
Typed by				X	X
Signed by	X	X	X	X	
Made up by		X	X	X	
TO MAILING DEPARTMENT					

Fig. 13.1. The two-way flow of correspondence.

the reason why management does not always give the department the attention it requires. A study by experts could often increase the department's efficiency. Also, efforts are rarely made to ensure that the most economical methods are used. This is surprising when companies complain loudly about the cost of postage.

13.3   Mail Inward

Methods of dealing with inward mail differ between businesses, largely because of the differing quantities of mail received. The procedure adopted by a football pools promoter, for example, will obviously be considerably different from that used by a local solicitor. A common factor, however, is that mail would be delivered to a central point convenient to the postman. Except where large deliveries are the norm this would be the Reception Office. Unless the business is small the mail must then be sent to a mailing department. This means that measures must be taken to ensure that the transfer is made promptly and safely.

In most cases, only a small staff will be required at this stage. The nature of their duties will depend upon the practice of the business but the following principles generally apply.

Initial sorting

A proportion of the mail will not be opened at this point because regular correspondents will address letters to departments or officers and these can be forwarded unopened. There is no point in opening every envelope containing an order, for example, because all such communications can be dealt with only by the appropriate department. Any letter addressed *personally* should certainly not be opened.

The first stage therefore would be to sort into categories mail which is not to be opened, and to place it in baskets marked with the names of the addressees.

Opening Mail

Mail which it has been agreed must be opened should be dealt with systematically.

A letter-opening machine could be used if there was a sufficiently large volume of mail to be opened. This machine removes a thin edge of the envelope so as to not damage the contents.

Every removed letter should be date-stamped.

Enclosures should be firmly attached to the letters. A letter may be quickly perused to see if an enclosure is mentioned in the letter. If it is and there is no enclosure the attention of the supervisor should be drawn to the omission and an appropriate note made on the letter. Alternatively, it may be decided that speed is a prior consideration and staff should not be required to carry out this check.

Any remittances should be noted on the accompanying document and entered in a **remittances inward book** or on a cash sheet. The record should show the name of the sender, and the amount and form of the payment. When all the post has been opened the cashier should check the remittances against the entries and sign the book or sheet as acknowledgment of his having taken custody of the money.

An **inwards mail register** should record only such documents as are prescribed. To enter every item takes up much time and serves no purpose. Rules should therefore be made as to which items *must* be listed. According to the type of business these could be legal documents, manuscripts, etc., but it must be remembered that most of these would be addressed to particular persons and therefore would not be opened in the Mailing Department. In appropriate cases it is usual for departments to keep their own records of the receipt of certain documents.

Sorting and Distributing

The letters and enclosures would be sorted into the baskets holding the unopened mail. Where there is some doubt as to who should be sent a particular letter the decision should be made by the supervisor. Practice varies between businesses as to the method of dealing with communications which appear to require the attention of more than one person. For example, a customer may send a settlement of his account and at the same time raise a query which should be dealt with by the Sales Department. An inflexible rule is that any remittances must be disposed of first, so that that letter must first go to the cashier.

There may be a rule that the Mailing Department should write the names of all the addressees on the letter or attach a circulation slip showing the routing of the document. A more usual practice is to leave it to the common sense of the first addressee to redirect the letter after he has finished with it or to forward a copy so that he can retain the original.

Another example is the procedure to be adopted if a letter of complaint was received from a member of the public. It should not be the responsibility of the mailing clerks to decide who should deal with the complaint, particularly as more than one person may have to be involved. Such a letter should be sent to whoever appears to be the logical person to deal with it; in this case, probably the Public Relations Officer. It will then be the responsibility of that person to deal with the complaint himself, pass it to a more appropriate person or circulate it for the views of those involved.

Considerations such as these underline the principle that although the Mailing Department is expected to be efficient (particularly as regards security), its prime objective should be to distribute mail *quickly*. Executives and departments require to have their correspondence as early in the day as possible. This will not be possible if the Mailing Department has to spend a lot of time on routines which serve little useful purpose. It must also be remembered that the department is usually manned by fairly junior staff who should not be required to take decisions which could have serious consequences.

Having been sorted, the mail will then be distributed or departments may be required to collect it.

13.4   Organising Outward Correspondence

Outgoing correspondence will emanate from almost all areas of the business but it must all end in the Mailing Department. This department will work to a timetable so that all mail is ready for posting by a specified time. There must therefore be a time schedule reaching back from that time. The department will know how long it usually takes to prepare the post, so a rule must be made as to the latest time by which correspondence must reach the department. This in turn means that every executive and department must ensure that typed letters are collected and signed early enough to meet that requirement. It must be understood that any letters reaching the Mailing Department late will be held over to the following day. Also, letters typed after a certain time would have to be dated for the next day because they will be among that day's signing.

This process can be aided by a system of collecting points from which mail may be taken to the Mailing Department. Pressure on the department will be eased if there are several collections during the day. Any special despatches, such as a large circulation, should be dealt with *during* the day, leaving the routine postings to the usual time.

Any special instructions about airmail postage, recorded delivery, etc., should be indicated on the envelope in pencil by the writer. If first-class mail is to be used it should be so indicated by being typed or rubber stamped on the top left-hand corner.

13.5   Mail Outward

It is at the outgoing mail stage where it is most likely that efficiency and economy can be improved. The Post Office can assist in both respects by providing courses for the efficient running of mailrooms. The most useful source, however, is the *Post Office Guide* because it will often indicate the economies which can be effected by a judicious choice of the services offered.

Cost-saving Equipment

Franking machines. Machines which will quickly frank mail have been in existence for more than 50 years and the saving of time they provide is well proved. They range from small desk models for ordinary correspondence to units capable of handling large circulations.

A so-far inescapable disadvantage is that franking machines have to be taken to the Post Office for resetting of their meters. Developments now current will soon make this unnecessary by the use of a computer-linked system. The user will be able to telephone, quoting his account and meter number, when the machine is due to be recharged. A voice response will then give him an individual setting code which will enable him to reset his own meter.

Circularising equipment. The issue of a large number of standard documents, with each envelope containing several papers, can present a formidable task. An advertising campaign, for example, may require each addressee to receive a package of papers, not all of them of the same size. These must be collated so that each addressee receives a complete set, requiring the contents to be folded to a standard size, inserted in pre-addressed envelopes and the envelopes sealed. Without mechanisation this means that a number of people have to work at long tables, the whole operation being tedious, time-consuming and open to all sorts of errors.

Equipment is available which will automatically sort up to 20 sets of documents into bins. Other equipment will fold, crossfold, count and insert into envelopes. One system will not only carry out those operations but will also seal, frank and stack the envelopes at a speed of up to 3,500 pieces an hour, using just one operator.

(The use of **addressing machines** for circularising is mentioned on page 125.)

13.6 The Typing Force

Classes of Typists

The classes of typists may be identified as follows:

(*a*) *Copy-typists.* These are typists with no knowledge of shorthand. It has to be accepted that the standard of many copy-typists is not high. This derives from the under-supply of typists so that desperate employers are often compelled to accept staff who are not wholly satisfactory. Currently, this is one of the facts of business life and the only (partial) solution is to reduce routine typing as much as possible. Another uncomfortable fact is the high labour turnover of typists.

(*b*) *Shorthand typists.* The shortage of efficient shorthand typists makes them expensive to employ. This has led to the development of processes which make shorthand unnecessary.

(*c*) *Audio-typists.* These type from recorded dictation. Because of the cost of shorthand typists and the benefits of using dictating equipment an increasing proportion of typing personnel comes in this category.

(*d*) *Personal secretaries.* These are shorthand typists who usually work for one executive and who may reach the status of being regarded as personal assistants. Typing is usually only part of a personal secretary's duties because she may be responsible for organising appointments, dealing with matters in the absence of the executive, interviewing, 'guarding' the executive from unwelcome visitors, etc. Many such employees are very efficient and make a valuable contribution to the running of a business. In some cases, however (through no fault of the secretary), her cost is not justified. Having a personal secretary is sometimes a 'status symbol'—something which is added at a certain stage of promotion, even when there is no justification for it. Because of economic pressures, such an attitude is now much less prevalent. Increasingly, the practice is for private secretaries to be shared between two or three executives or to combine the duties of secretary with more managerial work.

Economic Division of Work

Because typists are expensive to employ, the various kinds of typing skills which are available must be combined in the most economical proportions. Basically, each sort of typist should be fully employed in providing the skill relevant to that sort. If a copy-typist spends part of her time doing the less expensive work of filing it must be borne in mind that she is costing the firm a *typist's* salary. The situation becomes even more wasteful if a shorthand typist does a large amount of copy-typing.

The composition of the typing force will be largely determined by the relative volumes of different types of work. A company employing a lot of correspondents will require a larger than usual number of typists who can transcribe. The reverse will apply if most of the work consists of typing forms.

The dictating methods used will also have an important bearing on the kinds of typists employed.

With a large typing force the most efficient and economical way of dividing the work could be as follows:

Audio-typists—routine correspondence.
Copy-typists—repetitive documents.
Senior copy-typists—complicated documents; display work.
Shorthand typists—private secretarial work; confidential matters; reporting meetings.

13.7 Typing Pools

This term can relate to one of two systems. In the strictest sense, a typing pool is a collection of typists in one department whose services are available to departments generally. Therefore, instead of a department using typists on its own staff it will use those in a central department. It can also refer to a system otherwise known as 'centralised dictating' (see Section 13.8).

Advantages

Pooling enables a more even distribution of work to be achieved. For example, a department typist may sometimes find she has little or no typing to do, while at the same time a typist in a neighbouring department is over-worked. The flexibility derived from pooling also makes it easier to cope with staff absences.

The system brings with it the benefits of specialisation in that the girls concentrate on typing instead of filling in time by filing, answering the telephone, etc. The accommodation is also specialised, being designed especially for typing work.

A typing pool often serves as a training centre for typists. Because it will have a supervisor, the standard of work should be improved.

Disadvantages

An important disadvantage is that typists dislike pools. If they do only copy-typing they have no contact with the writers of the correspondence, and working for everyone means there is no personal interest in any one aspect of the work.

The current policy to reduce this disadvantage is to set up specialist pools. These, of course, are smaller than central pools, which makes them more attractive. The principle is that the typists in any one pool deal with a section of the total work so that each typist has a closer identity with the work and those engaged in it. It also benefits the company in that the typists become more specialised and therefore more knowledgeable in certain areas. When a girl in a central pool has been largely engaged in typing for the Sales Department she may produce some startling letters if she has to produce them for, say, a chemist! If she is in a smaller pool she may write a lot of letters for chemists and other technicians and would thus produce more sensible letters.

A further reason for the unpopularity of pools is the general one that the congregating of a large number of women in one place is disliked.

13.8 Centralised Dictating

This relates to a pool of audio-typists. The principle is that all those who need to dictate have access to a dictating centre, either on a PBX system or a separate circuit, by speaking into a handset. The material is then recorded on disc or tape in the central department—that is, the author does not have the dictating machine at his desk. If the **bank system** is used the recordings are allocated by the pool supervisor. The **tandem system** links the dictator to an individual typist to whom he can talk if necessary. Each typist has two machines, one being available for recording while the other is being used for transcription. A third method is **direct link**, which uses a continuous tape loop allowing long dictation periods and enabling the typist to transcribe while the dictator continues to speak.

13.9 Dictating Equipment

There is a considerable number of dictating machines on the market offering a variety of methods, but the basic principle is the ability to record on material which can be used by someone else to type from. Models range from the pocket memo type and the desk-top type to the centralised dictating system.

The **pocket type** has considerable advantages in certain circumstances. Surveyors and engineers can use them while they are actually 'on site' making estimates and reports; visible stocktaking is possible without having to write anything down; a salesman can dictate orders as he receives them.

An executive away from his office can make recordings on a **portable machine** and post the recording media to his office for typing. It is possible to telephone recordings from any distance direct to a centralised dictating point.

Desk-top models can be self-contained or, as shown above, the author can be linked directly to a typing centre.

Advantages

Dictating equipment in general provides the following advantages:

(*a*) The working times of dictators and typists do not need to coincide, because dictation can take place when convenient to the author.

(*b*) Typists' time is not wasted by dictation being interrupted by telephone calls, visitors, etc. A survey has shown that the average secretary produces only 76 lines of type in a day. With centralised dictation a typist can average at least 600 lines a day.

(*c*) The author can dictate at his own speed, play back and correct without taking up the time of a typist.

(*d*) Fewer typists are needed. It has been claimed that centralised dictation can double the output of a typing pool.

(*e*) Typists do not have the problem of transcribing from rough notes submitted by the authors. Unless dictating machines are used, site engineers, for example, may hand in work of this description.

Disadvantages

The possible disadvantages are as follows:

(*a*) Dictating is an acquired skill. Not all authors make successful dictators (*b*) The loss of a personal secretary can sometimes be interpreted as a loss of status.

(*c*) Machines can break down.

13.10 The Cost of Letter-writing

Possibly the largest single item of expense in letter-writing is typists' salaries. Other labour costs are those relevant to time spent on dictating and those of mailing and other supplementary staff. There is also the considerable rent-cost of space occupied by staff and equipment. Added to this must be the cost of buying and maintaining machines, and of postage and stationery.

Estimates have been made that the cost of a single letter produced by traditional methods is something in excess of £5. Recognition of this startling fact accounts for the many innovations adopted in order to reduce costs.

13.11 The Typewriter

Undoubtedly, the one piece of office equipment known to everyone is the typewriter. In spite of revolutionary changes in office work in recent years, the typewriter remains the fundamental and most widely used machine. Although there have been technical developments, the basic mechanics of typewriters remain unchanged. Because typewriters are so familiar it is necessary only to identify some of the refinements introduced in recent years.

Electric typewriters are electrically assisted—that is, the usual manual process of touching keys is still necessary but only to the extent required to overcome inertia. Consequently, such machines are less tiring to operate than manual machines. Because of the unvarying pressure of the key heads the typed work always has a uniform appearance. A number of other operations, such as carriage return, are automatic.

An electric typewriter may print by the normal 'type-bar' method or the 'golf-ball' system may be used. In the latter case, instead of a basket of keys the machine uses a spherical head (about 1 inch in diameter) on which are moulded the characters. By depressing a key the head spins and tilts so that the selected character strikes the ribbon. The carriage is fixed and the ball travels across the face of the paper.

This system has the additional advantage of enabling a variety of typefaces to be used. This is because the golf-balls are easily interchangeable. It is thereby possible to produce a document with more than one typeface so that the product has an appearance approaching that of printing.

Electric typewriters cost about twice as much as manual machines. This additional cost can be set off against the increased production capacity, which is reckoned to be 33 to 50 per cent higher than that of a manual machine. As with all machines, however, this gain will not accrue unless the machine is fully employed. In order to justify their greater cost electric machines should be used in conditions of high employment, such as a typing pool. It may flatter a private secretary to give her such a machine but it is economically unwise to do so unless her daily output exceeds a certain amount.

Continuous stationery equipment can be fixed to a typewriter. Where long typing runs of standardised forms are necessary a lot of time can be spent feeding in and withdrawing each form, particularly if carbon paper has to be inserted. The solution is to print the forms on a continuous roll. With the use of this equipment the roll is fed into the machine from a concertina'd pack and after typing the forms are separated by tearing across perforations. Carbon paper can be automatically inserted, although a more satisfactory method is to use carbonless paper.

Ribbon cartridges simply slot into typewriters which are designed to accept them. The often frustrating operation of fitting a new ribbon is thereby avoided.

Varityper is a term relating to any system which can provide a variety of typefaces.

13.12   Word Processing

One of the most significant developments in recent years has been 'word processing', the justification for which is the high cost of typing. A skilled typist is capable of producing 60 to 70 words a minute but it is estimated that on average she produces only 15 words a minute. There can be a variety of reasons for this. For example, the incidence of typing errors must, obviously, reduce output; material may have to be retyped because of revisions made by the author; it takes longer to produce tabulated data. Word processing considerably reduces the effects of such incidents.

A further justification is that typing frequently involves a considerable amount of repetition. For example, the Contracts Department of a business may have to type a lot of legal agreements. There may be a large number of clauses which appear in all the contracts; other common clauses may appear in, say, half of them. As any contract must contain a high proportion of text which is standard there will be a considerable amount of repetitive typing. The principle of word processing is that in making out an agreement all that has to be typed is the information which refers only to that contract. All the standard terms and phrases would be typed automatically.

Another function of word processing is to enable any number of standard letters to be written with only one typing. For example, a sales campaign may require a letter to be sent to every customer. The only difference between one letter and another may be the names and addresses of the customers. Once one copy of the text of the letter has been typed further copies are produced by automatic typing, including the typing of each customer's personal details. If an additional or alternative paragraph has to be included in some of the letters, or a paragraph has to be omitted, this can also be done automatically. All these letters will be written at speeds considerably in excess of that of human typing.

The Equipment

A self-contained unit consists of the following equipment, occupying an office desk, as shown in Fig. 13.2:

(*a*) *The keyboard.* There is an electric typewriter with a normal keyboard layout but with separate function keys.

(*b*) *A visible display unit.* This displays, immediately above the keyboard, the words being typed.

(*c*) *A magnetic text storage unit.* This holds the typed information. It also holds a store of frequently used standard information which can be automatically introduced where required. It is situated to the typists's right.

(*d*) *The printer.* This can produce automatically at a rate of about 550 words a minute. It can accept information from the screened typing and from the standard information store. In the illustration it occupies the right-hand desk.

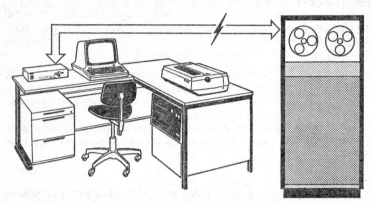

Fig. 13.2. Word processing computer-linked unit.
(By courtesy of Philips Electrical Ltd.)

A unit can be linked to a central computer, as shown in Fig. 13.2, so that data can be called up and then stored and processed. Also, a number of processors can be linked by telephone, allowing for automatic transfer of texts, even when the receiving processor is unattended.

The Process

The typist types a letter in the normal way but it is not recorded on paper at this stage. Instead, what she types appears on the screen. She types as though she were writing a continuous line; moving to a new line is done automatically on the screen and without breaking words. Any corrections can be made simply by overtyping. Where necessary, text can be inserted, deleted or moved to another position. Any other adjustment to layout, such as column widths or line drawing, can be done merely by operating keys.

The screen will usually display one page of text, A4 size—28 lines of up to 80 characters per line. Other models will record larger documents, any part of which can be displayed by 'scrolling'.

Much time and labour can be wasted when the author of a document is not satisfied with what he has written. When he receives it in type form he may realise it could have been better worded or laid out. He may also reject it because it contains typing errors. Without word processing the document would have to be typed again. To edit a document, using word processing, a print is made of the original and the author would then mark it with his corrections. The tape from which the print was made is then fed in and the function keys are used to make the alterations which are necessary to produce the new draft. An illustration of this process is given in Fig. 13.3. At the top is shown the original typing and the subsequent editing. The amended draft

From the Sales Director

To Branch Managers   15th March 19..

Introduction of Model DX

~~*Following*~~ ~~(~~Fallowing~~)~~ the meeting we had on the 12th/I wish to/emphasise
the decisions then made. ·

March   *again*

The project is to be reclassified as "Possible" instead of
"Probable".

Underline and indent left & right

No communication whatsoever is to be made in response to any
enquiries from customers or the (press) Any enquiries must be
referred to me.   *Press*

New specifications will be issued (as) as soon as circumstances
make it possible.   *delete*

From the Sales Director

To Branch Managers   15th March 19..

Introduction of Model DX

Following the meeting we had on the 12th March I wish to again
emphasise the decisions then made.

> No communication whatsoever is to be made in response
> to any enquiries from customers or the Press. Any
> enquiries must be referred to me.

The project is to be reclassified as "Possible" instead of
"Probable".

New specifications will be issued as soon as circumstances make
it possible.

Corrections: The typing error in the first line was corrected by over-typing.
'Press' was given an initial capital.

Insertions: Two insertions were made in the first paragraph and the lines were
automatically extended.

Moving: The second paragraph was moved to its new position.

Indent and underline: New left and right margins were set, with the whole paragraph automatically rearranged. The whole was underlined automatically.

Deletion: The word 'as' in the final paragraph was deleted and the text closed
up automatically.

Fig. 13.3. Editing by the word-processing system.

as finally produced is then shown, followed by an explanation of how the
changes were made.

Amendments can also be made *before* printing if the author examines the
draft as displayed on the screen and then has any amendments made. He can
thus 'play around' until he can see a picture of an acceptable product. The
assistance this can give in composing display work is obviously considerable.

When the screen shows the accepted version the material is magnetically recorded and fed into the printer. Any number of copies can be produced. The saving of time is considerable because, first, the draft does not have to be retyped and, secondly, the final typing is done automatically while the typist gets on with other work.

Other Automatic Processes

The time of a typist is considerably reduced by various automatic processes. For example, the tedious task of typing statistical work is made easier by the facility to move columns of figures across the screen, either to space them evenly or to change their position. Decimal alignment is automatic.

In addition to the examples of editing shown in Fig. 13.3 spacing between paragraphs can be altered to give a more balanced appearance; right-hand margins can be justified so that the text appears in print format; the text can be arranged in columns instead of page width. It is possible to draw lines so that the drafting of charts is comparatively easy.

It is even possible for the processor to search a document to find certain words and to substitute new ones. For example, if a catalogue is now to use the phrase 'high grade' instead of 'de luxe' for one of the products, the new phrase can be inserted in place of the old one so that new catologues do not have to be retyped.

It is also possible to sort data into any required order, such as alphabetical, numerical or datal.

Discs or tapes holding standard information are filed in an identification system. A complete index of all the files can be displayed on the screen and the files can be renumbered, renamed or rearranged as required without going into the store.

13.13   The Economics of Word Processing

One of the reasons for a company to adopt word processing would be to reduce the cost of employing typists. To obtain an estimate of the saving which should result it is usual to write off the cost of the equipment over a period of five years and to assume annual maintenance costs to be 10 per cent of the capital cost. If that set of figures plus the cost of employing a reduced number of typists is less than the present labour costs, then, obviously, investment in a word processor is economically viable.

As with all forms of mechanisation, however, this concept is acceptable only if there is a certain minimum of work which is relevant to the word-processing system. Unless the typing work includes a large amount of repetitive matter, installation may not be justified.

To make the process viable there must be some reorganisation of administration methods. It must be arranged for the system to be fully occupied and this will usually entail taking some typing away from secretaries. The total of automatic typing must be organised under a responsible person so that work can be programmed, allowing the advantages of the system to accrue to as many aspects of the business as possible.

In calculating the cost in relation to the benefits one must take account of work other than letter-typing which word processing can do more efficiently.

There is a tendency to forget the time which can otherwise be spent on such jobs as updating price lists, indexing and listing, drafting display work, etc. It must also be remembered that while the printer is producing copies at high speed the typist can continue with other typing. This must also incidentally eliminate the costs of the duplicating which may otherwise be necessary.

Key Points

1. The **Mailing Department** must be recognised as being a *vital* and *specialist* function area. All other departments rely on its efficiency.

2. The prime concerns in dealing with **inward mail** are *security* and *speed*. Procedures should not be introduced which make those objectives more difficult to achieve.

3. The following 'deadlines' should apply concerning **outward mail**: letters—

   (a) ready for signature by—

   (b) signed by—

   (c) at Mailing Department by—

4. For *economical use of typists* the **composition of the typing force** should be determined by:

   (a) the volume of different kinds of typing work; and

   (b) the dictation methods used.

5. **Typing pools** have the following

   advantages: economical use of labour; flexibility; specialisation.

   disadvantages: unpopularity with typists; lack of specialist experience of dictators' work.

   A (partial) solution can be the establishing of *specialist* pools.

6. The use of **dictating machines** provide the following

   advantages: typists fully engaged in typing; dictation at authors' convenience; tapes can be mailed; fewer typists;

   disadvantages: possibility of poor dictating skills; machines can malfunction.

7. **Word processors** are justified where:

   (a) there is much *repetitive work* with variations within batches of otherwise uniform material;

   (b) when *display work* is required.

   Other advantages include the following:

   (a) Amendments and corrections can be made to the master before it is printed.

   (b) Any number of copies can be made.

   (c) Automatic typing is very fast, leaving the typist free for other work.

   (d) Standard information can be stored and programmed to be input at required points.

   (e) Economically justified after a certain level of output by reducing typists.

   (f) It can update lists, etc., automatically.

14

COMPUTERISATION

14.1 The Computer Revolution

The development of the computer over the past quarter century has had revolutionary results. Because of its ability to carry out complex calculations at very high speeds it has been of considerable help in almost all areas of scientific research. It has extended the process of automation in production, which in turn has resulted in reactions in the field of industrial relations. It has made possible the compiling of vast 'data banks' capable of holding extensive information about people, and this has given rise to some moral concern. Where the revolution has been most obvious, however (and the one with which this book is concerned), is in the office. It has led to changes in procedures which strike at the very roots of administration; it has resulted in shifts in the pattern of office employment, bringing in new skills and disposing of others; it has forced a change of attitude by management.

Whatever the reactions of any one person to computers, the fact is that they are here, that they play a large part in office life and that they will increasingly do so in the future.

In the days when computers were first introduced into office work there were some unhappy experiences and these have contributed to some of the adverse reactions which remain today. Installation was very expensive because of the size of the equipment and the cost of building special rooms to hold it. Some managers were over-enthusiastic (including those who regarded a computer as a prestige symbol) and reacted adversely when the computer did not solve all their problems. Other managers were luke-warm, were persuaded to accept a computer and then, peevishly, did not give it the facilities necessary for its success. There was a shortage of experienced staff, so that programming was not always efficient. Business associates resented the loss of the 'personal touch' when dealing with computer owners. Employees were reluctant to adjust to new procedures.

Most of these disadvantages have disappeared, partly because computerisation has been extended to more areas of work, bringing with it a better understanding. Another reason is that although the use of computers has increased considerably in recent years, installations of large computer complexes have declined dramatically. Smaller computers can give most businesses the service they require at very much lower costs. The single factor leading to this development has been the introduction of semiconductors. Silicone chips, with their ability to hold an enormous amount of circuitry in a tiny space, have made **microprocessors** an almost common form of office equipment. Dramatic though the development of computers has been, the advent of chips has had results which may fairly be described as sensational. They relate not only to computers; reference is made elsewhere in this book to automatic invoicing systems, word processors, etc. All these and an increasing number of other operations are made possible by the use of semiconductors.

Computerisation is now accepted as a way of life. Managers, many of them trained in the 'computer age', have a better understanding of the system. Competition among suppliers has resulted in simpler and more efficient equipment being produced. There is an increasing (although still inadequate) workforce of programmers, operators and technicians.

14.2 What is a Computer?

'To compute' means 'to count', so that, strictly speaking, a computer is anything that counts. Even in the generally accepted understanding of the word it can have more than one meaning. A pocket calculator is a computer, as is a complex in which the machinery alone can cost over a million pounds. However, any computer in the common usage of the word has certain characteristics, which may be listed as follows:

(*a*) It operates on electronic pulses, which accounts for the extremely high speeds at which it works.

(*b*) Data which have to be processed must first be in a form the computer will accept.

(*c*) It will obey instructions, allowing it to

(*i*) perform any required arithmetical function;
(*ii*) select and carry out alternative courses of action;
(*iii*) move to another operation from a preceding one.

(*d*) It can bring in data stored elsewhere and update with new data.

(*e*) It can transfer data to store.

(*f*) It can produce computer material suitable for feeding into a subsequent operation.

(*g*) It will check the data it receives and produces.

(*h*) It will produce data in a readable form.

A large computer is capable of carrying out in parallel several unrelated operations in accordance with predetermined priorities. It will change from one routine to another, either automatically or by asking for instructions from the operator.

14.3 The Degree of Automation

The high efficiency of which a computer is capable depends upon the accuracy of (*a*) the **data fed in** for processing and (*b*) the **processing instructions** it is given.

These two areas are the only ones where human participation is necessary, *but they are vital*. Provided both tasks are performed correctly the rest of the work can safely be left for the computer to do. Administration is therefore concerned with devising systems which will provide input data accurately and instructions which will produce the required results.

The necessity to provide accurate instructions is less daunting when it is realised that most computing operations are standard ones. A computer will be engaged on such routine jobs as compiling the payroll, dealing with orders, maintaining ledgers, etc. Once systems have been designed to provide each of these operations the instructions rarely have to be radically changed.

The input of *data*, however, is more prone to error because no item will be standard. There can be inbuilt checks, as part of the instructions, but the main safeguard must be a system of verifying the accuracy of every item before it is fed in. This point is discussed further later in the chapter.

14.4 An Outline of the Computing Process

A simplified explanation of the process is possible by relating it to what would have to be done if a ledger was posted by hand.

(1) The posting media would be assembled and sorted into a logical sequence.

(2) The ledger sheets to be posted would be brought from a 'store' (or the ledger pages selected) and related to the relevant posting media.

(3) An operating routine would be decided on.

(4) The items would be posted to the relevant ledger sheets or pages and updated to show the new balances.

(5) The ledger sheets would be sorted back into ledger order and the ledgers returned to store.

(6) A list of all the postings would be available from a Day Book.

(7) The new totals of the ledger balances would be transferred to another account (Debtors' Account or Creditors' Account).

(8) Totals would be transferred to Purchases (or Sales) Account, Discounts Account, etc.

(9) Any other required information would be produced, such as sales analyses, comparisons with other data, etc.

(10) Control accounts would be posted and proved.

These operations are reflected in a computer processing. Before making a more detailed study of each stage involved it is necessary first to outline the complete process. The stages are related to the parts of the computer. These are listed below and should be read in conjunction with Fig. 14.1.

(*a*) At the **input stage** the information to be processed (i.e. the posting media, but now known as the **source documents**) must first be converted into a form acceptable to the computer. (The processes and the forms are described in the two following sections.) These and the instructions (known as the **program**) are fed into the Central Processing Unit.

(*b*) The **central processing unit (CPU)** is the nerve centre. It contains the **immediate access store (IAS)** which holds the data being worked upon, the program or part of the program, and standard information frequently required for processing. The CPU carries out the series of operations programmed until the whole process is completed.

(*c*) The **backing store** contains data stored away from the CPU. Because of the high cost of storing data in the IAS, much of it, including parts of the program if necessary, is held in the backing store and is transferred to the CPU when required. Records in the backing store are known as 'files' and are updated by feeding in the data being processed. There is therefore a two-way flow between the central processor and the backing store.

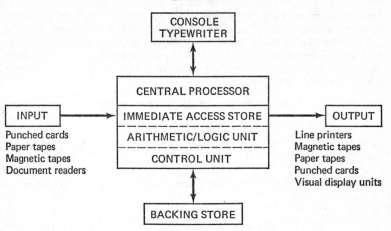

Fig. 14.1. Integration of computer functions.

Backing storage uses magnetic tape, discs and drums. **Tapes** are described on page 154. A **magnetic disc** consists of circular tracks containing a considerable number of recordings. Programming allows any item on a disc to be located in a fraction of a second. **Magnetic drums** operate on the same principle as discs except that the recordings are around the circumference of a cylinder.

(*d*) The **output stage** presents the processed data in the required form. It may be printed on paper or displayed on a screen. It may also provide data in an acceptable form (i.e. on cards, discs or tapes) as input for a subsequent computing operation. (The output equipment is described in Section 14.7.)

(*e*) The **console typewriter** can be used to instruct the computer at appropriate stages of processing.

The following terms are relevant to the above description:

Hardware is a collective term for the computer equipment.
Software refers to the programs which instruct the computer.
Configuration means the combination of equipment in a particular computer system.

14.5 Data Preparation

Data to be fed into a computer frequently have first to be converted into 'machine-sensible' form. If the information appears in written form (such as a copy order or credit note) it must be translated from that source document into a form which is acceptable to the computer. As previously stated, any system of data preparation from source documents must allow for verifying the accuracy of the conversion (see Section 14.6).

Not all input data, however, derive from source documents. As a by-product of a computing operation, output material may be automatically produced which can be fed in for another operation. For example, a computer 'run' for posting sales ledgers can incidentally provide input material for another run, such as one for relating sales to sales costs. Similarly, a suitably designed accounting machine may produce punched tape as a by-product of a posting operation so that it is then available as input to a computer (see page 158). Where systems such as these produce input material automatically there is no necessity to verify, but where data are converted from source documents verification is essential.

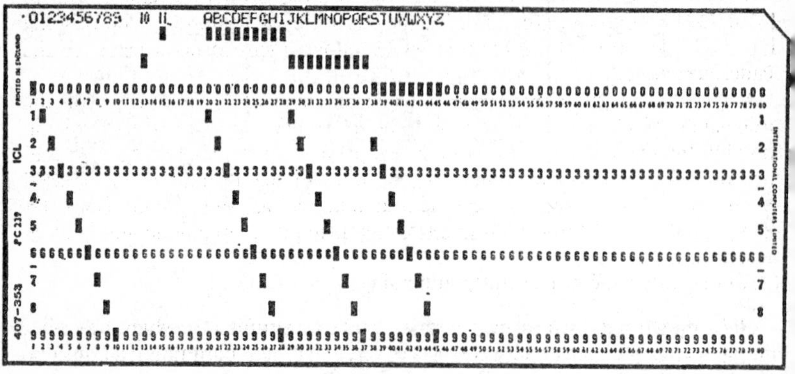

Fig. 14.2. A punched card.

14.6 Input Equipment

Punched cards were the earliest forms of input but they are now less popular for this purpose because of the time which has to be spent in preparing and verifying them. They are more frequently used as by-products of computer runs because, as already stated, they do not require to be verified and they are produced automatically. Items of information to be entered are recorded by punching holes in numbered columns (see Fig. 14.2). Punching is usually done automatically by placing the cards in a frame and depressing keys, the equipment being known as a 'key punch'. To verify the accuracy of the punchings the cards are repunched from the original documents. Where a second punching does not agree with the first punching of an item the machine locks to indicate that a discrepancy must be investigated. The system has the advantage that the cards can be automatically sorted into any required order but they are expensive, they occupy a lot of space and machine-reading of them is comparatively slow.

Paper tape is also punched but instead of the holes being made at numbered positions, as they are on cards, the binary system is used. Where a hole is punched it represents the binary digit 1 and where a position is not punched it represents 0. Most tapes have eight lines across the width. Again, verification is necessary by repunching. Paper tape is less expensive than cards, it occupies less storage space and machine-reading is faster. Paper tapes are similar to cards in that they operate on the principle of 'sensing' through perforations.

Magnetic tape is a more efficient method of input. It consists of plastic tape on to which data are recorded in the form of magnetised dots. It has the largest capacity of any method, one tape being capable of holding 10 million characters. They can be read and processed at extremely high speeds. If data have to be entered from source documents an 'encoding machine' is used. The information is keyed in by using a typewriter style keyboard and verification is achieved by repeating the process. Magnetic tape **cassettes** are used in mini-computers.

Document Readers

Equipment is available which can read printed or written characters on documents and convert the data for processing by a computer. The original data must be written by a method which allows them to be 'sensed' by the reader equipment.

A method which most people have experience of is that used for the processing of cheque transactions. The reference number of the person drawing the cheque and other details are printed on the cheque by a special method so that after presenting it to a bank it can be automatically processed through the clearing system. The method is known as **magnetic ink character recognition (MICR)**, the characters being printed in magnetic ink and in special founts.

Among other methods are the following:

Optical character recognition (OCR) refers to equipment which can read characters printed in special founts. They can read line by line or they can be designed to read selected parts of a page.

Mark sensing allows for a source document to be marked by a special pen and for a 'reader' to sense those markings. It is particularly useful for obtaining information from non-clerical staff in that the compiler is required to merely place marks on appropriate sections of a specially designed document. Fig. 14.3 gives an example of a market survey form to be completed by a

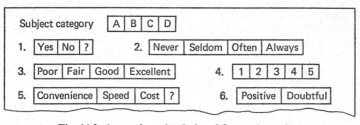

Fig. 14.3. A questionnaire designed for mark sensing.

researcher at an interview. 'Subject category' relates to the social/age group of the interviewee as determined by an agreed coding. The other items record answers to questions which are referenced by number to a standard list held by the researcher.

Light pens can be passed over **bar codes** on source data. They read the information and store it to provide keying-in data. Stock can be controlled by this method if each item has an identity code on it. It is used in shop check-out points by being linked to a cash register. An extension of that system automatically adjusts stock levels as each sale is made.

14.7 Output Equipment

The most commonly used equipment for producing the result of data processing is the **line printer**. This prints the information on to continuous rolls of
paper or continuous interfolded stationery. This can be done at speeds in
excess of 2,000 lines per minute, each line having a maximum of 132
characters.

As mentioned above, a computer can produce material ready for use in
another run. Magnetic tape can also be on microfilm for storing. This is known
as **computer output on microfilm (COM)**.

Where pieces of information are required, a suitably designed computer can
be 'interrogated'. The question is put by using an automatic typewriter and
the answers appear on a visual display unit. Examples of the use of this
facility are given in Section 14.10.

14.8 Programming

The hardware (i.e. the equipment) provides the advantages of speed and
accuracy, and the ability to carry out complex operations. But a computer is
mindless; it has to be told what to do. Its flexibility can be exploited only if it
is given instructions. These are known as 'programs' (the software).

To write a program requires a person who not only has the necessary
expertise but who also has a thorough knowledge of the processes which are
to be computerised and the results which are required. Thus, for programming
many clerical operations an understanding of accounting principles is necessary, both in general and as they apply in the particular situation.

The process is complex. New data must be assembled, possibly converted,
and then fed in; they must be related to existing data which must be transferred from store at the right stages; the required calculations must be made;
the end of one process must signal the beginning of a logical successor; items
for analysis must be extracted and finally printed; files must be updated with
the new data; extracted information in computer form for subsequent input
may have to be produced. The whole must therefore be arranged in logical
steps, one building on the other.

Writing a program can be a lengthy operation but many users of small
computers have found that with a short period of training they are themselves
able to write comparatively simple programs. For those operations which are
common to most firms (such as payroll, stock control, ledger posting, etc.)
it is possible to buy **packaged programs**. These provide a considerable saving
in that the cost of employing programmers is avoided. More specialist
programs can be designed to order by suppliers.

The instructions must be written in a style the computer understands. This
is achieved by the use of **programming languages**. Instructions are keyed in,
using one of the standard languages. These are then translated into machine
language within the computer. Some languages use code letters or mnemonics
mixed with plain words. A plain word language frequently used for commercial
operations is COBOL (Common Business-Orientated Language). In a payroll
exercise, for example, it is necessary to calculate the taxable pay to date. To do
this by hand the following steps would be required:

(*a*) Establish from tax tables the tax-free pay for the current week which is relevant to the employee's code number.

(*b*) Add this week's gross pay to the accumulated gross pay to last week.

(*c*) Deduct tax-free pay from the gross pay to date.

(*d*) Enter taxable pay to date.

In COBOL language this would be written a

COMPUTE (GROSS + TOTALGROSS)−(TAXFREE × WEEK) = TAXABLE

14.9 A Data-processing Operation in Outline

It is now possible to outline the operational stages in a normal computer run.

(1) Assemble source documents into a logical sequence.

(2) Convert and verify source documents into machine form.

(3) Input:

    (*a*) transaction data;

    (*b*) output from earlier runs (where relevant);

    (*c*) program or part-program.

(4) Process first stage.

    (*a*) Take in relevant store data.

    (*b*) Merge transaction data and store data.

    (*c*) Process as instructed.

    (*d*) Move to next stage.

(5) Repeat for following stages.

(6) Update file records.

(7) Output to:

    (*a*) line printer;

    (*b*) input for later runs.

14.10 On-line Processing

This relates to a system in which terminals are connected to a distant processor, providing a two-way flow for processing and interrogating. Such systems are being used increasingly. For example, a branch of a building society can immediately update a customer's savings account held at the head office when a branch transaction takes place; it can ask the head office to search its computer for information; the head office can send messages to the branch.

Such information can pass back and forth by being displayed on screens in response to messages sent by automatic typewriters. Tour operators, for example, can inform enquirers as to the availability of a particular tour and actually make the booking—all by displaying screened messages. Brokers can have visual display contact with their colleagues on the stock exchange floor so that 'conversations' can be held and decisions made.

The cash dispensers offered by many banks provide another example. A customer can insert his card and by keying in his personal number draw the amount of cash he indicates. This is made possible by each point being connected to a central computer. The processor checks the customer's account to see if there is sufficient credit and if there is it issues the cash and debits the account. If required, it will inform the customer of his balance.

Airline reservations can be made and confirmed visually within seconds. When passengers arrive at the airport the system can again be used to check them in. The clerk types in a reference number from the flight ticket and a central processor confirms the reservation. The clerk has much other information available if it is required. She can be given the passenger list for any flight and can even adjust the seating arrangement to suit a passenger. All the information provided by the clerk about any particular flight is printed out for use by the cabin crew so that they are aware if, for example, they are to receive a handicapped person or an unaccompanied child.

14.11 The Choice of Computers

Deciding on the type of computer to be used depends upon many factors, including the volume and complexity of any one type of work. Another factor is the extent to which computerisation is decentralised. In a system known as **distributed processing** much data processing is done under local management. Links are established with a central computer as a control and as an information source, but much of the work is completely localised. This provides the advantage of speed in that data do not have to be sent away for processing. There is also an increase in security because a decentralised system will not come to a halt if there is a failure in one unit.

The most obvious way of classifying computers is by size.

Mainframe computers. These are the large installations. Their processing power may not be any larger than that of a small computer costing considerably less. The advantage of a large computer, however, is its ability to meet a large number of different requirements, each demanding separate program development. Its versatility may therefore justify its higher capital cost. A large computer is economic where the volume of traffic is high and where many of the processes are very complex.

Mini-computers. This is the type used by most small businesses. It has capacities for input, storage and output similar in operation to those of main frame computers but it may be small enough to occupy an office desk top. In this growing market competition by suppliers is intense and this, in conjunction with improving technology, is keeping prices reasonably low. Such equipment is particularly acceptable for performing standard operations, such as those relevant to sales and bought ledgers, wages and salaries, stock control, etc., because (*i*) packaged programs can be bought or written to order, and (*ii*) it can be operated by non-specialist staff.

Visible record computers. These are *accounting machines* in which all the operations are performed electronically, as contrasted with a mechanical accounting machine. A feature is the use of **magnetically coded ledger cards**. When such a card is fed into the machine it is automatically aligned to present the next space for printing. If the wrong card is inserted the machine will lock. The current balance is magnetically recorded as well as being written on the card. The posting of a new entry updates both the magnetised and the written record so that a new balance is automatically available for the next posting.

They have the advantages of high operation speed, large internal storage capacity and programming facility. The only expertise required of an operator is the ability to use a keyboard. They can produce tape for subsequent computer input. They can cope only with standard routines and therefore do not have the flexibility of mini-computers. They are particularly useful where the volume of work to be carried out is not large enough to justify the cost of a mini-computer.

14.12 Examples of Computerisation

The use of computers is expanding so rapidly that examples of their employment are now superabundant. One may first mention those standard clerical operations which have been computerised for some time. Invariably, this has brought with it such advantages as more efficient costing, improved methods of forecasting and analysing, and firmer management control.

The following list gives only some of the considerable number of less orthodox uses of computers:

Stock ordering by branches. Orders by supermarket branches are entered on punched cards and sent to the warehouse. The computer then provides the following documentation: (*i*) a list of items to be 'picked' by the warehouse for delivery to each branch each day; (*ii*) the adjusted stock levels of each item; (*iii*) 'reorder lists' of stock to be replenished; (*iv*) 'invoices' of stock delivered to each branch; (*v*) analyses of slow-moving and fast-moving stock; (*vi*) delivery van loading and route schedules.

'Tag re-ordering'. Every standard item sold by a chain of stores has a code number allocated to it, indicating its type, size and colour. The codes are magnetically marked on tags and attached to the goods at the manufacturing stage. The goods are sent direct to the branches from the manufacturers. On arrival, the tags are detached and posted to the head office. There they are fed into a computer in daily batches. The computer then automatically prints out, on a weekly basis, further orders, indicating the amounts and the delivery addresses. The orders are sent to the manufacturers with cheques to cover the cost, so that no invoices or statements from the suppliers have to be checked.

Salesmen's orders. Instead of a salesman posting his orders to his head office at the end of each day, he dials a number on his home telephone. This connects him with a computer and he then lists his orders by pressing buttons on a keypad. Each order is acknowledged by 'voice response' (that is, by a recorded voice), either to confirm acceptance of the order or to inform the salesman otherwise. (For example, he may be referring to a 'special offer' which is no longer available or to a discontinued line.) The data are collected on magnetic tape and processed the following day.

14.13 The Effectiveness of Computerisation

Where the expense of installing a computer is justified the following advantages will accrue:

(*a*) *Speed.* Data can be processed and information produced at extremely high speeds.

(*b*) *Management information.* It is possible quickly to obtain complex information which would otherwise take a very long time to assemble. In fact, computerisation will often produce information which it would be almost impossible to obtain by any other method. It can not only provide sophisticated forms of analyses but it can also calculate probabilities, thereby contributing to more effective planning. It is capable of helping to solve problems by constructing mathematical 'models'.

(*c*) *Accuracy*. Any 'computer errors' are almost entirely *human* ones, due to inaccurate input or faulty programming. The accuracy of a computer is virtually total.

(*d*) *Staffing*. If input to a small system is by keying and program packages are used, operation by semi-skilled staff is possible.

(*e*) *Information networks*. Some of the disadvantages of decentralisation are lost because of the ability of computers to transfer information immediately between outlying stations and the centre.

Against the undoubted advantages of computerisation it is necessary to set other factors in order truly to evaluate its effectiveness:

(*a*) *Rigidity*. Because of the automatic nature of computerisation all the procedures must be strictly adhered to. Where there is no computerisation it is possible to cope with an unusual event or even a crisis by altering the procedure. For example, a transport strike may make it essential to switch suddenly to unorthodox methods of moving some of the goods. In a manual system this could possibly be done by rapidly selecting certain orders for special treatment. Computerisation, however, involves a strict sequence of operations which cannot be departed from, so that it would be impossible to suddenly adapt.

A computer will provide only that information it is programmed to give. A program is designed to give all the information it is anticipated will be required, but in practice there is sometimes an unexpected demand for other information. This can usually be satisfied by manual analysis but information stored in a computer is 'locked in' and cannot be released unless it is programmed to do so.

(*b*) *The cost of programming*. The cost of a packaged program is a one-time expense, but this applies only to small operations. More complicated systems will require individual programs and this will entail the employing of systems analysts and programmers. Compiling a programme is time-consuming, particularly as it must take account of the consequent alterations to the current system. It is frequently the case that once writing a program has commenced unexpected problems arise so that adjustments are necessary. Having been written, a program must then be tested in real conditions and this often makes further adjustments necessary. Consequently, the time elapsing before a process can be established is frequently far longer than was anticipated. Not only is this costly in terms of salaries and incidentals but, also, inconvenience may be caused by the delay in changing to computerisation.

(*c*) *Implementation problems*. The transfer to computerisation, even if only part of the work is affected, can present considerable problems. There will probably have to be an extensive or even complete alteration of the existing systems. This can affect not only the process being computerised but also those related to it. For example, computerisation of the Sales Order Department will alter the documentation used by field salesmen as well as others. The difficult period when the running down of one system coincides with the running in of a new one is usually accompanied by 'teething troubles'. These may be due to inadequacies in the new system as thrown up by its operation and by the inexperience of those who have to use it.

Having considered the merits and demerits of a computer one must recognise what it is *not*. It has a mathematical brain but it is not capable of exercising intuition, discretion or creativity; nor can it make moral or strategical judgments. If a problem can be mathematically posed or if it can be structured in a logical series of questions, then a computer will provide answers with remarkable speed and absolute accuracy. But *real* decisions, particularly those involving social implications, must be made by people. A mathematically viable solution is sometimes not acceptable when account has to be taken of such intangibles as moral attitudes, human and political responses and the vagaries of economic forces.

14.14 Introducing a Computer

Before deciding to buy or hire a computer the following questions should be asked:

(*a*) *Is a computer required?* This must appear to be an obvious question but there have been instances where other methods would have achieved the desired result without incurring the expense of a computer and the reorganisation its installation demands.

(*b*) *What is the computer required to do?* Unless the objectives are clearly defined there is a strong possibility of the computer being inadequate. Sometimes at a later stage it is realised that more than the original objectives is required. Unless the computer is sufficiently flexible to allow it to be adapted the user may have a machine which does not fully earn its cost.

(*c*) *Is it anticipated that more processes will be computerised in the future?* If the answer is in the affirmative then the first configuration must be one which is capable of being expanded.

(*d*) *To what extent will computerisation require alteration of existing procedures?* Invariably, many changes will be necessary. A considerable amount of documentation will be scrapped and new forms introduced. Some interdepartmental processes may be abandoned because instead of work flowing from one department to another much of it may be coordinated by the computer. The new administration structure and its procedures must be designed before the computer is ready to take over, preferably with the help of the suppliers.

(*e*) *Will computerisation provide all the benefits required at an economic cost?* For example, if it enables invoices to go out 24 hours earlier than previously, is that sufficient benefit to justify the cost? To answer such questions realistically often requires a cold examination of the claims of suppliers' salesmen.

(*f*) *Will it be necessary to employ new staff or train present staff?* A large installation will require a company to employ programmers and system analysts as well as operators. Because of the rapid development of computerisation there is a shortage of experienced specialists, a consequence of which is that they are expensive. It is frequently possible to man small installations by training some of the present staff for the new duties. (The effects of increased automation on staffing are discussed on page 220.)

Key Points

1. **Computers** cannot eliminate human fallibility. *Converted input* must be verified; *programming* must be accurate.

2. **Input equipment** includes:
    (a) punched cards (usually as previous output material);
    (b) paper tape;
    (c) magnetic tape;
    (d) document readers, such as MICR, OCR, light pens and mark sensors.

3. **Output** can be in the form of:
    (a) line printers;
    (b) COM;
    (c) visible display units;
    (d) input material.

4. The **central processor** accepts:
    (a) source data which have been converted and verified;
    (b) output data from a previous run;
    (c) the program (or part program).
    It can accept data from the backing store and pass to it.

5. **Distributed processing** is a form of *decentralised* computerisation.

6. **On-line processing** connects sundry terminals to a central processor.

7. The main types of computer are:
    (a) **mainframe**—large complex; housed in specially designed rooms; multi-functional; requires expert staff;
    (b) **mini-computers**—desk-top; standard operations or for one special function; non-specialist operators; simple or packaged programs;
    (c) **visible record computers**—accounting machines using magnetically coded ledger cards; standard routines; can produce tape for computer input.

8. The **benefits** of computerisation include the following:
    (a) Fast processing of complex operations.
    (b) As an aid to forecasting.
    (c) Accuracy.
    (d) Widespread input and distribution of data.

9. The possible **problems** of computerisation are that:
    (a) the user is committed. He is forced to use a specified procedure and may be unable to cope with unanticipated events;
    (b) information is 'locked in' and cannot be released unless programmed to do so;
    (c) complex programs are expensive and time-consuming to write;
    (d) 'teething problems' can be extensive;
    (e) a computer cannot make judgments.

10. **Computerisation viability.** Relate the *true costs* to the benefits, allowing for other factors such as staffing, reorganisation of procedures, etc.

15

EFFICIENCY IN THE OFFICE

15.1 The Departmental Concept

The office work of a business is divided into departments, so that when we speak of efficiency in the office we are referring to efficiency *within* each office and efficiency in coordination *between* offices. Office work provides a service, each department serving a particular aspect of the business and the total of the departments serving the business generally. In this chapter we are concerned with efficiency within a department—that is, the proficient accomplishing of those functions which are specific to it.

Although the functions of any one department differ from those of others, certain principles are common to all departments. Before considering the factors which contribute to or detract from office efficiency these principles must be understood:

(*a*) A department has a specific objective and to that extent it is a self-contained unit.

(*b*) A department also has relationships with other departments, however, so that it does not, in fact, operate in complete isolation.

(*c*) Although a department has a degree of autonomy in managing its own activities,

(*i*) it must conform to top management directives and operate within any prescribed budget;

(*ii*) any of its activities which affect another department must be accomplished by a procedure which does not conflict with those of the other department. For example, if a department, having completed its part of an operation, has to pass documents to another department, those documents must be in a style acceptable to the second department's routines;

(*iii*) some of its work may be done centrally, e.g. typing, duplicating.

(*iv*) its procedures and forms may be dictated by an Organisation and Methods section (see Chapter 16).

(*d*) Within each department there is a hierarchy within which the principles of direction, delegation, responsibility, accountability and control automatically operate. Thus, the management principles discussed in Section 1 have relevance to even the smallest department as they do to the largest organisations.

15.2 Personal Efficiency

The degree and the type of efficiency required of a person depend upon the nature of that person's work and the extent of his or her responsibility. The following broad divisions may be made:

(*a*) A person engaged in work which is *entirely routine* will be required only to have the expertise necessary to carry out that work. For example, a punch card operator would be required to do her work accurately and that would be the extent of the demands upon her.

(*b*) Few jobs, however, even the most junior, are entirely routine. At almost every level *a certain amount of organising* is necessary. For example, a copy-typist will probably type a number of different letters and forms, and each will require a different treatment. The inflow and outflow of her work must be organised, particularly if she has to decide if any one sort has to have priority. Her equipment and materials must be arranged in the most convenient way. Thus, added to technical expertise there must be organisational ability This is demonstrated below in Section 15.4.

(*c*) At certain levels *judgment* may have to be exercised. A clerk replying to a letter, answering a telephone call or speaking to someone face-to-face must use discretion. The tone or content of any response he makes may have an important effect on the firm.

(*d*) *Responsibility* exists at every stage. An accounting machine operator is responsible for the accuracy of her work; a telephonist is responsible for passing on messages left by callers; a counter clerk is responsible for maintaining good relations with the public. Every clerk is responsible for completing his or her prescribed stage of work. At the top, the manager has overall responsibility for each subordinate's work and the attainment of the department's objectives.

The total of a department's work is done or controlled by human beings, so that the efficiency of the whole is the sum of the individuals' efficiency. The effectiveness of a department therefore depends upon:

(*a*) the proficiency of *overall* planning and direction; and
(*b*) *individual* attributes of

   (*i*) technical expertise;
   (*ii*) managerial ability; and
   (*iii*) conscientiousness.

15.3 The Office Manager

The manager heads the departmental hierarchy and has his place in the total organisational structure. Consequently, he has delegated authority and responsibility for carrying out the work of his department and is answerable in that respect to his superiors. Within the department, therefore, but subject to any constraints imposed on him, he will plan and implement the work of his department. His objective must be maximum efficiency, which entails:

(*a*) completing the work within the prescribed time;
(*b*) reducing costs as much as possible;
(*c*) achieving a very high level of accuracy.

To do this places the following requirements on him.

(*a*) *To devise and implement systems*. He must decide on the best ways of dealing with routine work. He must study the routines in operation, make any amendments which may be necessary and check on the results. Such routines must, where relevant, take account of varying workloads so that 'peaks' of work are coped with and 'troughs' of work are not idle time. His systems must have sufficient flexibility to deal with unusual events.

(*b*) *To allocate work.* Each type of work should be given to those with the requisite abilities and aptitudes. Allocation to those with specific expertise will be obvious, but it is more difficult to decide who should be given different degrees of responsibility. Understanding of people is therefore essential. It is dangerous to force responsibility upon those who cannot exercise it or who do not want it, but it is also unfair to deny it to those with initiative.

The principles of delegation mentioned in Chapter 6 are always applicable. In particular, a manager's responsibility does not end when he has delegated. He retains responsibility for his subordinates' work and there must therefore be some supervision, exercised with such degree of discretion as is advisable.

(*c*) *To aim for harmonious working.* His most difficult task is to handle people. The most efficient of systems will collapse if there is friction between the staff. Work must be allocated evenly; account must be taken of personality characteristics; discretion must be exercised constantly and firmness frequently. A manager must be fair and seen to be fair. It is therefore possible for a department head to be a good organiser in the technical sense of the word and yet be a failure as a manager. (In this chapter we are concerned with the *technicalities* of office working; because the question of human relations is so important it is dealt with more fully later.)

15.4 Personal Methods of Working

Experts may be called in to alter a procedure in the interests of efficiency, as explained in Chapter 16. They would, however, be unlikely to change a small 'self-contained' part of a procedure or dictate how it should be done. For example, an expert may design a form and decide the route of its subsequent distribution, but the organising of the typing of the form would be left to the typists concerned. The efficiency of the typing operation will therefore differ between typists because some will have greater organisational ability than others. Thus, one typist may arrange her work area differently from another. This can be explained when it is shown what the operation demands:

(*a*) Forms must be typed from some information source. There must therefore be a place for the source material and one for blank forms.

(*b*) Most forms require copies. A place must be kept for copy forms and, unless they are in carbon-back sets or on non-carbon paper, for carbons.

(*c*) There must be a station for accepting new work and another for assembling completed work (including originals and copies).

The most efficient typist (assuming all typing abilities are the same) will be the one who arranges her work in the most labour-saving way, because labour-saving means time-saving. An expert typist working in a muddle (or who, at least, is badly organised) may produce less work of an acceptable standard than an inferior typist with a systematic approach. (The practical aspects of personal arranging of work are discussed on page 198.)

15.5   Dealing with Priorities

The above operation is a routine one in that the typist types only one kind of form. Where she has a variety of work, however, it is necessary to take organisation further. An inflow of different sorts of work will mean more piles of inward and outward material and varying treatments. She may have to cope with more than one kind of form and perhaps compile lists and type letters as well. In addition to the increased variety of work this may also mean having to deter-min priorities of work. Some of it may have to be done by a certain time and she must decide which is the more urgent. So far as possible she would do the work in batches of the same category because if, for example, she concentrated on the forms for some time her output would be higher than if she constantly moved from forms to lists to letters, but the urgency of some work may make this impossible.

The determination of priorities is a frequently occurring feature of office work. Most standard routines require work to be done by a certain time but office work is not entirely routine. For example, management may unexpectedly ask for figures to be produced at short notice; something may have 'gone wrong' with a customer's order; there may have been a fundamental error which must be corrected before a routine can continue. These are 'emergencies' and a decision must be taken as to what work must be delayed in order to cope with the non-standard event.

But priorities often have to be made in circumstances which do not qualify as 'emergencies'. For example, it may be known that certain documents must be ready for a meeting, the date of which has been announced. There may be regular 'peaks' of a certain operation (such as sending out monthly statements); official documents may be due on a certain date (such as annual returns to the Inland Revenue concerning PAYE). If such demands means giving them priority over other work it is possible to plan ahead so that they can be absorbed into the routine work and, where necessary, less important tasks can be postponed.

In facing the problems of determining priorities the following guidelines will therefore apply:

(*a*) If a priority can be anticipated then forward planning will reduce the difficulties.

(*b*) Where there is a conflict of priorities the one with the most important consequences should have preference. If, for example, top management requires data in order to make an important decision this should be attended to before, say, giving an executive figures to be produced at a meeting. In extreme circumstances, the second priority may have to be sacrificed.

(*c*) Routine work comes lowest in the priority list because it is usually possible to 'catch up'.

(*d*) What may appear to be a low-priority item to a department may be a high priority to another which is waiting for the first department to take action. The first department must take this into account in determining the level of priority. If giving priority to one part of a department's work results in delays in other work reaching another department, the decision must be taken by the person with overall responsibility for the first department.

(*e*) The determination of priority between work done by one person (such as the typist mentioned above) may be done by that person. If, however, the decision will affect the department's responsibility then it must be made at a higher level. Again taking the example of the typist, she may consider that the essential task is to complete the typing of the forms but the department's prime task may be to complete the lists.

It is sometimes necessary to decide if a priority has to be determined at all. For example, a cashier department may fail to balance its cash at the end of the day. Should identifying the discrepancy be a priority? If searching for the difference is going to delay completion of other work beyond the set time then it should not be given priority. Preference is due elsewhere and the problem of the discrepancy should be tackled as soon as time allows.

15.6 Work Planning

Planning of work is necessary for the following reasons:

(*a*) **Routine jobs** usually have to be completed within set periods. For example, all invoices dated one day may have to be posted the following day; the procedure for paying weekly wages may have to be completed by the end of every Thursday; monthly statements may have to be despatched by the 3rd of the following month. All such work must therefore be planned to be done within the prescribed periods so that for each job there will be uniform starting and ending times. Such jobs are the easiest to cope with. There would be tried and proven procedures and the volume of work would probably be fairly steady. The department would therefore have the staff and equipment which experience has shown to be adequate and suitable.

(*b*) **Peaks of workload** may be anticipated. Thus, it will be known when extra work will have to be done. For example, if the trade is seasonal it will be possible to predetermine when the pressure will be highest; the company secretary will expect to be busier in the period running up to the annual general meeting; the accounting department will know its 'deadline' for preparing the annual accounts. The departments concerned will therefore operate on an annual timetable, allowing them to programme the work in advance. This will require them to absorb the extra work into their routine work, which may entail using more staff, employing extra equipment (e.g. booking computer time) and perhaps deferring less important work.

(*c*) **Unscheduled peaks** may occur. These would be events outside the normal periodic routines. If a sales campaign is to be launched which is not a regular event it will put pressure on those involved. It may be decided to hold a large conference; some routines may be changed because of the introduction of a machine; the company may move its offices. Although these would be unusual events there would be some warning of their occurrence. Plans could therefore be made in advance, although the extra work would have to be assimilated into the regular work. The planning must therefore provide not only a timetable and procedure for the new operation but must also allow for the continuation of normal work.

(*d*) **Emergencies,** however, do not allow for pre-planning. They are unanticipated events and therefore cannot be programmed in advance. The emergency may be a comparatively minor one, such as the breakdown of an accounting machine or an epidemic among the staff. No immediate alternative action may be possible in such instances; the business will simply have to catch up on its work when conditions are back to normal. The effects of more fundamental emergencies will depend upon their nature. A strike by suppliers may mean searching for alternative supplies, switching to production which does not require those supplies or merely waiting. In any event, reorganisation must be urgently undertaken.

15.7 Seeing a Task Through

For those doing other than entirely routine work it is usual for them to be engaged in a variety of matters of a continuing nature. An action taken today may result in another action having to be taken at some future date or it may have to be kept 'under review'. For example, if an executive writes to someone suggesting they meet at a certain time he not only has to keep that time free but he must also ensure he gets a response from that person. He therefore needs a system which will allow him to check if the appointment has, in fact, been accepted.

Most executives have to 'juggle' with a number of matters in progress and it would be fatal for them to rely on memory. An obvious solution is to use a diary. This is usually in book form but it can be a display chart or date-indexed cards. It should aim to show not only what must be done on a certain day but also, where necessary, to give a prior warning. For example, if a report has to be submitted on a certain date there must be an earlier reminder so that there is time to write the report.

The following notes are in explanation of the diary extracts shown in Fig. 15.1:

Feb. 1 is a 'follow-up' note. Millstone has been offered a contract and the executive wishes to check if it has been accepted. If it hasn't, he will communicate with Millstone or follow up a few days later. Unless a note is made the matter may be 'lost out of mind'.

He is due to meet Brownlow for lunch on the 3rd, so on the 2nd he wishes to prepare himself by studying the relevant papers. He has to report on his interview to the Managing Director after the lunch meeting.

The Chief Accountant has advertised for a new accountant. There is a follow-up note for the executive to telephone on the 4th to see if the appointment has in fact been made.

On the 5th there is a reminder to take home and study over the weekend the papers concerning Smithers. The executive is due to discuss the matter with the Legal Officer on the morning of the 8th and to report on it to the Managing Director in the afternoon.

The note of the 9th is to remind him to prepare a report on the Basildon Branch for the Executive Committee meeting. He is also reminded to send the report on the 11th and to attend the meeting on the 12th.

He is reminded that his secretary will be away on the 10th.

On the 12th he has promised to attend a party for Miss Mills who is leaving the company.

FEBRUARY	
Mon 1	Millstone contract accepted ?
Tue 2	Brownlow data.
Wed 3	Brownlow — Royal Hotel 1. MD re Brownlow 4.
Thu 4	James — new accountant ?
Fri 5	Take Smithers papers.
Sat 6	
Sun 7	
Mon 8	Thomas re Smithers 10. MD re Smithers 3.
Tue 9	Exec committee report re Basildon—due 12th.
Wed 10	Jane away.
Thu 11	Submit Exec committee report.
Fri 12	Exec committee 11. Board room. Miss Mills farewell 4. Canteen.

Fig. 15.1. Extract from an executive's diary.

15.8 Operation Scheduling

Planning and controlling a task, particularly if it is a 'one-off' operation which is complex, can be facilitated by scheduling. This is a form of time-tabling, setting out what has to be done at specified times. The object is to arrange for a logical sequence of events in such a manner as to allow the operation to be completed smoothly and by the agreed date. Fig. 15.2 shows a schedule for moving the Invoice Department from its present office to another which is presently empty.

Such a plan usually requires one person to be in charge. Difficulty is sometimes experienced in getting people to cooperate fully and the controller must be given sufficient authority to ensure compliance. In the example given it is possible there may be some 'feet dragging' by staff who are resentful at being moved. The tradesmen involved must be given a realistic period of time to prepare for the operation. None of the jobs in the example could be done without a reasonable amount of notice. The planning could not therefore be completed until the contractors have accepted dates, but having been given those dates the controller would be advised later to obtain confirmation that the appointments will in fact be kept. This latter action has been time-tabled for June 20th.

Many of the stages are dependent upon the completion of other stages within stipulated periods and a timetable failure in one area can upset other areas or even destroy the whole plan.

The principle in drafting such a schedule is to start with the completion date, once it is known that that date is feasible. One can then work backwards so that the events running up to it can be timetabled. All foreseeable contingencies must be allowed for at the initial planning but it is often found that other eventualities have later to be taken into account. The importance of

<u>Removal of Invoicing Department from B3 to D7</u>

June 1	Confirmation by today: Blackstone clean and decorate D7 by July 1 and B3 July 6 – 12 Thomas & Co. fit carpets July 3 Removal by Office Movers 8.30 a.m. July 5
20	Check contractors
21	Advise all staff of move and new extension number
23	Advise Invoicing to pack and label by July 4. Provide material.
July 1	Advise Reception to send Invoice mail to D3 on 4th and 5th. D7 decorating completed.
2	Check Invoicing
3	Carpeting D7
5	MOVE
6	Invoicing collect mail from D3. Resume normal working. Check Blackstone re decorating B3
12	B3 ready for occupation

Fig. 15.2. An operation schedule.

checking on the progress in the various areas has already been mentioned, but it is also essential to advise outside parties of the change and (in this case) the interim disruption. Where necessary, as in the example, allowance must be made for the period when normal working is not possible.

As mentioned earlier in the chapter, some major operations are annual events. They must be planned but such operations are made very much easier because they can be based on past experience. Examples are stocktaking, paying dividends, staff sports days, etc.

15.9 Allocating Work

A department manager will know the nature of the operations for which he is responsible and the normal volume of work within a period. It will be his task to achieve his objectives by dividing the various tasks between the staff available to him. Some allocations may be obvious because of the specialist expertise of some members, e.g. computer operators. In other cases they will not be so apparent. For example, a department may not require a full-time filing clerk, so that at different times filing may be done by different people.

The matter of status must be considered. Within the staff there will be levels of seniority which would result in supervisory levels being established. The personal attributes of the staff will differ so that some will be capable only of routine work. The age and experience of each member will differ. The problem will usually be complicated by the expectations of some junior staff to be promoted to more responsible work. It may suit the manager to have much of the routine work done by juniors but this will lead to many of them ultimately resigning because of boredom and frustration.

For other than a small department it is therefore necessary to have a plan so that the efforts of the staff are integrated in the most efficient manner. The success of such a plan is dependent upon the following objectives being attained:

(a) *Staff should be sorted into process groups.* Those engaged on the various stages of one process should work as a team.

(b) *Working units should be small.* If the team mentioned above is fairly large it should be split into small groups. This makes supervision easier because each unit would have a leader but, equally important, small groupings promote a feeling of unity. A person has difficulty in having a sense of 'belonging' to a group of more than, say, 12 people.

(c) *Similar skills should be grouped together.* Those engaged entirely on typing, for example, should be a defined group. This would, in the case of a large number of people being engaged on one process, be a subgroup of the team. Such an arrangement also makes work-sharing easier.

(d) *Some flexibility may be necessary.* A manager working to an annual plan will anticipate periods of pressure in some areas and he must therefore be able to move staff between groups when necessary.

(e) *Staff attitudes must be considered.* Allowances must be made to move staff who have the ability and desire to change to more responsible work. It may also be necessary to transfer people who have proved to be unsuitable in their first position.

(f) *The hierarchy structure must function efficiently.* There must be provision for section leaders, supervisors, etc., in the chain of command.

(g) *Individual qualities must be recognised.* Work must be allocated to those best qualified to do it. Some staff welcome routine work and others dislike it; some are better able to handle people than others; only some have qualities of leadership; some work best under pressure, while others tend to 'panic' in such conditions.

15.10 Activity Analyses

After work has been allocated it is possible to calculate the proportion of time spent by each member on each of his various tasks. This may indicate some anomalies which may not otherwise be apparent and this is the justification for the exercise.

The process requires that a count be taken of the hours each person spends on each task. Several counts are necessary because the composition of work in any one week is unlikely to be exactly similar to that in every other week, but

```
Job title: Junior/trainee typist        Miss P Ryan

Department:  Sales


        Activity                    Hours per week
Inward mail                              2
Outward mail                             4
Filing                                   6
Classifying sales returns               13
Switchboard relief                       5
Typing training                          5
                                        35
```

Fig. 15.3. Activity analysis of a clerk.

over a period averages can be deduced. It must also be remembered that complete accuracy is impossible. In real life a lot of unscheduled events happen which consume time, such as a long telephone call with a difficult customer, time spent at meetings held at irregular intervals, various 'crises', etc. Any figures produced must therefore be recognised as being not fully representative.

First, the work of each clerk is analysed into tasks on a time basis. The result of one such exercise is given as an example in Fig. 15.3.

An overall picture of the division of work in the department can be obtained by combining all the individual analyses in a tabulated form. Fig. 15.4 gives an example of part of such a form. Although it does not relate to the whole of

Department: Sales	Hours per week analysis			
Activity	S/visor Ms Adams	S/typist Ms Taylor	A/typist Ms Jones	Junior Ms Ryan
Inward mail			2	2.
Outward mail			4	4
Classifying sales returns	4			13
Filing			2	6
Switchboard				5
Typing training				.5
Sales analysis	10		15	
Audio-typing		8	12	
Shorthand transctiption		10		
Dictation	18	17		
Meetings, etc.	3			
Hours per week total	35	35	35	35

Fig. 15.4. Activity analysis of part of a department.

the staff, certain deductions can be made from it. For example, the shorthand typist transcribes shorthand for only 10 hours, she spends 17 hours receiving (or waiting for) dictation and 8 hours as an audio-typist. The audio-typist spends only 12 hours on audio transcription and 15 hours copy-typing sales analyses. Eight hours are spent on very junior work. In both cases, therefore, there is a waste of fairly expensive time. Efforts should be made to allocate work more closely in line with the attributes (and cost) of those available.

A full table would also show the total number of hours spent on each task. The example may indicate that an inordinate amount of time is spent on dictation, so that the use of other methods may be worth studying. Attempts may be made to reduce the time employed in analysing sales.

15.11 Work Measurement

It may be possible to use techniques to measure:

(*a*) The amount of output of a group and/or of a person.
(*b*) The ratio of errors to output.
(*c*) The time taken to complete a task or a specified volume of work.

Measurement is not always possible but where it is it should not be done merely for its own sake. To say that a department produces 10,000 invoices a week may be interesting, but unless the measuring is applied to produce a meaningful conclusion it is pointless to undertake it. Any form of measuring is bound to be expensive and any such cost must be justified by the benefits it produces. Normally, measuring would be undertaken for the following reasons:

(*a*) To relate costs to productivity.
(*b*) To ascertain the reason for rising costs per unit.
(*c*) To compare existing performance with that which is expected to apply if the system is changed.
(*d*) To plan the allocation of work for a system which is yet to be installed.
(*e*) To identify the cause and cost of errors.
(*f*) To identify the incidence of 'idle time', either of people or machines.

Quantity Control

It must first be accepted that a high proportion of clerical work cannot be measured with any degree of accuracy. For example, it is possible to measure the number of ledger entries made by a machine operator but one could not measure the output of an accountant who has to perform mental work of a non-routine nature. A number of minor tasks arise at irregular intervals; consultations have to take place and decisions made; the volume and type of work may fluctuate frequently; 'emergencies' may have to be coped with. In general, therefore, the only work capable of effective measurement is that of a routine and continuous nature. This could include such jobs as card punching, posting ledgers, standardised typing, etc.

The objective would be to establish an acceptable standard of output—that is, the amount produced by a competent person working under normal conditions. Subsequent deviations from that standard would indicate the necessity to establish the reasons. This may be because of changed circumstances (such as an alteration in the system) or the inferiority of an operator's ability.

Measurement may be made by merely recording the actual amount of output. Thus, an operator could count the number of cards she has punched or a supervisor could record the number of cards she has allocated and which have been processed. Recording the number of letters typed will not give such an accurate figure because letters vary in length. It must be recognised, however, that there is very little difference in the time spent on writing a half-page letter and on writing a full-page letter. In each case the time spent not actually typing (in lining up the paper, sorting copies, dealing with envelopes, etc.) is the same. The only difference would be the amount of 'keytapping'. If some letters are particularly long it may be more accurate to count the number of page sides than the number of letters. Even so, this could be applied only to ordinary letters. It would not be possible to measure accurately where display work or statistical presentations are required.

Several counts must be taken and these must cover various periods. The output rate of any operator will not be the same throughout the day, so the counts must, in total, cover every hour. Also, in any one day a clerk will complete no more than the work she is given, so that her hourly production rate will fall if her daily load is below average.

Determination of the norm is often possible by asking an experienced operator what she considers the figure should be. The figure may have to be amended later but such an approach is often the most satisfactory one if the staff are reliable and of an acceptable standard. Responsible staff are unlikely to abuse this system because they prefer it to monitoring exercises.

Quality Control

This aims to reduce the incidence of errors. Mistakes can be very costly. An error in an originating document will be perpetuated throughout the subsequent stages; customer goodwill may be lost if errors affect them; time spent in correcting errors is unproductive time.

If errors occur to an unreasonable extent it is necessary to identify where and why they occur. Analysis of a procedure may indicate that most errors occur at a particular point. This may be due to the poor design of a form, for example, or there may be one stage at which the staff are under pressure. Identification will then allow for alteration of the system so that errors are reduced. Alternatively, it may be found that one operator has a higher error rate than the others. This failing can be identified only by individually checking the operators' work.

It must be decided to what extent reduction of errors should be taken. Apart from computer input, it is generally not economically wise to insist on 100 per cent accuracy. A high level of accuracy is essential, of course, but the cost of extensive checking to guarantee absolute accuracy is usually not justified. There should be established a 'tolerance level', so that investigation would be called for only if errors exceeded that figure.

Time Measurement

This can relate to the time taken to complete an operation. For an individual or a group engaged on the same work this merely requires dividing the volume of output by the time spent, so that a time/unit figure is produced. It can also relate to the length of time it takes to complete all the processes within a procedure—say, from the originating document to the end.

It can also have relevance to the analyses of activities mentioned earlier in the chapter. A person could keep his own record of the time spent on different tasks during the day or **activity sampling** could be used. This method requires that observations are made at random times of what a person is doing. To be effective, a considerable number of observations must be made and it is doubtful if the cost of such an exercise would be justified by the results.

15.12   Movement Diagrams

Frequently, a procedure in an office requires the work to be done in stages, each clerk or section completing a stage and then passing the work to the next stage. Thus, there is a regular movement of paper from one point to another. In such instances the office should be so arranged that paper moves, so far as is practicable, in a straight line, with the minimum of distance between each stage.

It is possible to chart such movements so that any wasted movement becomes evident. A scale plan of the room is drawn and a pin is driven in at each work station. The movement of paper is then portrayed by running a string from station to station along the course of the paper flow. The length of the string, when scaled up to actual size, will equal the distance each piece of paper travels. This deduction can be extended by multiplying the distance by the number of journeys made each day. If the room plan is then redrawn more logically a similar exercise will indicate the amount of movement saved.

For obvious reasons, such a chart is known as a **string diagram**. An illustration of the anomalies it can highlight is given in Fig 15.5. The procedure begins and ends with the supervisor, the flow from one desk to another being interrupted by detours to the filing cabinets and the duplicator.

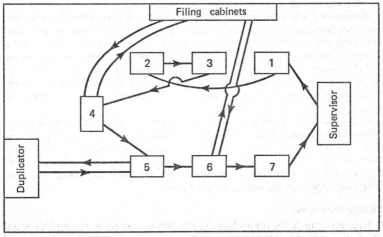

Fig. 15.5. A movement diagram (or string diagram).

The same principle can apply even when work is not of the 'production line' type. For example, if filing cabinets which are used by many people are badly sited there will be an unnecessary amount of human traffic, thereby wasting time and causing disturbance.

The logical layout of an office is therefore a factor which contributes to the efficiency of its performance.

15.13 The Question of Cost-Effectiveness

In deciding how effective an office is in relation to its costs one has to equate a positive figure to one which may be very much less so. The cost of a department will be known and will probably feature in a budget. It will include the cost of salaries, materials and rent, the depreciation of equipment, and overheads. The *effectiveness*, however, is usually not capable of accurate measurement except where there is an output of standard material. For example, how can one measure the effectiveness of a Personnel Department? It does not 'produce' anything and its activities have no measurable effect on staff relations.

However, whether or not measurement of effectiveness is possible, there is the necessity to reduce costs so that an acceptable standard of performance can still be attained. Department heads or higher management must always ensure that the resources available are combined in such proportions as to achieve the objective in the most efficient and economical manner possible. Standards may be maintained at a lower cost if, for example, the procedures were altered or mechanisation was increased.

The deciding factor may not always be the financial one. A more economical way of operating may lead to staff dissatisfaction to the extent that the new system is unworkable. It may result in a reduced service to customers, so that economy is attained at the cost of lower income. Sophisticated plans on paper do not always operate effectively in the cold light of experience.

Key Points

1. **Departmental efficiency** requires coordination of *individual* efficiency by *central* efficiency.

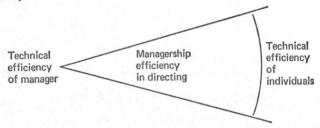

Technical efficiency of manager — Managership efficiency in directing — Technical efficiency of individuals

2. **Effective managership** requires *organisational ability* and *human understanding*.

3. **Work planning** means:
   (*a*) organising to complete routine work by set times;
   (*b*) anticipating known peaks of work;
   (*c*) making judgments in emergencies;
   (*d*) determining priorities.

4. In **scheduling an operation** the times of the various stages will be determined by *working back* from the fixed date.

5. Effective **work groups** require:
   - (*a*) grouping into process teams;
   - (*b*) grouping similar skills if there is sufficient to form a group;
   - (*c*) avoiding large groups;
   - (*d*) control by group leaders, answerable to the manager.

6. **Activity analysis** examines:
   - (*a*) what each person does; and
   - (*b*) how long he spends on each task in a normal day/week.

   This can be extended to a *departmental* activity analysis.

7. **Work measurement** is possible only for *routine* tasks. To justify the cost, measurement must serve a useful purpose.

8. **Errors** are costly and may be due to:
   - (*a*) a 'prone to error' part of a procedure;
   - (*b*) an operator's lack of ability.

   Identification of the cause indicates the corrective action to be taken. Aiming for *total elimination of errors* is usually unjustified but is essential for computer input.

9. A **movement diagram** is otherwise known as a **string diagram**. It charts the movement of people and paper in a department. The total distance equals the distance of one journey multiplied by the number of journeys in a period.

16

THE EFFECTIVENESS OF OFFICE PROCEDURES

16.1 The Necessity for Procedures

'Office procedure' is an alternative term for 'office system'. A procedure establishes a **sequence of activities** which are necessary to achieve a clerical objective.

A procedure should be designed; it should not just happen. In its most elementary form, however, a procedure is that method which is the most obvious way of performing a simple task. For example, the procedure for effecting a cash sale in a 'one-man' business would not require to be formulated, but for more complex operations where coordination of efforts is required then some drafting is necessary.

The person designing a procedure may be the person responsible for its operation. Thus, a manager may prescribe the systems necessary for carrying out certain operations in his department. Alternatively, procedures may be designed by specialists who are external to those departments which are required to implement them. This would be the case where procedures are drafted by an Organisation and Methods section. Unless there is some authoritative direction, confusion will be caused by every person 'doing his own thing'.

Prescribed procedures are therefore necessary so that **coordination of activities** is possible and in order to provide **uniformity of work methods**. This can be done only by planning and directing.

16.2 The Efficient Designing of Procedures

The following factors are relevant to the designing of procedures:

(*a*) *A procedure must be planned as a whole*. The completion of any one stage may 'trigger off' a subsequent stage or stages. Thus, when work on a form at one stage has been completed, it, or a copy of it, may have to be sent elsewhere for use at the next stage.

(*b*) *Suitable forms must be designed*. (The relevant principles are set out in Chapter 7.)

(*c*) *The fundamental principle must be simplicity*. (This is discussed below in Section 16.4.)

(*d*) *There should be extensive use of specialisation*. By increasing the number of stages in a procedure the scope of work in each stage is reduced. Every person thereby concentrates on a narrower range of work, with a consequent increase in efficiency.

(*e*) *Labour-saving equipment should be used as much as possible*. Used effectively, this not only reduces costs but also contributes to greater accuracy and speed.

(*f*) *Checking should be reduced to the minimum*. A checking operation is a stage in itself, adding to the time and cost of a procedure. Where possible, it should be eliminated. For example, if the top copy of a set of simultaneously produced forms is correct the accuracy of the others is assured. A computer system can include a self-checking operation.

(*g*) *Work should flow evenly.* The integration of the various stages must be so arranged that bottlenecks are avoided and waiting time is reduced to the minimum. Thus, the output of one stage must be equal to the capacity of the succeeding stage.

(*h*) *The 'exception principle' should apply.* This means that only exceptional items (which must be specified) have to be referred to a superior. This can be achieved if as much work as possible is of a routine nature.

(*i*) *Costs must be kept to a minimum.* There must be economy in the use of staff, paper and equipment. This requires the calculation of the 'true cost' of people and machines, which goes beyond salaries and the prices of machines. Altering the ratio between people and machines may reduce true costs.

16.3 'Over-systematisation'

A vital principle (which, unhappily, is sometimes forgotten) is that procedures are designed to *serve*. They are intended to make work easier, but this becomes reversed if a business allows itself to become 'over-systematised'. This can result from procedure-designing becoming an obsession, done for its own sake. A proliferation of systems and the making of rules about minutiae will increase costs instead of reducing them. It will also result in an organisation which is stifled by dedication to the 'rule book' and by the denial of initiative.

16.4 Work Simplification

In the early days of a business it will have systems which are capable of dealing effectively with the existing volume of work. As the business grows and its activities become more diverse, however, it is possible to reach a situation where the new systems which are required are simply added on to the original ones. With the increasing complexity of the business more and more adjustments are made to the systems so that a point is reached where there is a conglomeration of procedures, rules and directives, and costs are escalating. This can happen unconsciously because management is not fully aware of the effect of constantly 'tinkering' with old systems which are inappropriate to current conditions. If the business is not to be choked and impoverished by this burden there must come a time when a fresh look has to be taken at its procedures.

The classic example of this is provided in the history of Marks and Spencer Ltd. In 1956 the company Chairman realised that efficiency was suffering because of the vast amount of paperwork and that the attendant costs were rising rapidly. This led to the introduction of what became known as 'Operation Simplification'. Every aspect of every system was studied and in each case the questions asked were: 'Is it necessary?' and 'If it is, can it be made simpler?' Realistic answers resulted in some remarkable changes being effected. One of the many examples was that the system of booking goods into the branches was altered, so that 200,000 documents a week were saved. As a result of another exercise in simplification, invoices fell from 3,000,000 to 200,000 per annum. Manuals specifying the many procedures applicable to branches were abolished and replaced with guidelines, so that, for example, local managers no longer had to refer questions on every personnel matter to the Head Office. Information circulars and letters to branches were almost eliminated. A minor example of the company's new policy was the abolition of time clocks for the staff. This measure alone reduced clerical costs considerably.

These and similar changes throughout the company reduced the amount of paper by 26 *million* pieces a year. The policy not only cut material costs considerably but also allowed the work to be done by fewer people. At the end of the succeeding 12 years profits had more than doubled and the staff was 2,000 less.

This dramatic demonstration of the benefits of work simplification led to the policy of eliminating paper where possible and of simplifying those procedures which must be retained being accepted by business generally.

16.5 The Science of Organisation and Methods

The relevance of the above example to Organisation and Methods (O. & M.) is shown by the fact that the science is sometimes described as 'work simplification'. The word 'science' is used advisedly because techniques have to be used and the services of specialists are required.

The necessity for specialists exists for the following reasons:

(*a*) Those in charge of functions may not have the expertise for scientifically organising the operations for which they are responsible. Also, they should be freed of the necessity to do so in order that they may concentrate on their own duties.

(*b*) Business is constantly changing. The pressure to increase efficiency and reduce costs in order to combat competition and meet changing conditions means that frequent reviews of methods are essential.

(*c*) Mechanisation is used increasingly, requiring the creation of new methods of support.

(*d*) The introduction of new areas of activity within a business results in new systems having to be devised. The tendency of businesses today is to engage in an increasing variety of ventures. This can arise from internal expansion or be the result of mergers, so that increasing size alone also presents more problems to be solved.

(*e*) There may be a demand for more management information, particularly when management techniques become more sophisticated. This will call for the services of specialists capable of compiling new procedures.

(*f*) Only an independent person can draft a procedure free of the bias which may be held by the relevant department head. Department heads may be too close to their work to distinguish 'the wood from the trees'; an O. & M. officer is able to view more objectively. He can also more effectively relate the work of a department with that of associated departments and he will have a global view of top management policy.

16.6 The Aims of O. & M.

These may be summarised as follows:

(*a*) To ensure that a procedure fully achieves its objectives.

(*b*) To reduce clerical costs.

(*c*) To reduce errors.

(*d*) To complete an operation in the shortest possible time.

(*e*) To combine the use of staff and machines in the most efficient ways possible.

(*f*) To eliminate unnecessary operations or combine them with others.

(*g*) To make the most effective use of office space.

(*h*) To integrate related functions.

(*i*) To adjust the organisational structure where it is necessary to do so in the interests of efficiency. (This accounts for the use of the word 'organisation' in the name of the science. Methods of office work must of necessity be related to the staff structure of a department or of the business. Changes in procedures can result in alterations to staff composition.)

(*j*) To achieve uniformity in the use of forms.

(*k*) To provide management information as a contribution to budgeting, control and forecasting.

(*l*) To facilitate the measurement and control of clerical functions.

16.7 The O. & M. Department

This department provides a specialist service to the office as a whole. Primarily, this service is advisory. It has no executive control of any departments in which it carries out investigations. The O. & M. department will study an existing procedure and may advise that changes be made, but at that stage the changes will not be put into effect. The responsibility of the O. &. M department will be to make its recommendations to some authority; and if the recommendations are accepted it will be that authority which will direct the implementation of the proposals.

The activities of the department can be brought into being in the following circumstances:

(*a*) When invited by departmental or functional heads to investigate areas for which they are responsible. This may be for improving the effectiveness of a procedure, allocating work in a more efficient manner, using office space to better advantage, designing and redesigning forms, etc.

(*b*) When instructed by management to facilitate the integration of what are currently separate departments.

(*c*) When instructed to investigate areas where costs must be reduced, where there is a high incidence of errors, where complaints have been received about company service, where over-staffing is suspected, etc.

(*d*) When the introduction or expansion of mechanisation makes it necessary to devise new procedures.

(*e*) When the embarking upon an additional activity by the business requires the setting up of a completely new procedure.

(*f*) As part of a continuous review of procedures already in use.

16.8 The O. & M. Staff

The staff of the department must have a wide experience of office systems generally and of the operational features which are specific to the company.

Probably the most necessary attribute for an O. & M. officer to have is the ability to deal diplomatically with people. The activities of O. & M. staff often give rise to resentment and suspicion. Thus, a manager may bridle at the thought of someone 'telling him how to run his own department'; staff may be worried that there will be changes in the work they do or, at worst, that they will be made redundant. It is therefore imperative that an atmosphere of trust between the O. & M. officers and other staff be established at the outset. It should be stressed that the main objective is to make the work of the staff *easier*. If one aim is to reduce the number of errors then the point must be emphasised to the manager as being in his interests. Any proposals affecting employment should be made openly, with the support of the Personnel Manager where necessary.

Throughout an investigation there must be close consultation with those to be affected. The staff should be asked what difficulties they have and how they consider the problems can be solved. Alterations which are being considered must be put to the staff members in order to get their reactions. Although he is a specialist, an O. & M. officer must recognise that the people he is talking to are continuously and intimately involved in the work, and if he gets their cooperation they may mention points he would otherwise overlook. Such an attitude would also promote the participation which is so essential.

In an attempt to get the cooperation which is so very necessary, a preliminary memorandum, in a style similar to the following, may be sent:

From the Chief Administration Officer
To the staff of the Sales Department

Organisation and Methods Enquiry

I have asked the Organisation and Methods Section to review the procedures in your department. The aim of this memorandum is to explain why and how this enquiry will be conducted. Let me first assure you that the enquiry is in no way a criticism of your work. O. & M. enquiries are made periodically of most departments as part of our practice continually to increase efficiency. The O. & M. staff will be looking to see if it is possible to make your work easier and if the incidence of errors (which cause you more extra work than anyone else) can be reduced.

Your senior staff are responsible for planning work in the most efficient ways possible and I am well satisfied with their efforts. This takes time, however, and they are already fully occupied with controlling the day-to-day working of the department. They will therefore have available to them the services of staff who specialise in such work and who can bring with them independent minds and experience gained in other departments.

The enquiry must be a joint effort between you and the O. & M. officers. It can be valuable only if you fully cooperate. You, more than anyone else, know the working problems of the department and, accordingly, your observations and suggestions would be very welcome—and, indeed, are expected.

The enquiry will be concerned mainly with ascertaining facts. The O. & M. officers will be concerned with what is done, why it is done and how it is done. They may also need to measure work, e.g. to find out how much is processed in a week, how long a particular operation takes, etc. In so doing they will not be investigating *you*; it is simply that the only way of establishing facts is to ask questions.

Inevitably, the survey will interrupt your daily work to some extent, but you may rely on experienced officers not to inconvenience you unduly.

You are encouraged to speak freely to the officers. Any suggestions they may finally make will be put to you so that you may give your observations about them to the officers. If you should think it necessary, you could later discuss any proposals with more senior management.

John Baker and Barry Davis, under the leadership of Peter Brown, will commence the enquiry on the morning of Monday, the 15th of this month.

16.9 Outline of an O. & M. Exercise

An investigation to amend a procedure will normally follow the sequence outlined below.

1. The terms of reference are received

The O. & M. 'brief' should be in writing so as to remove any ambiguity and to provide the necessary authority. The area of the assignment must be specified and its objectives clearly stated. It must also serve to establish a working relationship with the function heads concerned so that their cooperation is clearly called for.

2. The existing facts are ascertained and recorded

The overall procedure must first be studied so that a broad view is obtained. This is usually achieved in informal discussions with the department head(s) and it is at this stage that the atmosphere of cooperation should be established.

A more detailed examination of each operation within the procedure is then made. This is done by asking questions of each staff member involved and observing them at work. It is necessary to record in respect of every operation:

(a) *What* is done, e.g. what entries are made on a form, to whom the form is passed.

(b) *How* it is done, e.g. by typing forms, by using writing boards.

(c) *When* it is done, i.e. the point at which the operation appears in a sequence of operations.

(d) *Where* it is done. A procedure may extend through more than one department or sections of a department.

(e) *Who* does it. This will have reference to the staff structure and take account of the division of activities.

(f) *Why* it is done.

Where appropriate, some of the work measurement techniques mentioned in the previous chapter may be used. Document flow charts may be compiled and then studied with copies of all the relevant forms. It may be necessary to itemise details of the machines used.

3. The existing facts are analysed

All the information obtained will then be analysed and, where possible, quantified. The data will differ between assignments but the following are some examples:

(a) *Documents.* The pattern of distribution; how many there are; their design and content; how they are compiled; the volume of output; the time taken to process them.

(*b*) *Personnel*. Who does what; categories of workers and their status; time spent on each operation.

(*c*) *Resources*. Machines and equipment; office space occupied; staff costs; services from outside the department.

(*d*) *Effectiveness*. Errors—their frequency and the areas of incidence; average backlog of work; costs compared with budgets; machine and staff idle time.

(*e*) *Organisational structure*. Effectiveness of span of control, direction, and division of activities.

4. Proposals for a new system are compiled

Having established where inefficiency exists it is then necessary to draft proposals for an improved procedure. Examples of the suggestions which may be made, following the pattern in paragraph 3 above, are as follows:

(*a*) Forms may be redesigned, others may be scrapped or combined; unnecessary copies will be eliminated or there may be additional ones if the information is to flow more widely. An estimate would be made of the daily output to provide a comparison with the current figure.

(*b*) Duties may be reallocated; new methods of work may be devised. The estimated times for completing tasks would be shown.

(*c*) Any changes in machines or equipment would be stated, giving comparative figures for output, cost, etc.; the office layout may be altered to give better work flows; changes in servicing facilities may be made.

(*d*) The anticipated effects on output, the frequency of errors, costs and machine utilisation would be estimated.

(*e*) Any suggested changes in the staff structures would be specified and justified.

5. The proposals are submitted

There should then follow discussions with the staff concerned so that their observations may, if necessary, be taken into account. There could be demonstrations of the new methods. Any objections should be freely accepted—partly to overcome any suspicion of 'steamrollering' and partly because some of them may be useful. (An O. & M. officer should never refuse to accept a viable suggestion.)

This should be followed by a written statement of the procedure for the staff to study. A report would then be made to whoever is required to authorise the implementation of the scheme. It is usual to invite written comments from the staff concerned. Discussions should then take place between the involved parties and management before a decision is made.

6. The new procedure is implemented

If the change is to be complex (as may be the case with extensive mechanisation) there should be a timetable for the implementation of different stages. In such instances it is not possible to effect an overnight change, so that the new system has to be phased in.

Provided the staff have had time to study the new procedure it should be left to them to start operating it, but with the O. & M. officers available to see it working and to provide any help needed. Where appropriate, the new system would be presented in the form of a manual to serve as a guide and reference to its operation (see Section 16.11 below).

Having seen the new procedure established, the O. & M. staff will move out of the area concerned.

7. *The procedure is followed up*

The O. & M. staff would be available for a certain length of time in case there were 'teething problems'. Experience of the new system will sometimes indicate that some adjustment is necessary. The terms of reference may require that a quantitative check be made after a reasonable period. Such data as volume of output, costs, etc., would be assembled and compared with the estimates made when the new procedure was drafted.

16.10   An Example of Redrafting a Procedure

The following is a demonstration of how a procedure may be analysed and an improved one compiled. It relates to the ordering of goods by the Purchasing Department of a manufacturing company following a requisition from the Stores. The distribution of documents in the existing procedure is shown in Fig. 16.1(*a*). An explanation of that procedure is as follows.

Goods ordered. Four copies of the order are made out by the Purchasing Department, the top copy being sent to the supplier and the second copy being retained in the department. The third and fourth copies are sent together to the Stores to inform it that the goods have been ordered so that the Stores may note on its records that requisition has been actioned. The Stores acknowledge receipt of this advice by returning the fourth copy to the Purchasing Department, retaining the other copy.

Goods received. The goods are delivered to the Stores which then makes out four copies of a goods received note containing particulars of the consignment. It retains the first copy and uses it to update its stock records. The goods are then sent to the Inspection Department with the second and third copies of the note. After the goods have been inspected they are returned to the Stores, together with the third copy which then contains the inspector's report. The second copy is retained by the Inspection Department. At the same time, the fourth copy is sent by the Stores to the Production Department to inform it that the goods have arrived.

Invoice received. When the Purchasing Department receives the supplier's invoice it checks that the amount on the invoice agrees with the quotation. A copy of the invoice is made and vouched to the Bought Ledger Section to authorise payment. The department retains the original invoice.

Criticisms

1. Copy 4 of the order is not required because the possibility of copy 3 not being received is remote. If the Stores does not get confirmation of an order having been made shortly after requisitioning the goods it would make enquiries of the Purchasing Department. The Purchasing Department does not require confirmation that its advice had been received.

2. There would be no necessity for the Stores to make out a goods received

(a) CURRENT PROCEDURE

PURCHASING ON REQUISITION BY STORES

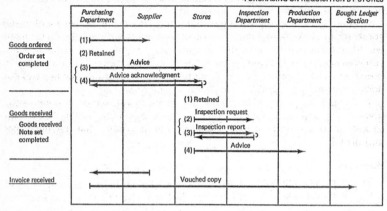

(b) PROPOSED PROCEDURE

PURCHASING ON REQUISITION BY STORES

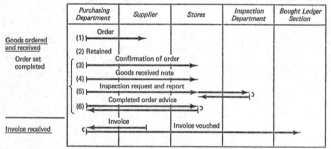

Fig. 16.1. Document flowcharts.

note if, as shown in the proposed alteration, it was in the form of a copy of the order.

3. Copy 3 of the goods received note is unnecessary. After inspection, the report could be made on copy 2 and returned to the Stores; the Inspection Department does not need to keep a copy of its report.

4. Copy 4 of the goods received note could be eliminated. The requisition had probably been made by the Stores merely in order to replenish its stocks and not to meet a particular requirement of the Production Department. *If* the Production Department had asked for goods not normally held in stock its request would have been made to the Purchasing Department. If, however, the Production Department had asked the Stores for goods which were temporarily out of stock the Stores would have informed it specially when the goods arrived. It is wasteful to prescribe forms which would not be required in most circumstances.

5. There is no provision for informing the Purchasing Department that the goods have been delivered. The department requires this information because

its records show only that the goods were ordered. It needs to be able to 'chase' the supplier (who would have promised a delivery date) if the goods are not received on time.

6. There is no provision for informing the Purchasing Department if the goods received are faulty, damaged or below standard. Also, the department would not know if the quantity received was less than that ordered. As a consequence, it could authorise payment of an invoice which should not have been approved. (This, of course, is additional to the fact that the department does not know if the goods have been received *at all.*)

7. There is no point in the Purchasing Department making a copy of the invoice. The original should be vouched. There is no need for the department to keep a copy because it merely has to note its records that payment was authorised.

Summary

(*a*) There is an unnecessary amount of documentation.
(*b*) There is a lack of control in parts of the procedure.

Redrafting the Procedure

The proposed amended procedure is indicated by Fig. 16.1(b). One set of documents is made out to cover what are the first two stages of the current procedure.

Goods ordered. Six copies of the order are made out in a set, only the first two containing particulars of the price. The first is sent to the supplier and the second is retained by the Purchasing Department. The other four copies are sent to the Stores in a set, each copy having a title indicative of its function. The first of the four copies is filed by the Stores and its records are noted that its requisition has been actioned. The other copies are held, pending the delivery of the goods.

Goods received. When the goods are received the Stores will complete copies 4 and 5 to indicate the *amount* of goods received and any apparent damage. It will file the first of these copies as its goods received note. The goods will then be sent to the Inspection Department with copy 5. After inspection, that copy, containing the inspector's report, will be returned to the Stores with the goods. If a clear report is given the goods will be taken into stock and the records updated.

The Stores will then return the sixth copy to the Purchasing Department, confirming, if such is the case, that the ordered amount of goods was received in good condition. The Purchasing Department will then note its records as a completed order. If the delivery was not satisfactory then the Stores would provide the details on the sixth copy so that the Purchasing Department could take up the matter with the suppliers.

Invoice received. On receipt of the invoice, then, assuming the goods were of the quantity and quality ordered and that the price agreed with the quotation, it would be vouched by the Purchasing Department and sent to the Bought Ledger Section for payment.

Summary

(a) Only one typing operation is required, involving only one department.

(b) The number of documents in circulation is reduced from ten to seven.

(c) There is an overall improvement in control.

(d) Fewer records have to be kept.

16.11 Specifying a Procedure

It is often advisable to commit a procedure to writing for the use of those who have to operate it. This is sometimes known as a **procedure manual** and it serves as a 'rule book' for carrying out the procedure. Fig. 16.2 is an example of part

Procedure to be adopted by purchasing officers after a purchase has received preliminary approval.

Activity	Documents and records
1. Receive purchasing requisition which has been checked and passed by a specified senior officer.	R1
2. .Check previous quotation and any subsequently notified changes by regular supplier.	Q5
3. Telephone supplier for quotation and delivery date.	
4. If reply is standard, confirm and ask for written confirmation. Note requisition and file.	R1
4a. If reply is not standard, hold and consult senior.	
5. Confirm order in writing. File copy.	F5
6. Enter in Orders Pending, noting delivery date. Diarise delivery date.	F7 D2
7. Confirm to requisitionist, quoting delivery date.	F8
8. File quotation when received.	Q6

Fig. 16.2. Part of a procedure manual.

of a procedure to be adopted by purchasing officers when placing orders which have been approved by a senior purchasing officer.

A **procedure chart** indicates the flow of documents by vertical lines and, by the use of symbols, the types of action taken at the various stages.

Flow charts showing the distribution of documents can appear as illustrated in this chapter or as shown in Fig. 7.9.

16.12 Efficiency Audit

Earlier in this chapter we saw that once an O. &. M. department is satisfied that a procedure it has installed is working effectively its officers play no further part. The fact that the department always acts only in an advisory capacity makes it essential it does not interfere in the day-to-day workings of any other department.

However, it is possible that an established procedure may, with the passage of time, have become less effective. The deterioration may be so gradual as to be imperceptible to those engaged in it so that there has been no call for it to be reviewed. The danger is that if the situation is neglected it may reach the point when inefficiency becomes too obvious to ignore. Meanwhile, there has been a period of undetected and increasing inefficiency.

Accordingly, the practice of some O. &. M. departments is to carry out periodic reviews of how the various aspects of the administrative work are being done. Such operations are known as **efficiency audits** or **methods audits**. There is a rolling programme whereby each area is examined at regular intervals so that over a period all the areas are studied. In normal circumstances a large proportion of the procedures will be found to be satisfactory, but there will usually be some instances where an improvement can be made.

There are a number of factors which can lead to a deterioration of a procedure. For example, the volume of work may have gradually increased so that, equally gradually, there has been an increasing strain on the procedure. It eventually becomes necessary to alter the system so that the increased amount of work can be handled effectively. Again, eventualities may have intruded on a procedure at some point in the past so that the system has since been less efficient. For example, a supplier may have changed his system so that the company in turn had to alter part of its system.

The audit would identify any such conditions and propose remedial measures. If the procedure being audited had a quantifiable element it would be possible to check if the original performance standard was being maintained.

Such an audit can also check on those aspects which support procedures. For example, the effectiveness of machines and equipment could be assessed. The competence of the filing systems could be checked. An exercise may be carried out to determine the cost of typing, duplicating, etc. The condition and suitability of the office furniture could be examined. The cost-effectiveness of lighting, heating, ventilation and cleaning could be calculated. Efforts could be made to improve office layout.

An efficiency audit is similar in its purpose to the regular inspection of safety precautions. Procedures must be checked regularly in the same way as fire hoses are examined at stated intervals, in case there has been a deterioration or they are inadequate in changed circumstances.

Key Points

1. A **procedure** establishes a *sequence of activities*. It should:
    (a) *simplify* tasks;
    (b) use *specialisation of functions*;
    (c) reduce *checking*;
    (d) reduce *costs*;
    (e) increase *accuracy*;
    (f) reduce *time spent*.

2. Systems become inefficient if they merely consist of encrustations on old systems. There will be a point when a system must be completely revised.

3. **Organisation and Methods:**
    (a) means '*work simplification*';
    (b) is a *specialist activity*;

(*c*) provides a service which is *advisory*;

(*d*) needs *cooperation* and *diplomacy* in order to be successful.

4. The stages in an O. & M. enquiry are as follows:

(*a*) Consult department head(s) to *establish overall procedure*.

(*b*) *Question* each clerk as to what he/she does and how he/she does it.

(*c*) Obtain copies of all *forms* used.

(*d*) Draft the *current procedure* and quantify where possible.

(*e*) Draft the *proposed procedure*, showing comparisons with the current procedure.

(*f*) *Discuss* the proposals with the staff.

(*g*) *Submit* the proposals to the authorising body.

5. A **procedure manual** is a *literary* description of a procedure.

A **procedure chart** is a *diagrammatic* description of a procedure.

6. An **efficiency audit** is a *routine check* of the effectiveness of systems, and may include a study of work allocation, machines and equipment, office layout, etc.

THE WORK ENVIRONMENT

17.1 The Importance of Planning the Work Environment

The environmental aspects of office work which must be the concern of management include the following:

(*a*) The apportioning to functional divisions of the total space available, so that:

(*i*) each division has an area which is appropriate in size and conditions to its function; and
(*ii*) the areas are in logical relationships with each other.

(*b*) The planning of the layout of each office in such a manner as to contribute to its efficiency.
(*c*) Taking account of human attitudes to the work situation.
(*d*) The provision of suitable furniture and equipment.
(*e*) Maintaining healthy working conditions.
(*f*) The provision of services, such as telephones, electricity, etc.
(*g*) Complying with legislation.

Proficient planning of the work environment is essential for the following reasons:

(*a*) Operational efficiency will suffer if work does not flow evenly and economically.
(*b*) Staff performance will be lower and less efficient if working conditions are not of a high standard.
(*c*) Staff will not work in poor conditions.
(*d*) The effective use of machines and equipment must be high in order to justify their cost.
(*e*) There must be economical use of space.

17.2 The Material and Human Considerations

In planning the work environment certain concepts have to be recognised. These can be grouped into two main categories.

(*a*) *Those based on economic factors.* As we have seen earlier, it is possible to plan work so as to increase its effectiveness and reduce its cost. This can be done by the use of techniques such as drafting work flow charts, calculating the cost-effectiveness of machines and equipment, replanning procedures, etc. These are *tangible* measures, the results of which can be quantified.
(*b*) *Those which take account of human attitudes.* No matter how extensive mechanisation may be, the influence of the individual remains paramount. It is not the case, as is sometimes contended, that people must learn to live with machines. The true relevance is that machines must be used to support *people*,

because human participation cannot be eliminated. In any circumstance, therefore, the attitude of humans must determine the success or otherwise of any function. We have also seen that no matter how sophisticated a procedure may be it will fail if the reactions of those to be involved in it are ignored.

Consequently, there is a vital factor to be considered which is not capable of a positive quantification as with techniques. This means that the work environment must be planned *so that people give of their best.*

Most people enjoy comfortable living conditions at home. They therefore expect there to be acceptable standards in the place where they spend such a large part of their time. A disgruntled staff is an inefficient staff, so that even for selfish reasons an employer must provide that minimum. But beyond that necessary standard it is possible to improve conditions so that performance is thereby improved. In this chapter our concern is with that factor—that is, *the effect of office environments on performance.*

17.3   Physical Conditions

The physical conditions which are conducive to efficient performance include not only such tangible aids as good lighting but also those things which contribute to 'atmosphere'. The major elements are discussed below.

Lighting

Apart from an employer's moral and legal responsibility, it must be accepted that a clerk subjected to eyestrain will suffer from irritability and mental fatigue to an extent which will reduce his output and increase inaccuracies.

So far as is possible, natural lighting should be used. Those whose work demands the best lighting should be placed near windows but not facing them. Generally, however, an office will be largely dependent upon artificial lighting. The most effective method of overhead illumination is fluorescent lighting because it gives an even light without shadows. Electric bulb lamps are suitable only if they give a diffused light by shining up to the ceiling and being reflected downward. Direct lighting by bulbs should be used for table lamps only where a high intensity of light is essential. Such occasions are rare and any such lamp must be well shaded.

Heating

Obviously, the ideal temperature must be not too high or too low. In practice, however, not all people in an office may agree as to what is the optimum temperature. Too low a temperature results in physical discomfort; the reverse produces drowsiness. In either case, personal efficiency suffers. One essential is even heat, so that panels are preferable to radiator units. Another requirement is that heat must circulate, so that heating must be combined with effective ventilation.

Controlling temperature by reference to the calendar is a common but unsatisfactory system. There can be cold days in the early summer and over-warm days in the autumn. The most suitable (and the least expensive) method is thermostatically-controlled heating. In addition to allowing for seasonal variations, this system will also deal with heat 'build-up' in a room.

Ventilation

This presents two conflicting problems. Staff complain about draughts and management is aware that a stuffy atmosphere reduces efficiency. Various methods can be used to reduce draughts but the only satisfactory solution is air-conditioning combined with, when necessary, thermostatically-controlled heating.

The decor

It is only in the last decade or so that the effect of colour has been fully recognised; it has now reached the stage of being a subject for expert study. The days are long since past when drab colours were used 'because they don't show the dirt'. Apart from the fact that dirt should not exist (visible or not), dull colours have a depressing effect. At the other extreme, vivid colours can be psychologically disturbing. The availability or otherwise of daylight is an influencing factor so that some rooms will require 'cool' colours and others will demand 'warm' colours. Light-reflecting colours and surfaces would be an advantage in a large office. Generally, colour schemes should have some relevance to the function of the rooms. It could range from a bright decor in a reception office to the quiet dignity of a board room.

The decision about colour schemes is one which should be made by an interior decorator who specialises in offices.

Cleanliness

Staff have the right to clean working conditions and a grubby office leads to slovenly work. There must be a regular routine of cleaning. This requires a daily programme of work and a periodic cleaning of walls, ceilings, curtains, etc. Often the most satisfactory method is to employ contractors. Desks should be so positioned as to make easier the task of floor cleaning; clerks should be responsible for keeping desk tops and drawers tidy; machines should be covered outside working hours.

Noise

Excessive noise is distracting and can set up emotional reactions. Every effort should be made to reduce noise to the minimum.

The structure of a building may cause sound to 'bounce back' from the walls and ceilings. This can be remedied by fitting sound-absorbent panelling. Carpets should be fitted to reduce reverberation. The cost of floor covering can be reduced if carpet squares are used because this allows for periodic renewal of only those parts which are subjected to the most wear.

A number of other remedies can be adopted, such as fitting doors with hydraulic stops so that they do not bang in closing; substituting buzzers for telephone bells; segregating noisy machines; installing double-glazed windows to reduce external noise; placing felt pads under typewriters, etc.

Safety

Precautions which must be taken to protect staff are prescribed by law (see Section 17.4) but other measures are necessary.

Polished floors frequently result in accidents and they should not be a feature in any office. Junior staff must be taught how to use machines which could be dangerous, such as guillotines. Staff must be warned not to overload lifts. 'Skylarking' must be dealt with severely. The condition of stairs and their lighting must be examined regularly. Fire drills should be carried out *thoroughly* and not be treated as light relief from the daily routine. Power and light plugs should be checked regularly. Telephone and electricity cables should not trail across traffic lines.

It is the duty of every manager to make his staff safety-conscious. He must recognise that people can be remarkably stupid. They stand on swivel chairs instead of using steps; they are careless with cigarettes; they leave objects on the floor for others to trip over; they leave naked razor blades in drawers; they pull out fully the top two drawers of a four-drawer filing cabinet.

Services

Offices require points for the input of electricity and telephones. Increased mechanisation and the more extensive use of telephones provides problems concerning cables. Inlet points are normally in the wall and therefore much of the equipment in a large office will be a long way from power sources. Cables can be run under the floors or, less satisfactorily, in ducts to the operating points. Where there is a bank of equipment (such as a series of desk computers) it is usual to have special desks which have hidden channels to hold the leads.

17.4   Relevant Legislation

The Offices, Shops and Railway Premises Act, 1963, contains detailed provisions concerning working conditions in those places of employment indicated by the title of the Act (see below).

The Health and Safety at Work, etc., Act, 1974, applies to *all* places of work and relates to the provisions of the above Act. It therefore includes regulations which do not relate to offices, but it establishes a principle which is of general application when it states: 'It shall be the duty of every employer to ensure, so far as is reasonably practicable, the health, safety and welfare at work of all his employees.'

The Act establishes a Commission and an Executive to assist in the implementation of the provisions of the Act. The Secretary of State has power to make regulations and grant exemptions. The Commission has authority to issue codes of practice. Enforcement of the Act may be by local authorities or the Executive as directed by the Secretary of State.

The Offices, Shops and Railway Premises Act, 1963

A copy of this Act must be displayed in offices for the information of employees. Its main provisions may be summarised as follows:

Cleanliness. Premises, furniture, fittings, etc., must be kept clean. Floors must be cleaned at least once a week.

Working space. There must be at least 40 square feet of floor space per person. This space includes that occupied by gangways, equipment, etc. If the ceiling is less than 10 feet from the floor the area must be 400 cubic feet.

Temperature. This must be 'reasonable', which is reckoned to be a minimum of 16 °C (60·8 °F).

Ventilation must provide 'adequate' fresh or purified air.

Lighting must be 'adequate' for the type of work. Windows must be kept clean and lighting equipment properly maintained.

Toilet facilities. The number of conveniences to be provided according to the number of employees is prescribed. The same ratio of wash basins must be provided. All facilities must be kept clean and well maintained. There must be hot and cold water, soap and towels. Adequate drinking water must be available.

Clothes storage. There must be accommodation for clothes not worn in the office and facilities for drying them.

Seating must be suitable in design and size.

Floors, passages and stairs must be fully maintained and be of sound construction. They must be free of obstructions and not have slippery surfaces. There must be handrails to stairs and stair-wells must be fenced.

Machinery. Any dangerous parts must be fenced. No person under the age of 18 may clean machinery if this would expose him to risk. No person may work a machine unless he is fully instructed about any danger.

Moving loads. No person may be required to lift, carry or move a load likely to cause him or her injury.

First aid. There must be a first-aid box or cupboard in the charge of a responsible person for each 150 employees or fraction of that number. If there are more than 150 employees there must be at least one person trained in first aid and who is available during working hours. That person's name must be displayed on a notice board.

Fire precautions. There must be adequate means of escape and appropriate fire-fighting equipment. Most offices are required to be inspected and certified as having adequate safeguards. Fire exits must be clearly marked and escape routes kept clear of obstructions. Fire alarms must be provided and tested regularly. Staff must be aware of the escape routine.

Notification of accidents. An accident which causes death or which disables a person from doing his usual work for more than three days must be notified to the relevant authority.

17.5 Office Layout

This relates to planning the positions of furniture, machines and equipment so that space is used with the maximum efficiency.

The method. It is necessary first to draw a plan of the area on squared paper. Account must be taken of immovable objects, such as windows, doors, pillars, etc. Others may or may not be movable, such as radiators, lighting and power points, telephone junction boxes, etc. It may be possible, if so required, to remove non-loadbearing walls or erect new ones.

Card or plastic templates of the desks and equipment will be made to the scale of the plan. These can then be moved about on the plan so that the most suitable arrangement is ultimately obtained.

The objectives. The aims of layout planning should be as follows:

(a) *Work must flow in the most logical and economical way possible.* Desks must therefore be arranged in a pattern dictated by the work flow, as explained in the previous chapter.

(b) *The movement of staff between work points must be easy.* This requires that traffic flows between desks and equipment should be as short and direct as possible. Gangways must be wide enough to permit easy passage without interference with those working at neighbouring desks.

(c) *Physical conditions must be of a high standard.*

(d) *Group-working must be attained.* In a large office, staff should be congregated in fairly small work-groups so that a sense of identity is achieved.

(e) *Supervision must be facilitated.* It must be possible for supervisors to be close to those for whom they are responsible. This is particularly so if the supervisors are also responsible for training.

(f) *There must be a degree of flexibility.* Allowance should be made for possible expansion or change of procedures.

(g) *Legal requirements must be complied with.*

17.6 Replanning a Layout

Fig. 17.1 demonstrates how replanning the layout of an office can improve its efficiency and provide better working conditions. The first diagram shows the original layout; the second shows the result of replanning.

There are six records clerks in the department. Each has at her left a visible index cabinet, holding the records for which she is responsible. A junior clerk sorts incoming documents at the work table and distributes them to the appropriate clerks. After the documents have been processed she collects them from the clerks and re-sorts them at the work table. In the original layout the incoming and outgoing work was placed on tables to the right of each records clerk.

The supervisor has two assistants. There are two typists whose work requires them to have access to the filing cabinets.

There were 15 filing cabinets and as space had to be allowed for opening and working at the drawers some of the area in front of the cabinets was largely wasted. The cabinets also limited the amount of light from the windows. These problems were solved by using lateral filing cabinets and placing them against the blank wall.

It was obviously unsatisfactory for the typists to work so close to the supervisor because the noise of their machines disturbed her. Therefore, they were moved and this provided the additional advantage of bringing them nearer to the filing cabinets and the duplicator (which was also moved). It also provided them with better lighting because they now had windows immediately behind them.

The position of the records clerks was unsatisfactory because not only were they facing the light from the windows but, also, they worked with their backs to the room, giving them a feeling of isolation. Their desks and cabinets were rearranged into a 'spine' formation so that incoming and outgoing work was placed on the spine instead of on individual tables. As a consequence, the clerks worked in a more sociable atmosphere. Servicing by the junior was made easier, particularly as her personal desk was moved from its previously remote position. It also improved her working conditions.

The assistants had been situated at the farthest possible point from the

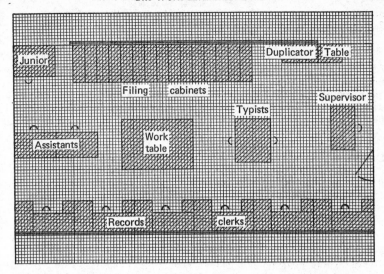

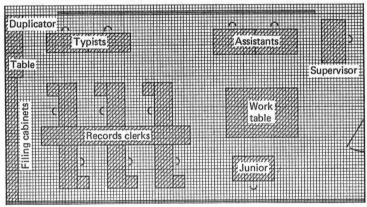

Fig. 17.1. Replanning an office layout.

supervisor. This was altered so that the three could work closely together. All benefited from improved lighting.

The work table, which is effectively the focal point of the department's operations, was made directly accessible to the three seniors.

The area immediately inside the door became free of desks, whereas previously the supervisor and one clerk had been in uncomfortable situations.

The replanning has had the effect, therefore, of

(*a*) grouping work into units;
(*b*) reducing traffic;

(c) saving space; and

(d) improving working conditions.

17.7 Furniture

An essential in the choice of furniture is that every piece must serve a specific purpose. To buy 'desks and chairs' is pointless (and wasteful). The requirements of the users must first be identified and then purchases can be made which will meet those requirements. For example, the top of a typist's desk is lower than one used for writing; a typist would find it tiring to use other than a special desk.

Desks

Any desk must provide:

(a) An adequate working area.

(b) Space for documents and equipment constantly in use.

(c) Storage space.

(These points have relevance to desk layout, as explained in the following section.)

Desks can be made up in units (as shown in Fig. 17.1). These are produced in standard designs and some can be assembled in a variety of combinations. They are generally referred to as **modular desks**.

The term **work station** relates to an L-shaped (or even U-shaped) configuration of desks with fitments which make it almost a mini-office. The side desk is usually used for typing or some other operation other than that carried on at the main desk, so that the operator, using a mobile swivel chair, can quickly move from one work point to another. The desks frequently have drawers fitted to hold files. Such an assembly is often backed by a screen which can be used to hold books, files, etc. Although such a screen provides additional space it can act as a barrier to communication and have a claustrophobic effect.

Work tops should be of metal covered with PVC or similar material so as to eliminate light glare and excessive noise.

A desk should always provide facilities for storing personal belongings (such as handbags) but, for obvious reasons, this should not be over-generous.

Chairs

Chairs for typists have always been adjustable but it is becoming recognised that this should apply to all chairs. The physical makeup of people varies considerably and in view of the amount of time a user occupies it he should be able to make his chair suit his requirements. The importance of this is proved when it is shown that the most common cause of absenteeism among office workers is back complaints.

Chairs should swivel and be on casters to allow easy access and egress from desks.

17.8 Personal Layout of Work

The importance of personal organisation of work was discussed in Chapter 15 so that the practicalities of desk layout can now be considered in more detail.

The elements of motion study apply in that it is necessary to so arrange work that:

(*a*) Both hands can be used simultaneously.
(*b*) Hand movements are reduced to the minimum.
(*c*) The most comfortable operations are those done most frequently.
(*d*) Work flows (for a right-handed person) from left to right.

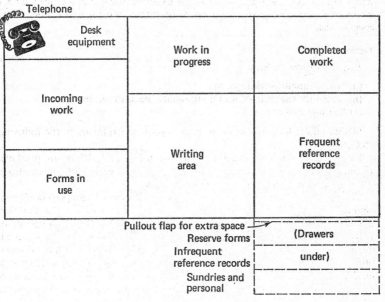

Fig. 17.2. Desk-work layout.

Fig. 17.2 shows that:

(*a*) The current work area immediately faces the sitting position. The imminent work is immediately behind the current work.

(*b*) Documents in constant use are immediately to hand on either side.

(*c*) The telephone is at the left hand and does not interfere with the work area.

(*d*) Records and materials not in constant use are readily available but do not occupy working space.

Work should flow across a desk in the most logical and energy-saving way. Orderly working economises in time and eliminates unnecessary effort. Consequently, output increases and the possibility of errors is reduced.

17.9 Specific-Purpose Offices

An office may be designed for one functional purpose, as would be the case with one department occupying a room. Here there would be a variety of work carried on in the room, but all of it directly relevant to the function of the department.

Other rooms may have specific usages for different reasons, such as the following:

(*a*) A room may be used only by those engaged in the same operational activity. This would apply particularly where that activity was centralised. For example, if a company has a large force of typists or machine operators they would probably be housed in offices which are restricted to such workers. This means that such offices could be designed specifically for one purpose. Thus, all the special requirements of typists for lighting, equipment, etc., would be met to the exclusion of others. This can be contrasted to the conditions which would prevail where a typist worked in a room which also contained others who were not typists.

Specialist functions such as mailing should also have specially equipped rooms. Another example of an environment specially designed for the occupants would be a draughtsmen's office. Those engaged on any work requiring concentration (such as mathematicians) would also require offices of a specific type.

(*b*) Those engaged on confidential work or where security is a factor must also have separate offices. This would include cashiers and wages clerks, legal officers and those in the Personnel Department. Again, the rooms would be planned and equipped to meet the special requirements of the work.

(*c*) Executives may have individual offices. These may be part of small suites to accommodate personal assistants and private secretaries.

(*d*) Most offices will have a reception area. This must have an individual style of furnishing and decoration. It is not a work area in the usual sense (except for the receptionist) so the emphasis must be on comfort and attractiveness rather than utility. It should provide facilities for informal discussions of a short duration.

(*e*) There should be a number of small rooms for interviewing. These should be furnished to provide a relaxing atmosphere. There should also be facilities for holding meetings of various sizes. Again, the furnishing should be appropriate.

17.10   Open Offices

In contrast to the 'closed offices' mentioned above there may be single-room accommodation which houses a large number of people carrying out a variety of activities. For some years there had been a tendency towards open offices, although, as shown below, this has more recently been tempered somewhat. There is much to be said in favour of the system and there are a number of valid arguments against it.

Advantages

(*a*) Employers first became interested in open offices because of the considerable saving in rent they provided. Far more people can be accommodated in an open space than if the same space held closed offices. The former has only four walls; it has fewer doors so that there are fewer opening spaces being wasted; there are no corridors connecting closed offices. A new building may have a sprung roof so that there are no supporting pillars taking up valuable space.

(b) Usage costs are very much less. There are savings on lighting (particularly if there are large windows, which would not be the case with small offices), heating and ventilation. The costs of decorating and cleaning are also lower.

(c) It has the advantage of flexibility. Desks and equipment can be moved to facilitate changes in work flow or to enable the room to be used for a completely different purpose. This can apply even where there is some physical division of sections because low partitions which can easily be resited can be used.

(d) Traffic is reduced between departments or sections which occupy the same room because there is no necessity to go outside it. Work-flow patterns within the office can be designed more efficiently.

(e) There is economy in the use of machines and equipment because they can be shared. A duplicator fully used in an open office will do the same amount of work as partly-employed duplicators in two closed offices because of the reduction in machine idle time.

(f) Supervision is easier.

(g) All grades of staff can be accommodated in the same room. As a consequence, officers work with their seniors who are no longer isolated behind doors. This promotes a more democratic attitude so that all levels are better able to make valid judgments of each other. Seniors can no longer rely on comparative inaccessibility to bolster their prestige and in turn they can assess their subordinates more effectively.

Disadvantages

(a) Carried to extremes it can result in a 'factory-like' atmosphere. Serried ranks of uniform desks can be daunting and lead to a feeling of impersonality.

(b) It is unsuitable for confidential work and the handling of cash.

(c) The increased movement and noise of people can be disturbing. This can have the effect of reducing performance.

(d) In general, social problems are more likely where there is a large congregation of people. Those working in smaller offices have a stronger feeling of 'belonging'.

(e) The effects of an epidemic can be swift and far-reaching.

(f) It is unsuitable for accommodating noisy machines, such as accounting and addressing machines.

17.11 Landscaped Offices

These offices (otherwise known as 'panoramic offices') are intended to retain most of the advantages of open-plan offices and to remove many of the disadvantages. The objective is to 'soften' the prospect by eliminating regimentation. Desks are angled instead of being in straight lines; working teams are grouped in 'islands' of desks. Staff thereby attain a clearer identity because they are more conscious of belonging to a smaller 'family'. The groupings can be made more positive by the use of low-level screens which also allow for some individuality in the immediate decor. The prospect can be made even more pleasing by the use of house plants.

Although the result is to improve working conditions it immediately sacrifices (at least partially) the main justification for open planning—the saving of space. Consequently, landscaping is not often applied to 'general offices'. The trend appears to be towards landscaping large departments or combinations of complementary departments. For example, a large Sales Department would lend itself to landscaping, as would the combination of a Public Relations Department and a Customer Services Department. Where this policy is adopted the remainder of the staff is accommodated according to its specialist expertise, such as in typing pools. Here again the principle of landscaping can be applied, although perhaps to a lesser degree.

Fig. 17.3 is a plan of the layout of part of a landscaped office. To the right is the manager's office, which has facilities for holding meetings. Immediately adjacent is the area occupied by his personal assistant. Three clerks and their work stations are grouped together. The four typists work near the filing

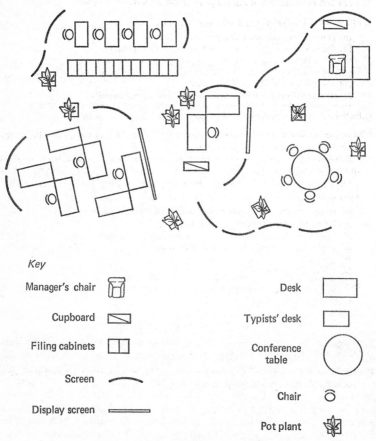

Key

Manager's chair	Desk
Cupboard	Typists' desk
Filing cabinets	Conference table
Screen	
Display screen	Chair
	Pot plant

Fig. 17.3. Layout of part of a landscaped office.

cabinets. Access to each area is possible without unduly disturbing those in other areas. The positioning of the screens 'softens' the boundaries of each area.

Key Points

1. **The effect of work environment on performance** is that if conditions are good staff will contribute more efficiently. This is because they are *able* to work better and are *willing* to work better.

2. Factors relevant to **physical conditions** may be summarised as follows:

    (*a*) *Lighting*—diffused, usually fluorescent;
    (*b*) *Heating and ventilation*—circulating heat; constant change of air;
    (*c*) *Decor*—bright but not 'exciting';
    (*d*) *Cleanliness*—should be scheduled;
    (*e*) *Noise*—largely a technical problem;
    (*f*) *Safety*—positive measures plus common sense.

3. Efficienct **office layout** must take account of

    (*a*) *Work flow*—forward straight-line direction;
    (*b*) *Human traffic*—economy and freedom of movement;
    (*c*) *Working conditions*—specific to the purpose and general;
    (*d*) *Supervision*—facilitating direction, control and (possibly) training;
    (*e*) *Flexibility*—adaptable to change;
    (*f*) *Social attitudes*—working in groups; personal identity.

4. **Furniture** must be *specific to its purpose.*

5. **Specialist rooms** should be *designed and equipped* for the individual functions; thus providing efficiency by specialisation.

    Separate rooms must be provided where *confidentiality* or *security* is required, and for *interviewing*.

    Open offices contain a *variety of activities*.

Advantages:

    (*a*) space-saving—fewer walls, partitions and door openings;
    (*b*) lower servicing costs—heating, cleaning, etc.;
    (*c*) flexibility;
    (*d*) reduction of traffic between departments;
    (*e*) equipment economy;
    (*f*) democratisation.

Disadvantages:

    (*a*) 'factory-like' atmosphere;
    (*b*) noise;
    (*c*) loss of departmental and personal identity;
    (*d*) danger of epidemics.

Office landscaping aims to *reduce regimentation.*

6. **Desk layout** has relevance to motion study in that it must be arranged so as to *minimise hand movements* and *reduce fatigue*.

SECTION 3
THE EMPLOYEE WITHIN THE ORGANISATION

18

EFFICIENT STAFFING

18.1 Personnel Policy

In the previous chapter we saw that the provision of good working conditions contributed to high morale within the staff and that this in turn made for increased efficiency. This, however, is but one principle which must be adopted by a company in respect of its employees when aiming for high performance. It must also operate satisfactory practices in other respects. The more important of these can first be summarised as follows.

(a) *Recruitment*. Staff of a sufficiently high calibre must be recruited. Specialists and those of management level must be experienced and efficient. Those at lower levels must be at least competent and reliable.

(b) *Labour turnover*. Pay, working conditions, career prospects and the attitude of top management must be such as to preserve a stable work force. An unsatisfactory employer will suffer from the disruption which results from a high turnover of labour. In fact, a rising rate of labour turnover serves to indicate that there is dissatisfaction among the staff.

(c) *Management succession*. There should be a defined policy of training and promotion so that the management structure is not weakened. This requires a succession of people who have been prepared so that they can fill positions vacated by their seniors and occupy newly created posts.

(d) *Remuneration and benefits*. The amount of remuneration is an important factor to an employee, of course, but it is rarely the only one. Certainly a good employer will pay at least the market rate for each job, but an employee will also be influenced by any 'fringe benefits' to which his employment entitles him. For example, a generous pension scheme is effectively an addition to salary. Other benefits may not be directly quantifiable (such as membership of a private medical scheme) but will nevertheless be very real.

(e) *Consultation*. There should be machinery to remove the damaging isolation which can exist between top management and the rest of the staff. There should therefore be established procedures which enable each side to put its views to the other and for both sides to work together in tackling problems which affect them both.

It is important that the matters summarised above are determined. Top management must have a positive attitude to them. For example, to ensure management succession someone must decide how it is to be achieved; it is not something which will just happen. The practices of top management concerning all matters relevant to staff should therefore be formulated. When this is done it is known as a **personnel policy.**

In a wider sense, the phrase can be said to also refer to practices which are *not* set out. As explained below, the attitude of top management can be shown by its behaviour.

18.2 Top Management Attitudes

Whether or not a personnel policy is specified, the staff will be aware of its nature from personal experience. If, for example, a company offers poor career prospects, that failing will soon be known by those who are affected by it. The personnel policy in that respect will be apparent, even if it is not published.

Something which cannot be formulated but which can be fundamental to personnel relationships is the attitude of top management as it is shown in day-to-day human contacts. Boards of directors have group character traits in the same way that individuals have. The lives of employees can be affected by the nature of their directors just as children are affected by the behaviour of their parents.

The state of human relationships at every level of an organisation is determined, to a considerable extent, by the attitude of those at the top. If those attitudes are 'hard-line' or if they are 'easy-going', the same attitudes will percolate down the line. The purpose of a directorate is, as the word indicates, to *direct*. If, instead, it *dictates*, it will bear down heavily on its senior executives. As those executives are answerable to the board for the activities of their subordinates, they, in turn, will adopt a similar attitude. This will be extended down the chain of command, each person protecting himself from his superiors by the attitude he adopts towards his subordinates.

If 'hard managers make hard under-managers' it also follows that slack control at the top produces a weak organisation at all levels.

18.3 Avoiding the Extremes of Management Attitudes

The similarity between a firm and a family has been expressed as a human relations theory. This states that in any well-run family there must be a balance between the influence of the father (who should motivate his children) and the mother (who should protect them and provide reassurance). If the father's influence is too powerful the children will be intimidated. If the mother's influence is over-strong the children will be pampered and spoiled. Unless both influences are in balance the result will be a maladjusted child.

The same dangers can exist in a firm. An over-paternalistic management will degenerate into an authoritarian one. Merely because it provides employment, such a management will consider this to be sufficient to allow it to do as it wishes. It would not hesitate, for example, to close down a factory with no consideration of the effect on those employed there. An overmaternalistic management, on the other hand, would give way to the slightest challenge. It would refrain from closing down the factory merely in order to save jobs.

The ideal would be for the two influences to be well balanced. The paternalistic one would motivate the work force to give of its best. It would encourage and support responsibility and initiative, on the understanding that failure by those responsible for achievement would attract penalties. The other influence would offer secure employment and benefits beyond those provided by the average employer. The overall result would be that those people who wanted it and were capable of it would be able to accept responsibility, knowing they would receive support and recognition. Other staff would know that if they gave of their best they would be rewarded. All staff would enjoy the protection of a considerate employer.

The result of such an attitude is certain to provide a high level of performance. Part of the consequent profitability would flow back to the employees in the form of continued and extended benefits. This, in turn, would of course promote further effort and attract new staff of a high calibre. Business history shows that firms which adopt such policies enjoy benefits which are self-perpetuating.

18.4 Recruitment

Earlier in this book we saw that a manager must distribute the work of his department in the most efficient manner possible by taking account of the expertise and personal qualities of the staff which are available to him. If he requires an additional staff member or a replacement he will know what he requires of the employee. He will start from that point and look for someone who can meet his requirements. This demonstrates the basic principle of successful recruitment—people must be selected to fit jobs; jobs should not be made to fit people.

The Personnel Officer (or Recruitment Officer if the company has one) will ask the manager what he requires a successful candidate to have. To do this, the content of the job would be specified. This process is known as **job description**. Thus, there would be itemised the expertise required, the experience the applicant should have, and the degree of responsibility and initiative the job calls for, etc. (A study of the larger advertisements for vacancies will provide condensed versions.)

Knowing exactly what is required (which will be beyond what is specified in even the most extensive advertisement) makes it easier to select effectively. What each applicant can offer can be directly related to every itemised requirement.

A secondary but important advantage is that possible applicants can decide if they may apply with any hope of being successful. This also benefits the employer because he will not then have to go through a large number of obviously unsuitable applications. An employer who does not adequately describe a vacancy merely provides himself with unnecessary work.

Because a job description specifies the scope and demands of the job it has relevance to any system of job grading which may be operated (see below).

18.5 Job Grading

Most sizeable organisations have job grading systems. In companies employing very large numbers of clerks and in government departments the systems can be extensive.

Most schemes provide separate scales for the main classifications of skills. Thus, there would be different gradings of typists, of computer operators, etc. Such a system provides the following advantages.

(*a*) It makes balanced staffing possible, so that the work content of a particular area can be expressed in grades of workers. For example, a department may be entitled to two officers Grade B, six officers Grade C and 10 officers Grade D.

(*b*) It provides for more accurate recruitment because the requirement of a job is specified.

(c) It can be part of a promotion scheme whereby people can move from one grade to another.

(d) It can be directly related to rates of pay.

18.6   Merit Rating and Staff Appraisal

This is a system for assessing the performance of a person *within* the grading of his job. Such an assessment can be made only by using a method of staff reporting—otherwise known as **staff appraisal**. This means that a superior who has intimate experience of the employee's work is required to place a value on specified qualities and aptitudes. A form is used which lists such matters as attendance, accuracy, conscientiousness, etc., of which assessments have to be made in a form similar to the following:

Poor/Fair/Good/Very good/Excellent

Inadequacies of the System

Certain reservations have to be made about such systems, including the following:

(a) Such a system can never be wholly accurate and, in extreme cases, can even be unfair to an employee. The main reason for this is that any asssesment must be a very personal one. For example, a very demanding manager will be less generous in his judgment than a more considerate one; 'personality clashes' between assessor and assessed can, even unconsciously, give a biased evaluation; 'favouritism' will produce a false report.

(b) It is also possible to have an assessment form which is unrealistic. It is difficult to see the point of a question about, for example, 'company loyalty' or how it can be answered.

(c) Earlier in the book we saw that, with certain exceptions, it is impossible to measure clerical output in a meaningful way. A staff report, therefore, cannot give an accurate quantification.

Practical Value of the System

Merit rating is sometimes directly related to remuneration. An employee's pay would first be fixed within the range of pay specified by a job grading scheme. That is, for each job there would be minimum and maximum rates. An employee with a merit rating above a certain level would go higher in the scale or he may be put on the lowest pay rate for the next higher job grade.

Whether or not such a practice obtains, staff appraisal can have a bearing on promotion. Ambitious staff like to know that assessments are made, even though they are rarely published, because when promotions are available a favourable staff report in an employee's file will stand him in good stead.

18.7   Career Prospects

Unless a company can offer firm prospects of promotion it will lose most of its more valuable employees—those with ability and ambition. A company therefore needs to have clear policies about **training** and **promotion**. Those with potential for more senior work should be trained in preparation for such work. It must be a stated policy that, where possible, senior positions would be filled from within the company. Junior executives who see the next rank of posts going to 'outsiders' will be discouraged and become apathetic.

To Promote from Within or Not

If there is no one on the staff with the expertise required for a new post then, obviously, a company must go outside to find a suitable person. This could apply if the company is going to use different methods (e.g. computerisation) or is venturing into new fields of business activity. Where a company has a choice, however, certain principles may be relevant:

(*a*) A person who has worked with the company for a long time will be aware of the company's philosophy and can therefore usually be relied upon to continue it. A newcomer may, if he is in a senior enough position, upset the traditions of the company.

(*b*) A present employee will have an intimate knowledge of the firm's 'internal politics' and the strengths and weaknesses of his colleagues.

(*c*) An outsider may bring with him a wider view and new ideas. Those who have known only their own company may be blind to its faults and be too afraid to upset the ingrained pattern of relationships which has existed for so long. A company which promotes from within almost exclusively is likely to experience the sterility which results from inbreeding.

(*d*) The management will already be aware of the characteristics of a promoted member of staff. To some extent, a newcomer may be an 'unknown factor', who, after his appointment, may display unwelcome traits.

It is a dangerous policy to promote a person only for his loyalty. It has been said that this practice can result in a person ceasing to be promoted only when he is shown to be incapable of coping with his present job. (This is known as the **Peter Principle**, first propounded by Lawrence J. Peter.)

18.8 Consultative Committees

Further evidence of how performance is affected by morale is provided by the benefits which accrue if staff and management cooperate in dealing with problems which are common to them.

Morale is improved if employees feel they are being treated as people and not merely as cyphers. It is therefore necessary that top management confirms this by its attitude and that there are procedures to demonstrate it. The latter is usually achieved by establishing consulatative committees to enable the two sides to work together. The scope of such bodies and the principles which should apply may be summarised as follows:

(*a*) Staff should be consulted about management proposals which may affect them. Such subjects could well be discussed at an early stage at consultative committee meetings.

(*b*) Staff should be encouraged to put their suggestions to management. Employers who recognise that their staff may well have ideas of value to the company will thereby demonstrate their respect for their employees. If employers consider the views of staff about *management* suggestions and reciprocate when the *staff* put forward proposals, there is created a spirit of participation which can do nothing but good.

(*c*) There must also be machinery allowing staff to make requests or complaints to management. All too frequently, most of the business of consultative committees comes within this category. If management demonstrates its democratic principles in the ways mentioned above, however, there is less possibility of meetings degenerating into 'grievance committees'. Staff must also play its part by not neglecting to use the committees for purposes other than 'getting at the bosses'. It must be recognised that where consultative committees do not function in the right spirit it is not always the fault of management.

(*d*) Following the above remarks, it must be stressed that management must sincerely support the avowed spirit of cooperation. If management merely 'goes through the motions' of holding meetings simply because there is an agreement to meet staff in specified circumstances, more damage than good will be done. In the interests of the company, management cannot always accept suggestions and protests by the staff, but it must genuinely consider staff views.

Key Points

1. A policy of **management succession** is necessary:
    (*a*) to *ensure continuity* in the company;
    (*b*) to *offer career prospects* to competent employees.

2. The **amount of remuneration** is not the sole consideration for an employee. Others include:
    (*a*) 'fringe benefits';
    (*b*) security of employment;
    (*c*) career prospects;
    (*d*) management attitude.

3. **Personnel policy** establishes *positive practices* and indicates *attitudes of management*.

4. People should be **recruited** or **promoted** to *fit jobs*; jobs should not be fitted to people. This is facilitated by **job description**.

5. **Job grading:**
    (*a*) categorises levels of expertise and responsibility;
    (*b*) allows for staff planning;
    (*c*) can relate to promotion;
    (*d*) may be linked to pay scales.

6. **Merit rating** is a form of staff *appraisal*. It suffers from being *subjective*. It may be *related to remuneration*.

7. **Promotion**
    from within—rewards loyalty; ensures continuity of company philosophy; promotes morale; may result in resistance to change; provides an executive who is already known.
    from without—may result in new ideas; may upset company traditions; may cause resentment by existing staff; may introduce an unacceptable personality.

8. Effective **staff consultation**:

    (*a*) requires genuine endorsement by management;
    (*b*) promotes participation and encourages initiative;
    (*c*) does not provide only a complaints procedure;
    (*d*) is more efficient if operated by an agreed procedure.

19

MOTIVATION AND HUMAN ATTITUDES

19.1 Human Nature in the Business Environment

A business largely consists of a congregation of human beings. Human activity and the attitudes of people have a dominating influence on administration, even where there is extensive mechanisation. This must be recognised as a vital factor because the attitude of people influences the effectiveness of their work. Human effort is affected by the following:

(a) The *attitudes of individuals* to their work.
(b) The *inter-relationships* of people.
(c) The effect of *environmental conditions* on people.
(d) The *attitude of management* to other workers.
(e) Changing *social attitudes*.

19.2 Why People do the Work they do

If one was asked 'why do people work?', for most the answer would be that they have to work to provide the necessities of life. But work provides more than that. This can be shown when one considers why each person makes his particular choice of job. For most people there are options in types of employment, so we must ask what it is that people are looking for when they make a choice. In most cases this will vary between one person and another. The motivations can include the following:

(a) *Security*. Some will take a particular job because it offers a strong possibility of continuous employment. The attraction is that of certainty of income.

(b) *Challenge*. A person may accept a post because he knows it will present him with difficulties. Such a person derives satisfaction in tackling and, eventually, solving problems. A person in a very senior position may change occupations simply because he wishes to prove to himself that he can surmount new heights.

(c) *Prestige*. To some people, the status attached to a particular post may be an attraction. Social standing is not necessarily commensurate with remuneration and it is possible for a person to accept a position which provides personal esteem without being influenced by the amount of the salary.

(d) *Power*. This may be akin to the desire for prestige but not necessarily so. Such a motivation shows itself when a person strives for a position mainly because of the authority it will give him.

(e) *Exploitation of personal aptitudes*. This is part of almost every motivation. People are best at doing the things they enjoy most, which are usually those things for which they have a natural inclination. Statisticians are people with an inborn ability and liking for figure work; the gregarious are more likely than others to become salesmen; leaders usually have a natural ability to lead.

(*f*) *For social contact.* Not everyone has to work for financial reasons. A woman who has been 'house-bound' for some time may take a job largely because of the contacts with other people it will provide. Others will choose one job in preference to another because it offers more social intercourse. Thus, some typists prefer to work in a pool instead of for a small firm.

In practice, of course, choice is usually influenced by more than one motivation.

19.3 Attitudes to Work

The attitudes of people to their work differ because of their differing *motivations*.

Attitude to work has a bearing on *performance*.

A responsibility of management is to recognise different attitudes and to capitalise on that knowledge when allocating tasks. No business requires a staff consisting entirely of brilliant and ambitious people; there must also be 'hewers of wood and drawers of water'. Matching the various demands of jobs with the differing abilities and attitudes of available people is therefore of prime importance.

One can explain this by making two simple divisions between those who want and are capable of responsibility and those who do not want responsibility. Similarly, work can be divided between jobs demanding responsibility and initiative and those which do not. The art of management is to fit the right type of person to the appropriate job. This requires that the following points be considered:

(*a*) Much office work is routine and can be boring. An ambitious person with initiative would be frustrated in such a job. He wants to exercise self-expression and if he is in a routine job his performance will be low. Consequently, not only is he not deriving 'job satisfaction' but his employer also suffers.

Fortunately for employers, many people like routine work. There are those who do not want the worry of responsibility and those who recognise their limitations. Some of them may prefer the undemanding nature of purely routine work; some prefer routine work which requires a skill (such as typing) but which carries little responsibility. Much has been written about factory line production work being 'soul destroying' because of its monotony. The fact is that many prefer to stand at a factory bench, while others shun it in preference to doing work requiring initiative and responsibility, such as being a milk roundsman. It is not simply a matter of relative intelligence; it refers to differences in needs.

(*b*) Other jobs demand responsibility and initiative. To fill them, management must recognise those who have the appropriate attitudes. Thus, provided such persons appear to have the required ability, they should be encouraged and trained to accept more demanding positions. Failure to do this will not only mean that such a person's productivity will be low (as mentioned above) but, also, the company will be losing potential talent.

On the other hand, to thrust responsibility on to those who do not want it or who have not the ability to cope with it could well be disastrous for all concerned.

19.4   The Effects of Giving Responsibility

The results of giving people responsibility or additional responsibility vary considerably because of the infinite differences in people's characters. Some of the many human reactions which can follow are as follows:

(*a*) Promotion usually results in a person being responsible for more people and having to associate with more people. This can sometimes bring to light personal failings in social attitudes which were previously unsuspected. Because of the increase in social contacts, such characteristics as brusqueness, shyness, lack of discretion, obstinacy, prejudice, etc., may show themselves. Revelations such as these can upset the plans of management when it becomes apparent that such a person fails to 'fit in'.

(*b*) A person can become too conscious of prestige when he moves to higher levels. He tends to stand on his dignity too much and become obsessed by protocol.

(*c*) A person placed in charge of a department or an operation will sometimes deliberately inflate the apparent importance of his job. He may do this by ensuring he never has a clear desk; by adding unnecessary aspects to his work; by appealing for more staff, etc. Such an attitude usually derives from a lack of self-confidence.

(*d*) A regrettable instance is when a person breaks down under the weight of responsibility. This may be because events have shown he has not the aptitude for being a *manager*—that is, he is efficient at his work as a technician but is unable to organise efficiently or deal with people diplomatically. Often, however, the reason is that he is a 'worrier' and is unable to cope because of his nature. The tragedy is that he may be a worrier because he is particularly conscientious, so that a virtue leads to his undoing.

(*e*) In addition to the unhappy consequences mentioned above, there are, of course, the successful ones. It is frequently the case that a person develops because he has been given responsibility. He has then found his true position and will display talents which had previously been underestimated.

19.5   The Consequences of Group Working

The most efficient way of dealing with work is to organise staff into fairly small work groups. It is known that over-large working groups prevent the creation of team spirit and makes control difficult. In considering the consequences of forming work groups one may equate them to families.

(*a*) A person within a group has something to identify with. He becomes part of a body of people. He 'belongs'.

(*b*) A work group has certain objectives and responsibilities, as has a family. There may be personal differences between the individual members but they all have some things in common. Thus, a family's main objective may be to maintain a communal home to which the wage-earners have a responsibility to contribute; a work group's objective may be, say, to calculate and pay wages with the responsibility of doing so within a time scale.

(*c*) Members of a family may quarrel amongst themselves but they will usually unite to resist attacks from outside. Similarly, members of a department may have their disagreements but they will stand together if, for example, the department is accused of inefficiency or lack of economy.

(d) Members of a family must accommodate each other's personal failings. They may clash but they will usually 'learn to live with each other'. Only when and if the stage is reached when one member threatens the whole foundation of the family will that person be ejected. The same principle applies to work groups.

(e) Families and work groups can be critical of other associations. In business it is not uncommon for antipathy to exist between two departments. As with families, there is often no positive reason for the dislike. Frequently, it has a psychological basis and may be due to jealousy, a feeling of inferiority or some other indefinable trait.

Life in business is like life outside it, in that it consists of a continuous series of social adjustments. These are necessary in order to reduce internal friction and to cope with external pressures. As is shown below, conflict may exist within a group and conflicts may be imposed on it.

19.6 Personal Conflicts

Following up the analogy of work groups and families, one may consider the incidence of personal conflicts in business. In the business context, however, one must also consider the effect of personal conflict on performance. Where relationships are strained the amount and standard of output will fall, so that part of a manager's responsibility is to reduce the extent of conflict. The only way to do this is to recognise the cause of a conflict.

One cause can be the staff structure. One person may be jealous of another because that other person has been promoted. A person may resent being 'bossed' by another, either because he is a person who resents any authority over him or because the senior person is abusing his authority.

Social prejudice can be another cause of conflict. For example, a feminist may be resentful of 'male chauvinism' or a man may be biased against women generally. Differences between races and cultural backgrounds often cause dissension. There are numerous varieties of such attitudes but they are rarely personal attacks in origin; they stem from general prejudices.

Two people can be opposed to each other because one has characteristics the other has not. Extroverts and introverts rarely mix well; a person with a quick brain may be exasperated by a 'plodder's' obsession with detail; a charming personality may arouse resentment in those less generously endowed.

Where any conflict exists, attempts must be made to reduce the damage it can do. Tolerance should be advocated, of course, but a more practical measure would be, if possible, to reduce the incidence of friction by altering the work pattern.

As with a family, however, there may come a time when the only solution is to remove the major source of conflict. Whatever the cause of the trouble, if the situation cannot be remedied within the group a solution must be sought outside it. A person cannot be dismissed because he has a prejudice against someone else, so it must be hoped he will be more amenable in another group. This is the usual way of dealing with such a problem, but there are two reasons why such a solution may not be possible. First, there may not be a suitable position to which the person can be transferred. Secondly, the person may be a 'social misfit'. Although such a person may not be mentally unstable he is the sort who cannot associate amicably in any situation.

19.7 Conflicts Caused by Management

Management, sometimes even with the best of intentions, can be the cause of conflict. This can be the case when a major alteration to a procedure affects the staff. It can also arise from an organisational change, such as the division or amalgamation of departments. Some changes in policy can also have repercussions on the staff, such as an alteration in training programmes or working hours.

To reduce the possibility of conflict there must be *early and adequate communication* of the proposal and, where appropriate, *genuine consultation*. Failure to keep a staff 'in the picture' can have damaging results which could have been avoided by a more thoughtful approach. These are discussed in more detail below.

19.8 Communication by Management

Unnecessary trouble can be caused if management does not make an announcement of any proposal affecting staff at a sufficiently early stage. Offices, like any other human grouping, thrive on rumours. The 'grapevine' is a very swift method of passing messages but it is frequently an inaccurate one. Rumour feeds on rumour, so that distortion becomes acute. A rumour may generate fear (such as of redundancies) or resentment, but the truth is sometimes not a disturbing thing at all. Until the truth is announced, however, the staff have only the rumours to rely on.

A frequent problem is that when the rumour starts management is only 'considering' a proposal at a very preliminary stage. It can then justifiably claim that it had made no announcement because there was nothing to announce. The problem will arise if tentative discussions are 'leaked' so that rumours immediately start.

For any hope of success, the following principles should be applied:

(*a*) To prevent rumours getting out of hand, management should make an announcement without delay, outlining the proposal and stating at what stage consideration of it had been reached.

(*b*) The method of announcing is very important. The memorandum on page 95, although it does not refer to proposals, provides an example of how unfortunate wording can worsen a situation. Where any proposal will affect staff there must be an attempt to forestall conflict by using diplomatic wording. An example of such a communication is given on page 182.

(*c*) The announcement should be honest. It should disclose all the facts and the consequences of the proposal. (An exception would apply, however, if some information has to be kept back at this stage for security reasons. For example, if the company was considering entering a new branch of trading it may be unwise to be too forthcoming at that point in case it provided an advantage to competitors.)

19.9 Consultations with Staff

If an innovation is to affect staff there should be consultation between management and staff, preferably before an announcement is made. Relationships will be much more comfortable if staff are consulted at the very earliest stage. Top managers would, of course, first discuss the outlines among themselves and decide their attitude to staff representatives.

If there is machinery for consultation, as when a staff association has been recognised by the employers, then the set procedures must be followed. In other cases it would be sound policy if staff were invited to appoint their own spokesmen. This would be preferable to management deciding to whom they would talk.

When a staff association does exist there are usually other provisions as to when consultation can be demanded. As explained in the previous chapter, machinery should exist for occasions when the initiative rests with the staff. Also, there are often rules whereby staff representatives must be involved in matters of discipline. These often provide that an officer of the staff body may at an interview represent a member threatened with disciplinary action or at least be an observer.

19.10 The Effects of Mechanisation

The expansion of mechanisation is, of course, linked to the problems caused by alterations of procedures. The necessity of adequate communication and consultation, as already discussed, therefore applies, but consideration must now be given to the changes caused by mechanisation which affect staff.

Work Content

There is a certain amount of truth in the assertion that mechanisation reduces personal interest in work. This effect is, however, less than may at first appear to be the case. Mechanisation, by its very nature, can be applied only to routine processes or processes which can be made routine. It cannot replace the functions of planning and negotiating; salesmen still have to talk to customers; the method of answering the telephone is as important as ever it was; machines cannot compile final accounts. Therefore, the interesting jobs involving human contact, judgment and initiative, as well as those requiring certain skills, continue to exist.

Working with machines can be tedious, but in the main it replaces tedious manual jobs. Writing up ledgers by hand, sorting cards, adding columns of figures, etc., cannot be described as inspiring work. A person who has used the old and the new methods would probably have no difficulty in stating his preference.

Mechanisation therefore results in changes in the content of jobs, so that often the same person is doing the same job but by a different method. A fundamental requirement of a machine is that it be simple to operate. The consequence is that staff can usually be trained as operators.

Employment Levels

In the early days of computerisation there were fears that it would lead to redundancies. It is now generally accepted that computers have not, in fact, reduced the total level of persons employed. It has changed the types of employment, however. People were replaced by computers which took over their work but a number of different jobs were created. New professions came into existence, such as computer programmers and operators, systems analysts, designers and engineers. Peripheral industries were created, such as those engaged in making ancillary equipment, tapes and cards, print-out paper, etc.

The expanding use of semiconductors, however, may have more disturbing consequences. Because they are smaller, less expensive and more versatile than mainframe computers the effect of their increasing use is more far-reaching. There is less demand for programmers; because the equipment is mechanically simpler, fewer engineers are required; skilled operators are not usually needed. In respect of the last, some present staff can be absorbed by being trained as operators (usually within a few days), but there is already evidence of a substantial reduction of people employed in offices where semiconductors are used extensively. The transition is already in progress but certainly it will increase in pace and in its effects.

19.11 Mechanisation and Management

The problems for management caused by increased mechanisation include personal ones. Mechanisation must result in alterations to relevant procedures. This in turn often means that the staff structure is changed. Some people who were in charge of departments or held senior positions may find that their departments have disappeared because the work has been integrated into a system operated by a new department. As a consequence, a person may discover that what appeared to be a well-established place occupied by him in a hierarchy and the possibility of rising within it no longer exists. He may be found other work which he does not easily take to; at the worst he may be made redundant. On the other hand, the change may provide him with opportunities which did not previously exist. If he can cope with the new type of work he may find himself in charge of or occupying a senior position in one of the new departments. It is therefore usually the case that 'reshuffling' staff as a result of mechanisation on a large scale benefits some and damages others.

Those doing routine work will, in general, not suffer from loss of prestige or seniority because, as already stated, the only change for them would be the method of working. There may be cases, however, where semi-routine work becomes less attractive because it has been converted into wholly routine work. An orders clerk dealing with a lot of customers on the telephone may enjoy that work because of the personal contacts it brings and the satisfaction derived from solving problems and dealing with crises. Such a person may not take kindly to a system where a computer accepts and processes orders.

In both cases there will be the need to assimilate the people to be retained by consultations with those to be involved, by reallocating the work in the most judicious ways possible and by training. Again, however, the possibility of redundancies may exist.

A major changeover can be traumatic, although the effect is less disturbing if, as is sometimes the case, the change is made in stages. In any circumstance, however, the problems of management in relation to the staff are considerable. There is a need to exercise diplomacy and, above all, fairness.

19.12 The Changes in Employment Attitudes

Over the years there have been changes in the attitude of employees and employers. These need to be recognised and understood because of the effect they have on motivation and on employer/employee relationships generally.

(*a*) *Expectation of good working conditions.* We have already seen that people expect high standards of working conditions because their own domestic conditions are good.

(*b*) *Entry levels and social barriers.* Because of the improvement in education and its wider availability it is possible for a young person to bring qualifications to a new employer which will allow him to demand a place above the bottom rung of the ladder. These educational opportunities are available at all levels of society so that potential executives can come from any class. Accordingly, class barriers are less restrictive than they were in the past.

(*c*) *Emphasis on youth.* Ambitious and competent people expect to be given responsibility at a fairly early age. Such people are no longer content to spend years doing lower-level work in the hope that eventually they will occupy 'dead men's shoes'. Employers also recognise the value of fresh young minds and the dynamism that often goes with them, provided they are accompanied by mature judgment. There can be considerable physical and mental demands on those occupying high places in management and the ability to cope with such demands lessens after a certain age. The general trend, therefore, is for an increasing proportion of senior executives to be in the lower age brackets.

(*d*) *Reduced recognition of loyalty.* There is a tendency for ambitious people to change employers more frequently than in the past. It is usual for competent people to change employment as often as is required in the search for better rewards. An employer will, if necessary, try to persuade another company's executive to join his company, knowing that other employers may 'poach' to get his best staff. Neither employers nor employees regard such activities as being 'disloyal' as they may have done in the past. That the practice is generally accepted is shown by the increasing number of firms which operate as 'headhunters'—that is, they search to find specialists for employers who require them.

(*e*) *Elimination of subservience.* The master/servant attitude which existed for so long between employers and their staff has disappeared. This is an expression of changed social attitudes generally, which has been strengthened by legislation to protect employees.

Key Points

1. **Motivations** in the work situation include:

   (*a*) *certainty of employment*, e.g. civil servants;
   (*b*) *self-expression*, i.e. exploitation of natural aptitudes;
   (*c*) *prestige*, i.e. self-esteem and egotism;
   (*d*) *power*, i.e. a desire to dominate or, at least, lead;
   (*e*) *challenge*, e.g. an industrialist accepting a top post in a nationalised industry;
   (*f*) *social contacts*, e.g. a married woman no longer 'housebound'.

2. **Attitudes to work** differ because of differing personal needs. Different *types of work*

require different attitudes. Jobs should therefore be allocated in such a way as to satisfy personal needs.

3. **A work group** is like a *family*. It consists of individuals with certain common interests.

4. **Conflict** detracts from efficiency. It can arise from:

(*a*) interpersonal relationships;
(*b*) poor organisation of work;
(*c*) management attitudes.

5. **Communication** from management to staff on matters concerning them must:

(*a*) be *early enough* to dispel doubt caused by rumours;
(*b*) be *open and honest*;
(*c*) be linked to *consultation*;
(*d*) be *diplomatically worded*.

6. **Mechanisation** in its effect on staff:

(*a*) eliminates tedious manual work;
(*b*) changes job contents;
(*c*) may alter career structures;
(*d*) may reduce employment;
(*e*) demands diplomatic handling by management.

Appendix 1

ASSIGNMENTS

1. You have been given the task of conducting an opinion poll on a matter affecting students in your college. You have to get the separate views of six departments and from that calculate the result of the overall poll. You allocate responsibility to one person for each department. Each of those persons has an assistant to do the clerical work. Each leader conducts his own poll and reports to you. You then summarise the sectional results and the global result and report thereon to the committee which appointed you.

(a) Identify: (i) the sectional and global objectives; (ii) where delegation of authority and responsibility occur; (iii) the incidence of direction; (iv) the areas of accountability; (v) the division of activities.

(b) How would you establish: (i) coordination; (ii) communication; (iii) planning; (iv) control?

2. (a) Construct an organisation chart for your college department, relating its Head to the leaders of each discipline and those within each discipline. Take into account (if relevant) that some staff teach in more than one discipline area. Include the domestic and secretarial staff.

(b) As a group, discuss the questions: (i) 'Did it do any good to draft the chart?'; (ii) 'Did we find anyone accountable to more than one person and, if so, what problems can that give?'

3. Refer to Fig. 2.1.
Since that chart was made the business has grown. Mr Smith has appointed Mr Blue to be assistant manager. Mr Black has been promoted to the position of Stock Controller, responsible for checking stock and making orders. His position as storekeeper has been filled by Mr Tan. The office staff consists of Miss Primrose who is responsible for keeping the accounts and paying accounts and wages. Miss Brown has been made supervisor of the cashiers, who now consist of Miss White, Miss Amber and Mrs Olive. Two more shelf fillers have been appointed, Misses Stone and Pink.
Draft an organisation chart showing the new structure.

4. Refer to Fig. 2.6 and conduct a discussion on the following questions.

(a) Miss Jones, a sales assistant, considers she has been unfairly accused by her manageress of dishonesty. In which direction should her complaint go?

(b) Mr Smith, a buyer, purchased a consignment of toys which subsequently proved to be unsafe. Who would be involved in the investigation?

(c) The Marketing Manager has the opportunity of buying portable television sets from Taiwan. Who must be consulted about this and who will make the ultimate decision?

(d) Mr Smart has a business degree and has been appointed as a management trainee. Name, in order, the first five departments you consider he should work in.

5. As a member of a design team you are drawing plans for production of a food mixer. The aim is to make a product which is more flexible in its capacity than others in the market. It will not only mix food but it will also chop, liquefy and grind solids and beat at variable speeds. What problems are you likely to encounter is designing an acceptable product and how can they be solved?

6. A pharmaceutical company spends seven years in researching for a drug which would prevent the advance of lung cancer if used at an early stage. To date, no progress has been made in achieving this, but in the course of its investigation the company has discovered a product which, if mixed with tobacco, will considerably reduce the risk of lung cancer. It markets this invention at a high price while continuing with its original research.

Debate the proposition that the company was morally unjustified in making huge profits from an 'accidental' discovery.

7. A company sells four sorts of biscuits, types A, B, C and D. It has four sales areas: East, South, West and North. Each area has five branches and each branch has six salesmen. Outline a procedure to provide the sales target and performance for each type of biscuit, analysed into areas, branches and salesmen.

8. Debate the following question. 'Is there any justification for a company of cigarette manufacturers to sponsor a team of racing cars?'

9. The class should be asked to bring three pocket calculators, all different models but of about the same price. Conduct a market survey to determine what sort of calculator (not necessarily one of the three) students would prefer to buy. (Sample questions: does it give more data than you normally require; are the display figures sufficiently readable; is colour important; what is the ideal size; what is the cost and life of the batteries; is keying sufficiently positive?)

10. A buyer of a piece of electrical equipment made by your company writes you an irate letter saying that he recently received an electrical shock from it. He demands that under the terms of the warranty he must have a refund of the cost. He also claims damages. You ask him to return it to a local dealer. The dealer then reports that he had been faced with an abusive customer. After the customer had left the dealer found that a seal had been forced off the equipment, making it unsafe.

Write to the dealer and the customer. (If this is treated as a class project, the letters should be composed by groups of three. Each group's efforts should be read and discussed by the class.)

11. Who should interview applicants for the following posts and what qualities should be looked for in making each choice?

(a) A copy typist in a large sales department. (b) An assistant company secretary. (c) A commissionaire. (d) A wages clerk.

12. The head of the Accounting Department has the following work which he wishes to delegate to his staff: (*a*) Producing complicated financial analyses; (*b*) checking expenses returns from branches; (*c*) internal auditing of branch cashiers; (*d*) supervising machine postings; (*e*) instructing staff of branches about a new method of making returns. He realises that some training may be necessary for all the posts to be filled.

Who should be given each job from the following members of the current staff and what degree of training and supervision would be necessary in each case?

(*a*) Mr Grant. Aged 20. Has been a cashier at a branch and at head office. Currently assisting in the compiling of cash forecasts. Inclined to upset people because of his abrupt manner.

(*b*) Mr Smart. Aged 22. Has assisted in machine postings and is studying for an accounting qualification. Has an aptitude for figure work. Ambitious and somewhat aggressive. Currently engaged on analysing branch expenses.

(*c*) Miss Waverley. Aged 23. Originally a machine operator but because of an aptitude for figure work is now engaged on investment appraisal. Shy. Training to be an accountant.

(*d*) Mr Young. Aged 20. Joined the company three months ago. Currently assisting in machine postings. Cheerful and somewhat irresponsible.

(*e*) Mr Grey. Aged 25. A 'plodder' and rather dull. Proved to be conscientious in the Wages Department. Currently showing the same attitude to checking fees and commissions payable to outside persons and bodies.

(*f*) Mr Miller. Aged 25. Showed a marked aptitude for organisation and documentation. Has assisted in compiling a new system of branch returns. Currently on a course studying systems analysis. Intense and impatient. Has domestic problems.

(*g*) Miss Tilley. Aged 19. Assists Miss Waverley. Bright at figure work. Attractive and likes a 'good time'.

(For a group exercise, each student should contribute his opinions to a class discussion.)

13. A company employs representatives who sell to grocers. Outline a procedure and state the documents used to provide head office control of the following functions of each representative.

He collects orders and passes them to head office. Deliveries of goods are made direct. If a customer pays for the goods when he orders them or pays for an earlier delivery of goods, the representative pays the amount into a local bank for transfer to the company.

14. A fellow-student has been injured by a top window swinging down and striking him on the head. You had previously pointed out the insecure condition of the window. As a member of a group representing your colleagues, make a written complaint about the incident. Address your communication to the appropriate person.

15. You are one of the staff representatives who attended a meeting, the minutes for which appear on page 102. Write an *account* of the meeting for the information of those you represent. Make such assumptions as may be necessary for writing the account.

16. A Mailing Department aims to take the post to the Post Office by 5 p.m. every day. It takes up to 45 minutes for the department to prepare the post. The company has 20 departments which send correspondence. Draft a timetable which is applicable to dictators, department heads, secretaries and typing supervisors so that the mailing programme operates effectively.

17. Would computerisation be justified in the following circumstances?

(*a*) Currently, month-end statements are sent on the 4th of the following month. Using a computer would enable them to be sent on the 2nd.

(*b*) A company exports extensively to the Middle East. It requires to be able to make better forecasts about political changes which in the past have disrupted its export plans. The suggestion is that a computer could assess degrees of probabilities in a given situation.

(*c*) A company employs six investment analysts. If their work was computerised, only three would be required.

(*d*) A company circulates world-wide to stamp collectors, giving them information about available issues, pending issues, 'bargains', etc., and providing a newsletter. The company includes specific information about certain types of stamps to those with particular interests in those areas. This selection is done by classifying the customers according to their interests and making up 'packs' relevant to those classifications. The customers value this personal approach. The proposal is that a computer would handle the selection and circulation.

18. The head of a firm about to commence business has calculated that the loads of typing work will be as follows in a 35-hour week:

(*a*) There will be enough copy typing to require 50 typing hours.

(*b*) 10 hours a week would be spent on typing contracts and on circulars which are to be duplicated.

(*c*) Typing dictated letters would take up 30 hours a week.

(*d*) There would be some confidential typing from time to time.

What do you suggest should be the composition of his typing staff?

19. A typist is in charge of a four-drawer cabinet holding 1,000 cards in numerical order, each card measuring 6″ by 4″. There is a card for each customer. Each day she receives a list, in duplicate, containing an average of 200 names in alphabetical order but quoting the customer number. Against each name is an amount. Her job is to type those amounts on the relevant cards and return the cards to the file. On completion of the batch she files the top copy of the list in a lever-arch file. The duplicate list she signs and returns.

Set out the step-by-step stages for completing the whole operation and show how her desk should be arranged.

20. You arrive at your desk at 9 a.m. You know you have to see the Chief Accountant at 11 a.m. to give him some figures and that it will take you 30 minutes to compile them.

At 9.5 a.m. you receive a telephone message that your assistant will not be in because he is ill. You know he had an appointment to meet a client who is due to call at 11.15 a.m. You had arranged to telephone another client at 9.30 a.m. with some figures which are in your assistant's desk.

At 10 a.m. the Company Secretary telephones to ask if you can attend an emergency staff meeting at 11.30 a.m. At 10.15 a.m. your secretary asks you to check a five-page report she has typed for you. She wants to duplicate it so that it can be circulated that afternoon. She has no other work and asks if you can dictate replies to six letters on your desk.

On your return at 11.20 a.m. from seeing the Chief Accountant your secretary informs you that an important client had telephoned to ask if you would lunch with him at 1 p.m. that day.

Show, in chronological order, how you would cope with the morning's events.

21. Your college has decided to hold a chess competition. There are to be four teams, each of three members. The full-time students will have two teams, and the day-release and evening students will each have one team. There will be a draw to determine the order of team play. A session between two teams will consist of three simultaneous games, the winning team being the one with the most winning games. (In the event of a draw the decision will be made by tossing a coin.) The winning team in one session will play the final against the winning team in the other session.

The evening and day-release students will not be available during the day.

Draw up a time table to cover the tournament. This should commence from the time that invitations are issued.

22. At what rate are lunches served in your canteen? Produce an average figure by checking at different times on different days.

23. The diagram on page 228 gives an outline of a Purchasing Department.

When a requisition is received from Stores the junior clerk obtains from the stock library the file containing details of the item and the possible suppliers. This is then passed to the manager who decides on the supplier and approves the order. From time to time the junior returns the files to the library. Each requisition is passed to one of the clerks who telephones the supplier and agrees terms. These are noted on the requisition which is passed to the typists who then make out the necessary documents for placing the order. The manager signs the order and the junior distributes copies of it to the relevant departments.

An average of 500 requisitions a day are handled.

(a) Construct a string diagram, showing the movement of paper and people under this arrangement.

(b) Construct a diagram showing a more efficient arrangement of the desks.

24. Redraft the office layout in Fig. 15.5 so that there is a more economical movement of paper and people.

25. Management is worried about the number of complaints by its customers that they are sometimes not supplied with exactly what they ordered, that there have been delays in deliveries and that invoices are not always accurate. The O. & M. department has been instructed to investigate the procedures for dealing with orders so as to identify the causes of errors and to recommend corrective action. At the outset of their investigation the O. & M. officers

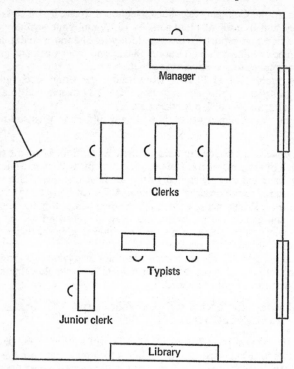

discover that salesmen are not always efficient in their paperwork. They also find that the manager of the Orders Department is very 'touchy' about criticisms of his department and strongly resents the 'interference' of the O. & M. staff.

What areas should the O. & M. officers investigate and what should be their attitude when interviewing the staff concerned?

26. Assume that a procedure had been changed in the way shown in Fig. 16.1(*b*). If an efficiency audit was carried out a year later, what aspects would the O. & M. team look at?

27. Staff can take remarkably stupid risks in an office. Draft a memorandum to staff pointing out what they can do to reduce accidents.

28. The Health and Safety at Work Act states that it is the duty of an employer to ensure the health, safety and welfare at work of his employees *so far as it is reasonably practicable*. Conduct a discussion, bearing in mind the above italicised words, on the following question.

How far (if at all) is an employer responsible if:

(*a*) an employee with a contagious skin disease uses a roller towel in the washroom;

(*b*) a typist, wearing high-heeled shoes, slips on some stairs;

(*c*) a window, recently renewed, falls and cuts a clerk badly on the hand;

(*d*) at an office party, held in the canteen outside office hours, an intoxicated clerk falls and injures his head.

29. To what extent do you think the Offices, Shops and Railway Premises Act sets *positive* standards? In particular, what do you think about the conditions relevant to working space?

30. Refer to Fig. 17.1. Replan the room on the assumption that (*a*) the volume of work made it necessary to employ a seventh records clerk and (*b*) management refused to buy lateral filing cabinets.

31. Your work is largely concerned with speaking to clients on the telephone and writing letters. In laying out your desk, where would you place: (*a*) the telephone; (*b*) the dictating machine; (*c*) record cards of the clients; (*d*) your inward mail; (*e*) your typed letters; (*f*) note pad; (*g*) diary?

(Carry out this assignment as a class exercise, using the blackboard.)

32. Mammoth Ltd is a huge corporation, with branches and subsidiaries in many parts of the world. It offers excellent working conditions and benefits to its employees. It rewards successful executives handsomely, but in return they are expected to 'live Mammoth and think Mammoth'. Hold a class discussion on the following questions:

(*a*) Do you know of such a company?

(*b*) How is the Mammouth philosophy likely to affect the lives of its executives and their families?

(*c*) If you qualified for a junior executive position, would you like to work for Mammoth?

33. Debate the following proposition: That management should not offer the possibility of top posts except to those executives who have proved themselves worthy of them by the age of 30.

34. Comment on the following staff assessment form:

Staff member................................

Department ....

Job title and grade ....

Give your assessment of each of the following by using one of these phrases:

Very poor/below average/average/above average/excellent

1. Punctuality and attendance   4. Initiative
2. Accuracy   5. Participation
3. Conscientiousness   6. Sociability

35. John Brown is 55 years of age. He is the senior accountant in a division and is the longest serving accountant in the company. The position of Chief Accountant has become vacant and Brown would appear to be the automatic choice for the post. Although he is very competent he has a somewhat abrasive manner. His relationship with the Finance Director, with whom he would have to work closely as Chief Accountant, is an uncomfortable one and the

director considers they would not make a good partnership. A year ago, Brown's assistant, Jack Smith, was promised Brown's post when he was promoted.

Form small groups. Each group should discuss the problem and produce a written statement to show how the situation could be resolved in the most equitable way. The statements should then be read and discussed in the class.

36. What motivations could be implied from the following changes in employment?

(*a*) From Managing Director of an oil-producing company to chairman of the National Coal Board.

(*b*) From junior partner in a firm of solicitors to the legal department of a local authority.

(*c*) From a nursemaid to a wealthy family to a filing clerk in an insurance company.

(*d*) From an accountant working for a partnership to Welfare Officer in a large company.

(*e*) From Chief Accountant to a scrap metal merchant to a middle management post with a merchant bank.

Conduct this assignment by means of verbal contribution from the class, bearing in mind that more than one motivation may be adduced in any of the circumstances.

37. Identify areas of possible conflict in a department consisting of the following people.

(*a*) John Mortimer is the manager. He is aged 55. He has held the same position for several years and considers he has been passed over for promotion on a number of occasions. He is efficient but very much a 'routine man'. He has little sense of humour and appears to be petty-minded in his relationships with his staff.

(*b*) Mrs Jane Wade is his assistant. She is 50 years of age and joined the department before Mortimer did. She considers herself to be a 'mother' to the staff but, generally, they regard her as being a gossip and something of a prude. She is divorced and has no children.

(*c*) Abraham Thomas is 21 years old. Born in London, he is of West Indian parentage. He is always very cheerful and is popular with the lady staff members in particular. He is competent but inclined to be careless.

(*d*) Miss Elsie Mills is 24 years of age. She is very efficient and has a passion for detail—she is a perfectionist. She is introspective and has few friends. She is usually quiet but is subject to outbursts of temper if she is faced with another's inefficiency.

(*e*) Jack Villiers is 22 years old. He has an attractive personality. He is particularly good at his work, dealing with it quickly and with little difficulty. He has solved several office problems and has virtually taken charge in a couple of emergencies. Management are considering him for promotion.

(*f*) Miss Rose Gaylord is aged 18 years. She is attractive, high spirited and has a full social life. She does her work well but with little interest in it.

38. Redraft the memorandum on page 95 in more diplomatic language.

39. June Baker, aged 19, joined the company as a typist three months ago. She has proved to be a sociable person and competent.

Since her arrival, her fellow-typists have suffered a number of small thefts. Articles have been taken from desks, handbags and coats left in the cloak-room. Another typist, Sybil Jones, once accused June of being responsible. The denial was so angry that Sybil regarded this in itself to be confirmation of her suspicions. Acting as spokeswoman for the other typists, Dorothy Clark insists that the supervisor takes up the matter with the Personnel Officer. The supervisor, Mrs Mary Duncan, agrees to do so.

Carry out an exercise in which class members act the parts of those present at the meeting with the Personnel Officer. These are Paul Thomas (the Personnel Officer), Sybil, Dorothy and Mary. In accordance with agreed procedure, Jack White, a clerical officer from another department, is also present as a Staff Association representative. He does not know June.

The purpose of the meeting is to enable the Personnel Officer to decide what action, if any, he should take. He had employed June at the request of a Probation Officer after the girl had been found guilty of shoplifting. Only the Personnel Officer knows of this incident.

Appendix 2

SUGGESTED FURTHER READING

Business Administration, L. Hall, Macdonald & Evans, Plymouth.

Business and Administrative Organisation Made Simple, G. Whitehead, Heinemann, London.

Business Equipment Guide, B.E.D. Business Journals Ltd, Wellington, Surrey.

Business Organisation, R. R. Pitfield, Macdonald & Evans, Plymouth.

Business Systems, R. G. Anderson, Macdonald & Evans, Plymouth.

Communication in Business, P. Little, Longmans, Harlow, Essex.

Effective Communication Made Simple, E. C. Eyre, Heinemann, London.

The Law and Procedure of Meetings, R. R. Pitfield and P. F. Hughes, Secretaries Journal Ltd, London.

Management: Its Nature and Significance, E. F. L. Brech, Pitman, London.

Management Made Simple, W. E. Coventry, Heinemann, London.

Modern Business Administration, R. G. Appleby, Pitman, London.

Modern Commercial Knowledge, L. W. T. Stratford, Macdonald & Evans, Plymouth.

Office Administration, J. C. Denyer and A. L. Mugridge, Macdonald & Evans, Plymouth.

Office Administration, E. C. Eyre, Heinemann, London.

Office Organisation and Method, G. Mills and O. Standingford, Pitman, London.

Office Practice Made Simple, G. Whitehead, Heinemann, London.

Office Procedures and Management, M. Symes, Heinemann, London.

Personnel Management Made Simple, S. Tyson and A. York, Heinemann, London.

Post Office Guide, Post Office Corporation, London.

Secretarial Practice Made Simple, G. Whitehead, Heinemann, London.

Index